Essays on twentieth-century poets

ESSAYS ON TWENTIETH-CENTURY POETS

George Fraser

Leicester University Press

1977

First published in 1977 by Leicester University Press
Distributed in North America by
Rowman and Littlefield, Totowa, N.J.

Designed by Douglas Martin
Set in Linotype Pilgrim
Printed and bound in Great Britain
by Richard Clay (The Chaucer Press) Ltd, Bungay, Suffolk

British Library Cataloguing in Publication Data
Fraser, George Sutherland
Essays on twentieth-century poets.
1. English poetry – 20th century – History and
criticism – Addresses, essays, lectures
I. Title
821'.9'1209   PR604
ISBN 0–7185–1156–5

Acknowledgment is made to the East Midlands Arts Association
for a grant in aid of publication

CONTENTS

To my wife
For thirty and more years
Of love and patience

PREFACE

This volume contains a selection from my longer essays on modern poets, over a period of about 30 years: the first of the two essays on W. H. Auden was first published in 1947, the final essay on Philip Larkin specially written for this volume in 1976. This volume, then represents half of my life and three-quarters of my working life (for I was publishing pieces which I at least took to be critical articles as early as 20). My social duties, in the last 20 years or so as a university teacher, and the claims made by family love and a luckily extensive network of friendships and affections have always had a first place with me. But certainly, and indeed well before many of these duties and claims had come into being, poetry has been the great abstract passion of my life. Why? It is partly a matter of competence. I have a very exact sense of rhythm but (I cannot sing in tune) a very poor sense of pitch. I am too short-sighted to get all that can be got out of landscape: I get much more out of pictures but my perception of colour is not perfect: there is a range of colours which I would hesitate whether to describe as blueish-green or greenish-blue. My short-sightedness and perhaps an excess desire to please makes me, unless I have some very special interest in them, a poor observer and inept judge of my fellow human beings; in my relationships with my fellow human beings there is a fairly regular sequence of initial enthusiasm and curiosity, growing disillusionment and boredom, and a final awareness that the inner dramas of my relationships with my fellows are largely subjective, and that he (or she) is not such a bad chap after all. Novels, therefore, are useful to me: at their best they provide a penetrating, exact, and detached view of life which 60 years on earth have failed to provide. At the same time, a more *rangé* person would be a better judge of novels. Next to poetry, I love that mixed art the theatre, but still, like a child, consider an evening at the theatre as a treat rather than an occasion for exercising critical acumen. That leaves poetry, I think, as the only kind of art or beauty from which I can derive the satisfaction of both the mind and spirit that others derive from music, the beauties of nature, the fine arts, the novel, drama. Here only am I on my own terrain.

I would like here to make a distinction between the proper pleasure of poetry and its therapeutic effects, rather like Aristotle's distinction between the proper pleasure of tragedy and katharsis. I take it by the way, with F. L. Lucas, that Aristotle meant by katharsis, a *tempering* of the excessive pressures upon us put by undirected pity and fear, rather than the *expulsion* of these emotions completely. No man would be human without those fellow-feelings for other human beings that include pity: no animal of any sort could survive without the constant alertness to danger which is triggered into drastic action by the emotion we call fear. But it is silly to spend hours a day weeping for the victims of starvation, civil war, and earthquakes, or never to go to bed without looking in all the cupboards for burglars. Aristotle's metaphor, anyway, was from blood-letting, an easing of hypertension : it was not from the effect of violent purgatives.

As distinct from the therapeutic effect, the proper pleasure of any kind of art lies in an excellence of which it alone is capable. The proper pleasure we find in a good poem lies in its finality and precision. The best prose remains unfinal, capable of being expanded or summarized, or having its meaning made more precise. A good poem means precisely what it says, no more, no less, and to expand it or summarize it even in a minimal way is to substitute some other thing for the poem. To expand or summarize prose, on the other hand, is merely to find a *fuller* or more *concise* way of putting the same meaning. But in the good poem (in the poem that succeeds in being a poem) the way of putting and the meaning, distinguishable in theory, are inseparable in fact.

Sensibility, on the other hand, can and ought to be appropriate. There is something badly wrong with a person who smiles happily when he sees a dead bird on the pavement and winces and frowns at the sight of apple blossom. As Mencius remarks, in a passage cited by I. A. Richards in *Mencius on the Mind*, we ought all to feel distressed when a child falls down a well, even though the child is no relation of ours, and not merely because of the unpleasant noise it makes as it bumps against the walls and the bucket at the bottom. Sensibility, as its connection with the word *sense* suggests, is not merely a feeling but almost a perception. It tends to increase our awareness, where our emotions tend to blind us. But the two must live together and poetry helps them to do so. We can display emotion about the failure of our sensibility to function properly (Coleridge: 'I see, not feel, how beautiful they are') or sensibility about our emotions and their possible inappropriateness (Ezra Pound: 'That the whole drama is subjective ...' and, much earlier, 'I had over-prepared the event'). Clearly a happy life for all of us depends on a well-balanced sensibility and much less on the strength or weakness of the emotions : except that one may be luckier to have weak than strong emotions, and perhaps an ideally good and happy man would be all sensibility and no emotion. Yet this ideal man, I somehow think, would be a saint, a sage, or possibly merely the best-liked man in the office, but not a poet.

I have never wholly understood, nor, I sometimes suspect, had the great poet-critic himself, fully understood what T. S. Eliot meant by that 'certain dissociation of sensibility' which 'set in', in England, somewhere around the middle of the seventeenth century : after they killed King Charles, perhaps. Clearly, from his context, Eliot was using the word 'sensibility' to mean something like 'total human awareness', something including sensibility in my own much more narrowly defined sense, emotion, and intelligence : especially intelligence working in a direct intuitive way, grasping a thought as directly as one senses the smell of a rose, as in Donne. Eliot said that a poet of our own century must be very intelligent. He was specifically referring to our time : in the time that Eliot admired, the age before that 'dissociation of sensibility', a beautiful poet like Thomas Campion did not need to be very intelligent except in his mastery of the sister arts of music and verse. The therapeutic task of Eliot and his contemporaries was to help to heal the inner fragmentation that afflicts us all. The therapeutic task, if one can think of him as having one, of Thomas Campion was merely to delight and soothe.

We have a poor vocabulary for the emotions (compare our vocabulary for distinguishing colours, and shades of colour). Perhaps a good poem is a new name for an emotion which has resisted articulation, which has tormented us but eluded our minds. Such emotions are social, not merely personal. The full aesthetic meaning of a poem is also its full social meaning. If one is interested especially in the character of the poet, that means that one is interested in his social formation (about which one can learn a great deal), not merely in his genetic mould, let us say his innate temperament (about which one can learn little or nothing). If a poem is a form abstracted from the world, it is also an important item in – it is part of the 'culture' of – the world it is abstracted from. Society, in the last resort, is the author of everything.

I am grateful to all the publishers, editors, and institutions concerned for permission to reprint, but particularly to Faber and Faber who very kindly returned me my complete rights in *Vision and Rhetoric*, 1959, at the same time expressing regret that they had not been able to keep the book in print. And for the British Council, which permitted me to print the then fairly recently published pamphlets from their British Book News Supplements series on Yeats and Dylan Thomas in that 1959 series (and have permitted me to print three essays from their briefer *Notes on Literature* series in this volume). I have much thanks, not only for that generosity, but for kindness over the years. Wherever possible I have given not only the year but the number and date of the periodical in which an article first appeared, but in the case of a very early article printed here, 'The poetry of Robert Graves', printed in the Harvill Press's *The Changing World*, I have not been able to track down a copy and have given only the year. Again, when an article (like that on Louis MacNeice) made use in an altered form of short reviews from periodicals, I have noted the fact, but not the dates of the short reviews. The introduction and the concluding essay on Philip Larkin were written for this volume and have their first publication here. The texts are as they originally stood except for the omission of such styles and titles as 'Mr' and such usages as 'the late' and for updating of punctuation conventions: indented block quotations, for instance, are here deprived of unnecessary opening and closing inverted commas. Provenances are given at the beginning of each essay. I have also, in revising proofs, put in a few new notes, correcting blunders or updating information. These are indicated by an asterisk in the text, and appear on pp. 254–5.

A final word of thanks; to the Board of the University Press, to kind, patient, and interested colleagues. Above all to my students who have taught me at least as much as I have taught them.

George Fraser   *Reader in Poetry, University of Leicester*   June 1977

1 · W. B. YEATS

Vision and Rhetoric, Faber and Faber, London, 1959; *British Book News* Supplements, Longmans for the British Council, 1954.

(1)

For just over ten years before he died in a hotel in the south of France, at the beginning of 1939, William Butler Yeats had been universally recognized by his peers as the greatest poet, writing in the English language, of this century. The recognition dates from the publication, in 1928, of his finest volume, *The Tower*. In June of 1939, he would have been 74. He had been writing verses since his 'teens and had been a poet of some reputation since his twenties. Since the turn of the century, he would probably have been mentioned by any critic in a list of the four or five most distinguished English poets, and, in any consideration of Irish poetry, he would have been head of the list. He had won the Nobel Prize for literature, he had done more than any other man to bring about the birth of the Irish theatre, and he had sat in the Senate of the Irish Free State. Yet every critic knows that these public honours are never the full measure of a poet's reputation. At regular intervals during his long life, shrewd critics had been convinced that Yeats was finished. To George Moore, in the Edwardian decade, it seemed that all Yeat's best poems had been inspired by his hopeless love for Maud Gonne; that love was never to find physical fulfilment,* and Moore thought that Yeats's lyrical gift would wither, like cut flowers in a glass. To the young T. S. Eliot, in the early Georgian era, Yeats seemed not much more than an interesting survival from the 1890s. The young Pound, sending some of Yeats's poems to an American magazine, took it upon himself to polish and improve them. The young Middleton Murry, one of the best critics of poetry of his period, dismissed *The Wild Swans at Coole*, which came out in 1919, as the work of a used-up aesthete. The interesting generation of writers who came to Oxford after the First World War thought little of Yeats. 'Surely,' wrote T. E. Lawrence to Ezra Pound, 'Yeats is no good?' Robert Graves, in the *Pamphlet Against Anthologies* which he wrote with Laura Riding, made jovial hay of 'The Lake Isle of Innisfree'. Thus, though Yeats had never been neglected, the full recognition of his greatness, like its full flowering, came very tardily.

To many critics, almost up to the last ten years of his life, it seemed that Yeats, wonderful as his gifts were, did not live wholly in the real world. Thus I. A. Richards, in *Science and Poetry*, 1925, commenting on Yeats's interest in magic, wrote: 'Now he turns to a world of symbolic phantasmagoria about which he is desperately uncertain. He is uncertain because he has adopted as a technique of inspiration the use of trance, of dissociated phases of consciousness, and the revelations given in these dissociated states are insufficiently connected with normal experience.' Quoting this comment, T. S. Eliot, in *After Strange Gods*, had even more severe things to say as late as 1934: '... Mr Yeats's "supernatural world" was the wrong supernatural world. It was not a world of spiritual significance, not a world of real Good and Evil, of holiness and sin, but a highly sophisticated lower mythology summoned, like a physician, to supply the fading pulse of poetry with some transient stimulant, so that the dying patient may utter his last words.'

The centrally important critical problem about Yeats becomes clear if we contrast these passages with the noble tribute which Mr Eliot paid Yeats on his death: 'There are some poets whose poems can be considered more or less in isolation, for experience and delight. There are others whose poetry, though giving equally experience and delight, has a larger historical importance. Yeats was one of the latter. He was one of the few whose history was the history of our own time, who are part of the consciousness of our age, which cannot be understood without them.'[1]

How are these pertinent strictures to be reconciled with this deserved praise? In what sense was the mental history of Yeats, which from a superficial point of view was so odd and eccentric, more profoundly 'the history of our own time'? Was Eliot, feeling that every truly great poet must in some sense be representative of his time, and feeling intuitively sure of Yeats's major qualities, merely making a formal claim that Yeats *must* be representative. Or can Yeats's representative quality be illustrated in detail?

(2)

When I. A. Richards, in *Science and Poetry*, suggested that a poet like Yeats, who took ghosts and fairies seriously, could hardly have anything quite centrally significant to say to the modern mind, he was making a crude but sensible point. The main debate of that mind, in this country, in the last 80 years, has been between an orthodox religious and an orthodox scientific attitude. Yeats was neither orthodoxly religious nor orthodoxly scientific; he had his own science, which was an occult one, and his own religion or 'sophisticated lower mythology', and in prose he sometimes reconciled them at the level of magic. In his better poetry, on the other hand, he often quietly jettisons both of them. The scientific attitude leads, in practice, to a kind of democratic humanitarianism. Yeats believed in aristocracy and, though his humane and fastidious temperament made him recoil from violence, he often allowed himself to romanticize violence, when it was safely set in a mythological past. The modern Christian attitude tends to lead to a preoccupation with sin. From this, Yeats was quite free. In the last ten years of Yeats's life, these two contrasting attitudes were well represented in this country by the work of Auden and Eliot. Auden, in the 1930s, was a kind of liberal semi-

---

[1] See 'The Poetry of W. B. Yeats' in *Purpose*, xii (1940), reprinted in *Southern Review*: Yeats Memorial Issue, April 1941; and in *Selected Prose* (1953).

Marxist, profoundly but not always obviously affected by a Christian up-bringing; Eliot was a Christian conservative, profoundly but not always ob-viously affected, particularly in his concern with social questions, by a liberal upbringing. These two poets, in fact, had much more in common with each other than either had with Yeats. Yet Auden, like Eliot, nobly saluted Yeats's passing:

> Earth, receive an honoured guest;
> William Yeats is laid to rest.
> Let the Irish vessel lie
> Emptied of its poetry . . .[1]

In saluting Yeats, neither Auden nor Eliot can have been merely saluting a great artist in verse. Both, in Yeats's work, given the deep seriousness of their critical attitudes, must have found a kind of wisdom, even though that expressed itself through ideas and gestures of which they disapproved. Yeats was as firmly set against Auden's attitude of the 1930s, which he symbolically described as 'Moscow', as against Eliot's, which he symbolically described as 'Rome'. Just as he was never a political democrat, never at all sympathetic with the

> . . . levelling, rancorous, rational sort of mind
> That never looked out of the eye of a saint
> Or out of a drunkard's eye,

so he was very much further, also, from any traditional Christian attitudes than many scientifically-minded agnostics are. What may be called his morality was neither that of a diluted and imperfect Christianity, nor that of a progressive humanitarianism. It could be better described as a morality of 'style'. It very much resembled (given that Yeats had a more genial and gener-ous temperament) the morality of Nietzsche. Yeats's instinctive sympathies were with the strong and proud, not with the weak and humble; with the brilliant rather than the stupid, with the exceptional rather than the average. They were not, however, like those of Nietzsche, with the oppressor rather than the oppressed. Yet, as an Irish nationalist, Yeats identified himself with the liberal wing of the Protestant Ascendancy, with those, like Swift and Grattan, 'who gave though free to refuse', rather than with the masses of the Irish people. Yeats's frank admiration for qualities like strength, beauty, reck-lessness, a dominating spirit, a 'proper pride', set him against the obvious superficial currents of our age. If he does, indeed, have the central represen-tatives that Eliot claims for him, one reason may be that this aristocratic or 'natural' morality – which is the morality of schoolboys, of film-fans, of soldiers, a morality based on the instinctive admiration we feel for those who excel us – is more firmly rooted in us than we think, and that when we

---

[1] W. H. Auden, in *Another Time* (1941); *Collected Shorter Poems* (1950).

find it nobly expressed we instinctively respond to it. More broadly, for all our preoccupation today with 'security', we still have hankerings after the heroic.

(3)

The case, however, for Yeats's representativeness has never been properly argued. The mere exposition of the meaning of many of Yeats's poems, as related to his personal history, to his social background, and to his philosophical opinions, is in itself such a complicated task that very little that can properly be called 'criticism' of his poems – criticism in the sense of concrete evaluation, of 'distancing' and 'placing' – has been written. Maud Gonne and Madame Blavatsky and the Abbey Theatre and Irish politics and the esoteric symbolism of *A Vision* tend to bulk so large in accounts of Yeats that they crowd out any consideration of his diction, his rhythms, his way of constructing a poem, the coherence and sensitivity of his responses. What John Wain wittily calls 'the Gypsy Petulengro approach' – the painstaking exposition, with diagrams, of what Yeats meant by gyres and cones and 'phases of the moon' – becomes so absorbing in itself, that mere literary criticism no doubt seems, by comparison, dull. This sketch is not primarily concerned with Yeats as a magician or a mystic. Miss Margaret Rudd may be perfectly right when, in a recent book about Yeats, she says that he is a rather inferior mystic, if we compare him with Blake. What is also true is that the Blake of the prophetic books is a rather inferior artist if we compare him with Yeats – these have to be approached, as even Yeats's book of occult philosophy, *A Vision*, need not be, with a primary extra-literary interest. 'Willie,' Mrs Yeats is reported once to have wisely said, 'you are a great poet, but you are no saint.' The great poet is our subject. He was, of course, no saint; but we may make out a case in passing that he had many of the virtues of Aristotle's 'magnanimous man' or of the *honnête homme* of the French seventeenth century. His representativeness for our own age does, as I have suggested, largely depend on the fact that he both possessed and praised what we think of as archaic virtues. He was the last quite whole-hearted spokesman of the aristocratic idea.

(4)

Yeats came from the outer fringe of the Irish Protestant Ascendancy, from a rather better family than Shaw's, and perhaps from not quite such a good family as Wilde's.* He spent his childhood between London and Ireland, and though in Ireland his family counted as minor gentry, in London, in so far as London bothers about such things, they probably counted as shabby-genteel bohemians. Yeats's father, J. B. Yeats, was an unsuccessful painter who wrote brilliant letters and had a genius for friendship. As a painter, he was influenced by the pre-Raphaelites and he handed down to his son the idea of a 'religion of beauty', and a romantic taste, that even in Yeats's youth was a slightly old-fashioned one, in art and literature. There are certain great writers, of the type of Ibsen, whom the young Yeats could never absorb; to the end of his days his attitude towards Degas and Manet was rather like that of Sir Alfred Munnings to Picasso. J. B. Yeats was also influenced in his ideas by the agnostic rationalism of Huxley and Tyndall, and against this side of his father the young Yeats violently reacted. As a boy, Yeats was dreamy and backward, fond of long solitary walks. To his dying day, he never learned to spell properly and diffidence about his scholarship prevented him from going to Trinity College, Dublin. This lack of a formal education is important in Yeats's development. He read very widely, but never systematically. He was bad at languages; in so far as the French symbolist movement influenced him at all, it was through translations made by his friend, Arthur Symons, and when in later life he said that he had 'almost forgotten his Hebrew', he meant that at one period, for some occult purpose, he had memorized a few words of that language. Even for himself, the map of what he knew and did not know can never have had very firm outlines. The young Yeats began writing verses very early. This early work shows much vividness of imagery, but it was some time before Yeats learned to write in regular stanzas or even to make all his lines scan. The first drafts of his poems to the end often show a surprising technical hesitancy – a trite choice of words, a flat shaping of the line; the poems were perfected by a habit, early acquired, of endlessly patient revision. The young Yeats was lucky in that his father encouraged him to go on with his poetry and even actively discouraged him from tying himself down to the drudgery of newspaper work. Yeats, however, soon became a fluent free-lance journalist, chiefly on topics of Irish folklore. By his early twenties, he had begun to make a reputation. In London, he became one of a group of minor poets, among them Arthur Symons, Lionel Johnson, and Ernest Dowson, whom today we tend to dismiss as 'decadents'.

If we compare the young Yeats carefully, however, with these friends of his of the 1890s, we notice important differences. Lionel Johnson and Ernest Dowson and Aubrey Beardsley were men of weak will, whom weakness drove to dissipation or perversity. They were men of essentially religious natures, hovering on the edge of conversion or despair. The possibility, ever present in their minds, of being damned gave them not a relish but a momentousness to sin. They tended to lack self-control (Dowson and Johnson were alcoholics). They did lack practical capacity. Yeats's early poems are full of melancholy, but they have little to say about sin. The young Irishman was not haunted by the fear of damnation. He was chaste and temperate – the greatest love of his life, that for Maud Gonne, was a wholly chaste one,* and his failure to win her did not drive him to prostitutes or drink. Shy and dreamy though he was, he was fundamentally a masterful man. Maud Gonne, dragging him at her heels on nationalist agitations, soon found that he was a natural orator and could easily dominate committees. His religion was, far more than that of his companions, genuinely a religion of poetry. Reacting against agnostic rationalism, he had not reacted in the direction of orthodoxy: 'I was unlike others of my generation in one thing only. I am very religious, and deprived by Huxley and Tyndall of the simple-minded religion of my childhood, I had made a new religion, almost an infallible church of poetic traditions, inseparable from their first expression, passed on from generation to generation by poets and painters with some help from philosophers and theologians.'[1]

How far there, one wonders, was he right about himself? Was he really 'very religious'? We wonder both about the word 'fardel' with its dandified air – the faded elegance of the 1890s – and about the word 'stories', which brackets off the question whether the 'stories' are true. The attitude is aesthetic rather than ethical or religious; in a sophisticated way, the young Yeats is playing a child's game of 'Let's pretend!' There are late poems of his, like 'Among School Children', that do express a properly religious attitude, one of mystical acceptance of a world experienced as contradictory; but the properly religious attitude that is often to be found in Yeats's poetry has little to do with – even tugs against – the pseudo-religious notions. It is not a playing with fantasies, but a response to the whole. The very fact that the young man could so easily concoct a 'new religion' for himself – out of Irish folklore and Blake and Madame Blavatsky and anything that came handy – is evidence of a rather unreligious nature; evidence of a blithe and irresponsible temperament, that of a young man sure of his genius, and unconvicted of sin. The note of the 1890s, the genuinely religious note, that is not to be found in Yeat's early poems is that of Lionel Johnson's 'The Dark Angel':

> Dark Angel, with thine aching lust!
>   Of two defeats, of two despairs:
> Less dread, a change to drifting dust,
>   Than thine eternity of cares.

Yeats's early religion, if it was properly a religion at all, was one without anguish or dread.

The charm of much of Yeats's early poetry is thus slightly equivocal – dreamy and melancholy, passive and self-indulgent, as indeed from this account of his poetical religion we might expect it to be. Riding's and Graves's attack on 'The Lake Isle of Innisfree' is, in fact, an attack on a poet for not being properly awake. In a poem from Yeats's volume of 1893, The Rose, a poem called 'A Faery Song', a modern reader is embarrassed by the monotonous doleful music, by the yearning that neither seems to have nor to seek for an object:

> We who are old, old and gay,
> O so old!
> Thousands of years, thousands of years
> If all were told:

[1] The Trembling of the Veil (1922).

> *Give to these children, new from the world,*
> *Silence and love;*
> *And the long dew-dropping hours of the night,*
> *And the stars above ...*

Even throughout the 1890s, however, there was a constant slow hidden growth in another direction. In *The Wind Among the Reeds*, the volume of 1899, the diction does indeed seem on the surface as formal and faded, the cadences as mechanically 'beautiful', as ever; and the symbolism also, growingly intricate but not growingly vivid,

> *... a coat*
> *Covered with embroideries,*

hangs now like a rich worn tapestry between the poet and the hard stone walls of the world. But the yearning has now an object, Maud Gonne. The individual words clutch more at particular objects. There is a movement towards active feeling, positive grasp :

> *I became a man, a hater of the wind,*
> *Knowing one, out of all things, alone, that his head*
> *May not lie on the breast or his lips on the hair*
> *Of the woman that he loves, until he dies;*
> *Although the rushes and the fowl of the air*
> *Cry of his love with their pitiful cries.*

Yeats, at some time after 1909, changed the 'dreamy Celtic' dying fall of the last two lines there to an arrogant rhetorical question :

> *O beast of the wilderness, bird of the air,*
> *Must I endure your amorous cries?*

The poem had enough latent strength to stand the change.

We should look, in the early poems, for that latent strength. Their weary, withdrawn note is a kind of protective colouring which Yeats had taken from his friends of the 1890s. (He was often, throughout his life, ready admiringly to imitate his minor, but never his major contemporaries. A natural leader, he liked to disguise himself as a follower even of small men.) There is, of course, a paradox here. Yeats made himself a major poet, starting with the equipment and apparently the tastes of a good minor one – with a chaste but excessively 'poetic' diction, with exquisite but trite cadences, with a tendency to use symbols in a way that was decorative, and even fussily so, rather than deeply exploratory, with a narrow and rather wilfully sad range of moods, always just on the verge of the literary pose or the 'stock response'. He started, also, without much grasp of the outer world; his early poems rarely make us *see* anything; we can weave our own daydreams round them, which is another matter. And though he acquired unique rank, among his contemporaries, as a visionary poet, it is probable that the merely *visible* world left him, to the last, rather cold. Usually he evokes it for us by a kind of trick, not describing the thing, but reminding us of our feelings about it :

> *A sycamore and lime-tree lost in night*
> *Although that western cloud is luminous ...*

> *Back turned upon the brightness of the sun*
> *And all the sensuality of the shade ...*

We remember our feelings about staring towards a fading distance at sunset, about sharp contrasts in a garden of light and shade. We ourselves, most of the time, *make* Yeats's physical world for him. We believe in it, because we believe in Yeats, and rather as we believe in a painted Elsinore when Hamlet is talking. We can, in fact, think perhaps more fruitfully of Yeats's poems as speeches made by him at crucial moments in a long noble drama. No poet lends himself so little to the cold-blooded examination of his poems as isolated objects; no poet gains more from being read as a whole, with a full knowledge of life. Yeats, as he grows older, acts, with growing assurance and spontaneity the difficult part of himself. The acting in the end, having gone through the stages of lyrical mime and heroic and satirical tirade, becomes almost naturalistic.

(5)

The Edwardian decade saw the masterful side of Yeats's nature coming to the surface. By 1908, when the first collected edition of his works came out, he had made a reputation not only as a poet and a dramatist, but as the man who had put the Abbey Theatre on its feet, who kept it going, and who had bravely defended Synge against local prejudice. Through Lady Gregory, who had become his patron, Yeats was now accepted by that 'Big House' society of which, in his childhood, he had only touched the fringes. He was becoming self-conscious about his ancestry. Some of the younger men in Dublin, and some older contemporaries like George Moore, thought him a mere shy ineffectual dreamer. He had resigned himself to unfulfilled love, and found public activity a distraction. Maud Gonne had made an unfortunate marriage, and though she was separated from her husband, she had become a Roman Catholic, so there was no prospect of her divorcing her husband and marrying Yeats. He and she, in any case, were becoming estranged in a deeper sense. She felt that the Abbey Theatre had tempted Yeats away from the national cause. She would have liked cheaper seats and plays that were straight nationalistic propaganda. Yeats, in fact, in the Edwardian decade, had become more concerned with the bigotry and bad taste, as he considered it, of his Dublin audience than with Ireland's wrongs.

The Great War, apart from the deaths of friends like Major Robert Gregory, hardly touched Yeats emotionally. But the Easter Rebellion of 1916, which took him by surprise (he was not in the confidence of any of the more extreme nationalists), made him regret his growing aloofness from the Irish cause. He remained a very moderate nationalist – he felt that England might still 'keep faith' – and indeed the 'troubles' of 1919 and after gave him a vivid sense of how violence can in a short time destroy values that it has taken law centuries to build up:

> *We had fed the heart on fantasies,*
> *The heart's grown brutal from the fare;*
> *More substance in our enmities*
> *Than in our love; O honey-bees*
> *Come build in the empty house of the stare.**

Yet he felt himself more profoundly identified with the Irish people than he had been for many years.

Yeats's long romance with Maud Gonne had meanwhile ended in a kind of comic fantasy. Her husband, one of the rebels of 1916, had been shot. Yeats felt he ought to ask her to marry him again, but was probably relieved when she refused. At the same time, he fell in love with her beautiful adopted daughter, who as a young girl had been half in love with him. The adopted daughter could not make up her mind. Yeats gave her a date by which to do so, and when her final decision was against marrying him, suddenly married another young lady, Miss Hyde-Lees. Not unnaturally, after such a complication of emotions, he was in a state of depression and anxiety after his marriage – even if there had not been the business of Maud Gonne and her daughter, he was a man in his fifties, weighed down by anxiety for his country, and marrying, after an unusually chaste bachelor existence, somebody much younger than himself – and it was partly to distract him that Mrs Yeats started the experiments in automatic writing that ultimately gave him the material for *A Vision*. In judging Yeats's occult philosophy, we should always ask ourselves how far, at a fundamental level, he himself took it seriously; and how far it was a necessary plaything for a powerful and distressed creative mind.

(6)

Many critics agree that it is on the volumes published in the last 20 years of his life, from *The Wild Swans at Coole* of 1919 to the posthumous *Last Poems and Plays* of 1939, that Yeats's future fame will mainly rest. The sharpening and hardening of his attitudes, the development of the tough, complex, and ironical 'later style' can, in fact, be traced further back, to the significantly named *Responsibilities* of 1914. There is even a hint of the new style in 'Adam's Curse' from a volume of 1904, *In the Seven Woods*:

I said, 'It's certain there is no fine thing
Since Adam's fall but needs much labouring.
There have been lovers who thought love should be
So much compounded of high courtesy
That they would sigh and quote with learned looks
Precedents out of beautiful old books;
Yet now it seems an idle trade enough.'

It can, however, be agreed that there is a remarkable new maturity, a new 'realism', in the works of Yeats's last 20 years; and this can be traced to several sources.

Yeats was now writing as a married man, a man with a house and children of his own, more rooted in everyday life than he had previously been. He was writing also as a man who had seen the dream of his youth, Irish independence, come true; and who was becoming aware of certain ironies, for him tragic ironies, involved in its coming true. His own personal dream had been of a free Ireland that would be a kind of replica, without the tensions or troubles, without the injustice to the majority, of the Ireland of Grattan's Parliament.[1] He wanted to go back to the eighteenth century rather than on into the twentieth. He hoped that the 'Big Houses' would survive, that the Protestant Ascendancy would still, because of their wealth, their wit, and their manners, constitute a dominant group. He thought of the local grandees patronizing poets and the peasants touching their hats. He was romantically innocent about politics. He found, of course, that what had come into existence was not a Protestant-dominated aristocratic Republic but a Roman Catholic farmers' democracy; and the farmers did not want to touch their hats to anybody. Some of the 'Big Houses' were burned in the 'troubles', others were deserted because they cost too much to keep up and because they, like even the nationalistic aristocracy, had outlived their social func-

---

[1] Until 1780, the Irish Parliament could reject or accept, but not amend, laws relating to Irish matters passed by the British Parliament. Irish patriots like Flood and Grattan took advantage of the American Revolutionary War (which involved war with France) to claim and secure legislative independence for the Irish Parliament. The Volunteer Movement – a kind of unofficial defence militia – ostensibly raised to resist invasion was in fact used to put moral pressure on the Viceregal Government. The Viceroy and his staff, however, retained practical control of Irish affairs by offering honours and sinecures to the pro-Government Parliamentary majority. The new Parliament did not represent the Roman Catholic masses of the people, or even their wealthier elements. Thus the short period of Irish Parliamentary independence – or really, of independence for the Protestant Ascendancy – ended in the bloody 'troubles' of 1798 and a little later in the Union, secured partly by lavish bribery, of the Irish with the Imperial Parliament. Nevertheless, the short period of Grattan's Parliament was marked both by splendid oratory and by a gay and brilliant social life in Dublin; and was thus often remembered nostalgically by Irishmen who saw Dublin, both socially and culturally, becoming more and more of a 'provincial' city.

tion. Yeats had hoped that Dublin, as the capital of a free Ireland, would become a great cultural centre; he saw the 'blind, bitter town' becoming more rather than less provincial. The Dublin City Fathers gave the freedom of the city to a retired Tammany boss, a Mr Croker, but rejected the suggestion of Dr Oliver St John Gogarty that they should also give it to Yeats. Sean O'Casey's tragic masterpiece, *The Plough and the Stars*, aroused as passionate an opposition from the Abbey Theatre audience as *The Playboy* had done. Yeats's growing bitterness comes out as early as *The Wild Swans at Coole* in one of his most powerfully sustained shorter poems, 'The Fisherman' :

> *All day I'd looked in the face*
> *What I had hoped 'twould be*
> *To write for my own race*
> *And the reality;*
> *The living men that I hate,*
> *The dead men that I loved,*
> *The craven man in his seat,*
> *The insolent unreproved,*
> *And no knave brought to book*
> *Who has won a drunken cheer,*
> *The witty man and his joke*
> *Aimed at the commonest ear,*
> *The clever man who cries*
> *The catch-cries of the clown,*
> *The beating-down of the wise*
> *And the great Art beaten down.*

Yeats, in this new Ireland, was not, in spite of the prestige that the Nobel Prize brought him, a centrally representative figure. He became a Senator, but found himself allied in the Senate, a little unromantically, with rich bankers and brewers; a speech which he made protesting, on behalf of the religious minority, against a proposal to make divorce illegal made him unpopular. The esoteric philosophy of *A Vision* is partly to be understood, as we have suggested already, in terms of Yeats's need for distraction. We should not take that book more seriously than Yeats took it. He had a long philosophical correspondence with Sturge Moore about hallucinatory cats, and other visions of this sort : are they real beings to which we have access only at privileged moments (Yeats would have liked to think so), or are they, on the other hand – hallucinations? It is interesting that in this correspondence he never refers to either the 'facts' or the 'arguments' of *A Vision* as having any relevant authority. He explicitly stated elsewhere that it was not very profitable to discuss the theories of *A Vision* in terms of 'belief'. Many of the ideas in the book, like that of eternal recurrence, are not new; they are in Vico and Nietzsche. Yeats, after he had written the first draft of *A Vision*, also found them in Spengler. Their truth, or otherwise, cannot be discussed here. They provided props for Yeats's attitude to life, which was becoming a kind of tragic stoicism. He sees life as tragic, but feels that it can be acted with the style of a tragedy. We can embrace our destiny joyfully: 'Hamlet and Lear are gay.'

It should be particularly noticed, however, that Yeats's attitude towards the supernatural was a profoundly ambiguous one. He wanted, from a world beyond ours, in contrasting moods, two apparently quite contradictory kinds of assurance; one that we are, in fact, bound, as the Buddhists tell us we are, to the 'great wheel of existence' and shall reappear upon this stage, in various roles, again and again; the other that, as the Buddhists also tell us, we can escape ultimately from 'the great wheel' — but not to non-being, a concept which never attracted Yeats, but to some kind of finite timeless perfection. He was not sure (as perhaps no Western man who studies Eastern thought ever is) that he really wanted to escape from the wheel. Thus in the face of the 'symbolic phantasmagoria', he retains the freedom of inconsistency. His images of a Byzantine heaven in which he would be transformed into a golden bird (the artist becoming an eternal work of art) symbolized his desire to escape from the disorder, the irony, the failure of life; but so also other symbols — as when he says he would like to live again, even in a 'foul ditch', as a 'blind man battering blind men' — stand for a craving for life, at any level, the 'lust and rage' of which he speaks in his *Last Poems*, that grew stronger in him as he grew older. Often he hated life for not being perfection. Sometimes, also, he feared perfection for not being life.

(7)

Yeats's early love poems are dreamily erotic, without being in the least consciously sexual; some of his later poems are so harshly sexual that they cease, in effect, to be erotic:

> *From pleasure of the bed,*
> *Dull as a worm,*
> *His rod and its butting head*
> *Limp as a worm,*
> *His spirit that has fled*
> *Blind as a worm.*

A glandular operation that Yeats underwent in his last years no doubt accentuated this tendency, but it was already there. It is best considered, however, as part of a more general tendency in his latest poems towards self-questioning, self-stripping:

> *These masterful images because complete*
> *Grew in pure mind, but out of what began?*
> *A mound of refuse or the sweepings of a street,*
> *Old kettles, old bottles, and a broken can,*

> *Old iron, old bones, old rags, that raving slut*
> *Who keeps the till. Now that my ladder's gone*
> *I must lie down where all the ladders start*
> *In the foul rag-and-bone shop of the heart.*

The man who wrote that stanza also wrote:

> *We were the last romantics – chose for theme*
> *Traditional sanctity and loneliness ...*

Anybody who wants to get the full range of Yeats must be able to respond to both kinds of statement – must be able to accept the tautness of a terrible great poet's sincerity. In that stanza from 'The Circus Animals' Desertion', Yeats has become aware that the symbols of his poetry have a Freudian meaning of which for most of his life he has been unconscious. But we should notice also that this stanza which bids farewell to the symbolist method is a triumphant example of it; for we 'know what the poet is saying' here, but we cannot 'say it in our own words'. A merely clinical interpretation will not work. Is, for instance, 'the raving slut/Who keeps the till' the Freudian Censor – is the money she will give us in return for old rubbish a release of Libido? Are the 'old iron, old bones, old rags' and the 'mound of refuse' symbols for the Freudian anal-erotic hoarding instinct? Is the 'foul rag-and-bone shop of the heart' merely the sexual imagination, with its accumulated scraps of lustful memory? Quite obviously not, and quite obviously what Yeats is saying here is something basically blind, grasping, insensate in all of us; something that hoards rubbish, that shuts doors, that hides away from the light. We climb up, but we never wholly get away. All that is still under our feet, in the cellarage. And the 'heart' is what grasps and is insensate, but also what loves and suffers, and the 'ladders' – the ways upwards and outwards, to the free air and the life of the spirit – do start there. And when we have said all this, of course, the stanza still retains, as all great symbolist poetry does, its eternal residue of mysterious suggestiveness.

The bare honesty of such poems, even more than the rich, dark mysteriousness of 'Byzantium' or 'The Statues', may partly account for Yeats's hold on the young. In his last volume he asks himself more frankly than most poets have done whether he may not have done as much harm as good:

> *Did that play of mine send out*
> *Certain men the English shot?*

Yet he can still strike a last grand attitude:

> *Cast a cold eye*
> *On life, on death.*
> *Horsemen, pass by!*

He would not, like Rilke (these lines were written out of irritation with Rilke) accept death as a final dark consummation. He would not accept life itself uncritically. And in the last thing he was working on, *The Death of Cuchulain*, the harlot (an eternal harlot, who has slept with 'Conall, Cuchulain, Usna's boys') speaks of the polarities and antinomies, of disgust and delight in physical love, of dread and delight in battle; speaks also of the Irish patriots of 1916, delighting in what they dreaded, who were always in Yeats's heart; speaks of gods and heroes whom we seem to embody, or who seem to stand behind us, in the crucial moments of our lives:

> *That there are still some living*
> *That do my limbs unclothe,*
> *But that the flesh has gripped*
> *I both adore and loathe.*

> (Pipe and drum music)

> *Are those things that men adore and loathe*
> *Their sole reality?*
> *What stood in the Post Office*
> *With Pearse and Connolly?*
> *What comes out of the mountain*
> *When men first shed their blood?*
> *Who thought Cuchulain till it seemed*
> *He stood where they had stood?*

(8)

Yeats felt that there was a tension between his life and his poetry. He thought sometimes of the poem as a kind of anti-personality which the poet builds up to compensate for or conceal personal weaknesses, of the poem as a 'mask'. This idea has something in common with Ezra Pound's idea of the poem as a *persona*. Pound is a poet who, according to one of his most appreciative but also harsher critics, Percy Wyndham Lewis, has no 'personality' of his own worth speaking of; he can function only by pretending to be somebody else, a Provençal troubadour or a Chinese sage. Yeats's masks in poetry are not of this sort; even in his earliest work his own personality seems to me to come over, or at least an important aspect of it, the 'poetic' aspect. Similarly, no doubt, at meetings of the Rhymers' Club in the 1890s, Yeats, fundamentally a very shy and diffident young man, put on a suitable 'literary dandy' or perhaps sometimes a 'dreamy Celt' personality. As Yeats's poetry matures, one of the things that happens is not so much that it becomes more 'personal', less of a 'mask', as that he gets more of his personality into it. He gets in things like irony, humour, arrogant irascibility, the coaxing manners of the professional Irish conversationalist, which in the 1890s he would probably have considered 'anti-poetic'; he gets in more of the prosaic detail of life, transformed by a poetic apprehension of it.

We might compare, even from *Responsibilities*, the generalized evocation of Maud Gonne,

> *...A crowd*
> *Will gather, and not know it walks the very street*
> *Whereon a thing once walked that seemed a burning cloud,*

with the prose bareness of a line and a half from 'Beautiful Lofty Things' in *Last Poems*:

> *...Maud Gonne at Howth Station waiting a train,*
> *Pallas Athene in that straight back and arrogant head.*

That line and a half evoke Maud Gonne, her setting, her bearing, her character (Pallas Athene, the goddess of wisdom, was severe and virginal). The more conventionally 'poetic' phrase about 'a burning cloud' tells us much about Yeats's feeling but does not evoke any image of a woman at all.

Often the force of the later poetry comes largely from this directness, like that of speech:

> *And here's John Synge himself, that rooted man,*
> *'Forgetting human words', a grave deep face ...*

> *Before a woman's portrait suddenly I stand,*
> *Beautiful and gentle in her Venetian way.*
> *I met her all but fifty years ago*
> *For twenty minutes in some studio ...*

> *Does the imagination dwell the most*
> *Upon a woman won or woman lost?*
> *If on the lost, admit you turned aside*
> *From a great labyrinth out of pride,*
> *Cowardice, some silly over-subtle thought*
> *Or anything called conscience once;*
> *And that if memory recur, the sun's*
> *Under the eclipse and the moon blotted out.*

There is no rhetoric in these passages; only in the last of them any figures of speech, and these so commonplace (a human relationship as a labyrinth, the sense of loss seeming to blot out the sun and moon) that they could occur unaffectedly in ordinary conversation. Common turns of speech are also sometimes exploited for irony. In *The Tower* we are told the story of Mrs French (it is in Sir Jonah Barrington's memoirs, 1833) and how a footman at dinner one day clipped off the ears of a farmer who was behaving boorishly and brought them to her in a little covered dish. It is with a delighted shock that we meet the lady again, in a summary of the characters in the poem, as

> *. . . Mrs French,*
> *Gifted with so fine an ear . . .*

Critics who have discussed to the verge of tedium Yeats's more obscure occult fancies might have discussed with more advantage this strong simplicity of his later style. Behind the strength is honesty of statement. The lines quoted above,

> *Does the imagination dwell the most . . .*

express a complex of feelings which most of us have experienced but which few of us have the courage to put on record: a complex of feelings that might be called remorse for compunction. Yeats speaks for what he calls, in a poem addressed to Von Hugel, the 'unchristened heart'; but with a dignity and passion that make it very unlikely that his words should ever cause scandal to Christians.

Yet if there were only pride and pagan courage and high art, only contempt for 'this filthy modern tide', only the obstinate 'lust and rage' of a 'wild, wicked old man' in Yeats, should we turn to him as we do, not only for distraction, not only for stimulus, but for wisdom and consolation? We look in poetry for love. All great poets are more profoundly capable of love than common men, and they may be terrifyingly more capable of hate, too. Yeats's capacity for hate distressed even close friends of his, like the Duchess of Wellington. It was there to the last, as in the poem, 'A Bronze Head':

> *Or else I thought her supernatural;*
> *As though a sterner eye looked through her eye*
> *On this foul world in its decline and fall;*
> *On gangling stocks grown great, great stocks run dry,*
> *Ancestral pearls all pitched into a sty,*
> *Heroic reverie mocked by clown and knave,*
> *And wondered what was left for massacre to save.*

But he could hate like that *because* he could love. And the 'touchstones' that I would choose from his poetry, to persuade an unsympathetic reader to reconsider it, all speak of love. I would choose these stanzas from 'A Prayer for My Daughter':

> *An intellectual hatred is the worst,*
> *So let her think opinions are accursed.*
> *Have I not seen the loveliest woman born*
> *Out of the mouth of Plenty's horn,*
> *Because of her opinionated mind*
> *Barter that horn and every good*
> *But quiet natures understood*
> *For an old bellows full of angry wind?*

> *Considering that, all hatred driven hence,*
> *The soul recovers radical innocence*
> *And learns that it is self-delighting,*
> *Self-appeasing, self-affrighting,*
> *And that its own sweet will is Heaven's will;*
> *She can, though every face should scowl*
> *And every windy quarter howl*
> *Or every bellows burst, be happy still.*

I would choose a line or two from the gentle minor elegy for Eva Gore-Booth and Con Markiewicz:

> *Dear shadows, now you know it all,*
> *All the folly of a fight*
> *With a common wrong or right.*
> *The innocent and the beautiful*
> *Have no enemy but time . . .*

I would choose the magnificent two last stanzas of 'Among School Children':

> *Both nuns and mothers worship images,*
> *But those the candles light are not as those*
> *That animate a mother's reveries,*
> *But keep a marble or a bronze repose.*
> *And yet they too break hearts – O Presences*
> *That passion, piety, or affection knows,*
> *And that all heavenly glory symbolize –*
> *O self-born mockers of man's enterprise;*
> *Labour is blossoming or dancing where*
> *The body is not bruised to pleasure soul,*
> *Nor beauty born out of its own despair,*
> *Nor blear-eyed wisdom out of midnight oil.*
> *O chestnut-tree, great-rooted blossomer,*
> *Are you the leaf, the blossom, or the bole?*
> *O body swayed to music, O brightening glance,*
> *How can we know the dancer from the dance?*

And (though Yeats is not on the whole a poet of striking single lines, of lines that impress us out of their setting) I might choose a line and a half from 'Nineteen Hundred and Nineteen':

> *Man is in love and loves what vanishes,*
> *What more is there to say? . . .*

Yeats's poetry I believe to be the centrally important part of his work.

His two best plays, *Purgatory* and *The Words Upon The Window-Pane*, are magnificently successful, but minor in scale; his longer plays seem to me all to dilute his art. He wrote very delightful prose and his reminiscences of the 1890s in particular, are a primary document for a fascinating period. He was not a good literary critic. His introduction to *The Oxford Book of Modern Verse*, like his selection of poems in that book, is strikingly odd and eccentric; but it has the wit and charm of everything he wrote, and here and there, among statements that seem quite absurd, it has extremely penetrating paragraphs – particularly, perhaps, about his friend Ezra Pound, whose qualities and weaknesses no subsequent critic has estimated so justly. But it was into his poetry that he put himself most completely. The poetry, however, is better poetry because he gave himself to so many other things. His patriotism, his public spirit, his capacity for staunch friendship and passionate love all enrich it. The sense, which grew so strong in him in later life, that every victory he had worked for implied a defeat of something he perhaps cared about more, lends almost all his later work a poise of complex irony. The characteristics which some of his contemporaries disliked, such as his arrogance or 'proper pride', are in his poems, too. Yet all true poets are fundamentally humble. Yeats was humble before the mystery of life. He never took either himself or his systems quite so seriously as some of his disciples have done. He was the last great poet in the English romantic tradition; and the only poet in that tradition, except Byron, with a genuine sense of humour and gift of wit. The true man, with the modesty and the generosity that underlay all his poses, comes out in the letters to Sturge Moore. Yeats is writing about the Nobel Prize:

> Yes, it will be a great help to me in several ways. Here especially it will help. I will find it easier to get the Government to listen to me on artistic things. I look upon it as a recognition of the Free State, and of Irish literature, and it is a very great help. People here are grateful because I have won them this recognition, and that is the distinction I want. If I thought it a tribute to my own capacity alone I, being a very social man, would be far less pleased.

All great poets tend to overawe us. They speak with 'something above a mortal mouth'. And they need their solitudes to withdraw into. But it is as a lover, as a friend, and as a patriot, as 'a very social man', that Yeats would like us to remember him. It is his broad and deep humanity that provides the substance of his art.

2·SEVEN POEMS BY YEATS

Notes on Literature, no. 10 (May 1962), and *Notes on Literature*, no. 63 (October 1966), issued by the British Council, London.

(1)

Yeats's 'The Wild Swans at Coole' was first published in *The Little Review* in 1917, and became the title poem of a volume he brought out in 1919. Its mood is a mood of what might be called clear desolation, and that mood pervades much of the volume in which it appeared.

In 1917, Yeats was a man of 53, an extremely famous but also an extremely isolated poet. Much of his energy as a writer had come out of, and in a sense gone back into, two sources. He had been in love with a beautiful political agitator, Maud Gonne. Since about 1900, he had put all his practical energies into encouraging the rise of a kind of cultural nationalism in Ireland, typified by the Abbey Theatre. By 1917, the long sighing for Maud Gonne was over. The harsh fanaticism in politics, which went so strangely with Maud Gonne's classical beauty, had always repelled him. But his efforts to encourage a more liberal and humane Irish cultural nationalism had met with little encouragement. The Dublin popular audience had shouted down Synge, Maud Gonne herself had wanted the Abbey Theatre to put on not works of art but straight nationalistic propaganda. The Dublin political nationalists whom he had come to despise, took Yeats completely by surprise.

He was even more out of touch with his English audience. Apart from the death in it of Major Robert Gregory, the son of his patroness, Lady Gregory of Coole Park, the war of 1914–18 had hardly touched Yeats's deepest feelings. To the generation of English readers who liked the Georgian poets, or more daringly the experimental poetry of the young T. S. Eliot and of Ezra Pound, Yeats looked like a survivor from the 1890s. Irish critics were unwilling, on the whole, to recognize his special distinction, his utter mastery of style and phrase. He belonged not to the Catholic mass of the people but to the liberal and national wing of the Anglo-Irish ascendancy; in a sense to a different stock from the mass of the Irish. Both devout Catholics and all-out nationalists were suspicious of a man who put art first, and in a sense made both his eclectic religion and his aristocratic politics out of art. He was a proud man, and George Moore had made fun of his pride; he lacked the warm, affectionate nature that made a much lesser poet, 'AE' (George Russell) universally beloved.

'The Wild Swans at Coole', therefore, should be read as a poem coming out of a very profound sense of the dedicated artist's isolation. Yeats when he wrote it must have felt that he had lost touch with his people, his 'own race', the harsh 'reality' of politics,

> To write for my own race
> And the reality,

with the time he was living in, even with the personal history, of vain love and vain struggle, of his own life. It is a high and dry poem, and the first lines set the note :

> The trees are in their autumn beauty,
> The woodland paths are dry ...

The lake at Coole mirrors a 'still sky' (all action, violence, human and natural drama are as far as possible drained away from the scene). On the lake in Coole demesne are 59 swans. It is 19 years, he tells us in the second stanza, since he first counted them; the 19 years in which he lived mainly at Coole, under Lady Gregory's patronage, more and more deprived of hope that Maud Gonne would finally accept his love, taken up with 'theatre business, management of men', his sturdy, bitter fight against the current for a renewed Irish culture. But these bitter years had been, also, years nobly dedicated to the pursuit of poetic beauty. (The swan traditionally stands for poetic beauty.) In the second stanza, the swans

> All suddenly mount
> And scatter wheeling in great broken rings
> Upon their clamorous wings.

It is not at all fantastic to think that as he looks at the swans, mounting and scattering about the sky, Yeats is also looking at his own poetic past, his past poems. These too are lonely creatures and there is only himself to admire them.

But he admires them sadly. They are as beautiful as ever, 'those brilliant creatures', but for him, since he first saw them and 'trod with a lighter tread', everything is changed. And the pathos is that nothing has changed, nothing seems to have changed for them (there is an echo of Keats's feeling about the nightingale : 'Thou wast not born for death, Immortal Bird!') 'Passion and conquest, wander where they will' attend not only on the swans, but on Yeats's own poems, on all achieved works of art. The phrase 'passion and conquest', if we bear in mind his own story, seems resonant with his passion for an unconquered Maud Gonne, his passion for a truly Irish theatre – and the unconquered Dublin audience. Even a phrase like 'wander where they will' has moving personal echoes. As a boy, we learn from his autobiographies, Yeats used to 'wander where he would', especially by trees and running water, dreamily making up poems and stories. But the life of a mature poet is what he elsewhere calls 'a sedentary trade' : for the last 20 years he had been tied to his desk, to a very high labour, but still with something of drudgery in it.

The last stanza is very gentle and moving. The swans are not only beautiful poems, they are the images of natural beauty, the natural symbols, out of which all true poetry is made. It is Yeats's privilege as a poet to respond to them, in a state almost of dream or trance, but even that privilege may not last for ever :

> But now they drift on the still water,
> Mysterious, beautiful;
> Among what rushes will they build,
> By what lake's edge or pool
> Delight men's eyes when I awake some day
> To find they have flown away?

The tiredness, the extreme fatigue, behind the poem is perhaps reflected in Yeats's contentedness with worn emotive counters like 'mysterious' and 'beautiful'; yet we cannot be certain of this for, though his diction in his later poems became much sharper edged, his rhythms more like those of passionate or witty conversation, he never wholly relinquished this poetic language of his youth. And, in fact, having gone out of fashion for a time, it now seems timeless : a line like 'Mysterious, beautiful' seems right because of its weight and cadence and because it is what Yeats would naturally say.

Yeats is saying, in fact, in this last stanza, that beauty is like the wind of the spirit which blows where it listeth; it may leave him high and dry, and he may awake some day to find that the swans have left him; but he cares more for beauty, for the fortunes of beauty, than for himself, and so the stanza seems not pettily repining, but movingly generous and noble. (I have seen it suggested that, after death, when he 'awakes' to Reality the swans, which however beautiful represent mere Appearance, will have vanished : no doubt this interpretation can find backing in *some* of Yeats's very varied and not always obviously consistent religious and philosophical ideas, but it seems to me dead against the current of feeling in the poem.) When the volume *The Wild Swans at Coole* came out, Middleton Murry condemned it as the work of a tired, cold, used-up 'aesthete'. He looks silly now, since Yeats went on to write such very great work; but he had, though in an unjustly censorious way, divined a central mood of this and other poems in the volume.

(2)

Yeats's 'Easter 1916', perhaps his greatest tragic poem on human politics, should be read alongside an earlier poem with a similar title, 'September 1913'. The earlier poem was written in a mood of disillusionment and with contempt for the character, particularly of the devout, shopkeeping Dublin Catholic lower middle classes. Yeats saw these as men born to 'pray and save', cautious, cold-hearted, indifferent to the romantic tragedy of Ireland's past :

> *Romantic Ireland's dead and gone,*
> *It's with O'Leary in the grave.*

The Easter Rebellion was an attempt by extreme Irish nationalists, while Great Britain was busy with the Great War, to seize some public buildings in Dublin, notably the General Post Office, and proclaim a Republic. Some of the leaders hoped that this might lead to a general rising. Others, knowing they would be defeated, realized the symbolic value, for a nation struggling for freedom, of a gallant defeat. The rebels surrendered after some days of quite heavy fighting. The English government court-martialled and shot 16 of the chief leaders, thereby creating new heroes for Irish legend. It was clear that romantic Ireland was by no means dead and gone.

The rebellion took Yeats completely by surprise. The main leaders, apart from one romantic aristocrat, Countess Marciewicz, came from the lower middle classes whom he had despised. Some were minor poets whom he had not thought much of. One was Major MacBride, who was the husband (though they had been separated for some years) of Yeats's beloved Maud Gonne. Yeats hated MacBride both for having married Maud and for having treated her brutally : MacBride was a coarse, hard-drinking soldier of fortune. Yet Yeats, with his extraordinary magnanimity, has to recognize MacBride too as a hero :

> *This other man I had dreamed*
> *A drunken, vainglorious lout.*
> *He had done most bitter wrong*
> *To some who are near my heart,*
> *Yet I number him in the song ...*

The title of the poem suggests that it is partly a retraction of, or apology for, 'September 1913'. Yeats is acknowledging that he had completely misjudged the character of the ordinary Irishman and the mood of contemporary Ireland.

The poem is in four sections, the first and third of 16 lines each, and the second and fourth of 24 lines each. The first, second, and last sections end with a line which has the effect of a celebratory refrain : 'A terrible beauty is born'. The third section ends with a line which has a very different effect : 'The stone's in the midst of all'. The rhymes in each section go in successive quatrains, a, b, a, b, c, d, c, d, but with a use of half-rhymes or off-rhymes, 'faces', 'houses', 'club', 'gibe', 'beautiful', 'school', 'hers', 'harriers'; the last two pairs there reflect Anglo-Irish phonetics, the first two pairs are to give an effect of casual conversational ease. The stress-pattern of the lines reinforces this conversational effect,

> *I have* met *them at* close *of* day
> Com*ing with* viv*id* faces
> *From* coun*ter or* desk *among* grey
> Eigh*teenth*-century houses ...

This is a pattern of three stresses to the line (two of them often stronger than a third, which might sometimes be better called a half-stress). Yeats had no theory of stress metre as Hopkins had and perhaps thought of himself as writing iambic trimeters, with very free substitution; the substitution is so free, that the poem appears at once exquisitely formal and a beautiful reflection of the natural stresses of Yeats's speaking voice. He can thus modulate amazingly from a plain, familiar style,

> *That woman's days were spent*
> *In ignorant good-will,*

to one of the utmost lyrical intensity,

> *That is Heaven's part, our part*
> *To murmur name on name,*
> *As a mother names her child*
> *When sleep at last has come*
> *On limbs that had run wild.*

A knowledge of Irish speech habits adds, in one's reading, to the expressiveness and beauty of many lines. In a word like 'nightfall', which the English pronounce as a trochee, '*night*fall', the Irish pronunciation is spondaic, '*nightfall*' : this makes possible the line,

> *What* is *it but* nightfall?

The Irish tend, also, to emphasize personal pronouns in speech more than the English : and this line,

> Her nights *in* ar*gument,*

should be read aloud with the stresses I have indicated, not as

> *Her* nights *in* argument.

These may seem trivial technical points to be making in the analysis of a poem whose greatness lies so much in its moral substance. But the most notable of all Yeats's technical gifts was his absolute mastery of rhythm, including pace and pitch and pause and variation of pace, pitch and pause; this mastery gives his poems their suppleness and life, and critics have paid remarkably little attention to it.

But the moral substance of the poem is certainly magnificent. In the first section Yeats describes the mood of lassitude, greyness, trivial jocular malice, which he had accepted as the permanent mood of Dublin, a mood of 'mocking' and 'motley'; he admits he was completely wrong:

All changed, changed utterly:
A terrible beauty is born.

In the second section he sets out to celebrate the leaders of the rebellion; the beautiful Constance Markiewicz, once the aristocratic beauty of her countryside, her sweet voice now grown shrill with political exhortation; schoolmasters and minor poets who might, just might, have come to something; MacBride, a drunken bully suddenly become a legendary hero. Apart from Constance Markiewicz (and in his heart he wishes, as we can see in his later elegy for her and her sister, that she had remained a gentle beauty and not become a heroic fanatic), they are people whom he would ordinarily find drab or disapprove of: but he humbles himself before them, as heroically transformed.

The third section is the most concentratedly beautiful part of the poem. It is a sustained long metaphor. The hearts of the rebels, 'hearts with one purpose alone', are like a stone in the midst of a stream where clouds are moving, horses are passing, birds are flying, everything is changing 'minute by minute' but

The stone's in the midst of all.

We feel the heroism of the stone, but also in the rest of the metaphor Yeats's wistfulness for the gentle changing peace that is life. Fanaticism is heroic, but it is also an image of death: and in the last section he underlines that,

Too long a sacrifice
Can make a stone of the heart.

He has the courage to ask whether perhaps this death was needless. Loyal to his own moderation, he points out that 'England may keep faith/For all that is done and said'. And it is no good saying that the heroes of 1916 have fallen asleep. They are dead. But even if they died in error ('bewildered') it was 'excess of love' for Ireland that bewildered them. They are dead, and there is nothing now but to name their sacred names, and celebrate them. They have become a part of the Irish legend, and they have transformed Irish history. Yeats makes his splendid gesture of salutation to heroic simplicity without surrendering the complexity of his own mind.

(3)

Yeats's 'Sailing to Byzantium' should be read alongside the later poem 'Byzantium', which treats the same theme in a richer and perhaps more exciting but certainly more confusing way. In comparison to 'Byzantium', 'Sailing to Byzantium' could be called almost a classical poem, but it has its own difficulties. I shall confine myself to the earlier poem, for it would be impossible to give even an adequate skeletonic analysis of both poems in a mere thousand words.

Byzantium was the capital of the Eastern Roman Empire, an Empire of Hellenistic Christian culture, which lasted much longer than the Roman Empire proper, from the third century AD to the fifteenth. It preserved itself by astute diplomacy more than by war, and was the centre of an extremely conservative civilization. For Gibbon and for most nineteenth-century historians, it was an image of stagnation, but for its great late-Victorian historian Bury and for the modern historian of the Crusades, Sir Steven Runciman, it represents a higher civilization than Frankish civilization, the in many ways very rough and ready civilization of medieval Western Europe. Yeats had never been to Byzantium (that is, to Istanbul, once Constantinople) but he had seen Byzantine mosaics in Ravenna and had been fascinated by accounts of the wonderful craftsmanship of the Byzantines, notably by a story of a golden clockwork bird that sang for the Emperor. He also in his otherworldly moods admired the otherworldly, anti-humanistic mood of Byzantine art and architecture. Obsessed with theology, liturgy, and an art and craftsmanship wholly devoted to religious subjects, Byzantine civilization seemed to him admirable as one concentrated on eternal rather than temporal things. In this poem, Byzantium stands largely for the permanence of art and thought as against the transience of mere animal life.

Yeats, however, always thinks in antitheses. The first stanza of the poem, beginning 'This is no country for old men' is not about Byzantium, but about the old Irish pagan country of eternal youth, love-making, fighting, diversion, which he had celebrated in his earliest long poem, 'The Wanderings of Oisin'. It is a country of love but also of 'dying generations'. Yeats talks of 'the salmon-falls, the mackerel-crowded seas' and we remember that these are rich, oily fishes (so suggesting sensuality), that the salmon can leap up over waterfalls (the energy of youth) but also that the mackerel goes bad very soon after it is caught (the transience of sensuality and youthful blind energy). If we fling ourselves into the transient we can merely praise the transient ('whatever is begotten, born, and dies') and we neglect the permanent products of man's mind, art and philosophy, for instance, 'monuments of unageing intellect'.

Nevertheless, though he realizes that the world of youthful sensual delight is no longer for him, Yeats in the second stanza notes than an aged man, without youthful physical energy, is a wretched thing unless

> Soul clap its hands, and sing, and louder sing
> For every tatter in its mortal dress.

Yeats is probably remembering these two famous lines by the Caroline and Restoration poet, Edmund Waller :

> *The soul's dark cottage, battered and decayed,*
> *Lets in new light through chinks that time has made,*

and the idea is basically the same : that physical decay should be counter-balanced by, and should lead to, new spiritual energy and insight. It is as a symbolic source of that insight that Yeats at the end of the stanza (having sailed over the rough seas of life) seeks haven in Byzantium.

In the third stanza, once in Byzantium, he addresses himself to the saints depicted in mosaic on the walls of churches ('O sages standing in God's holy fire') : the holy fire is partly a reference to the fires of purgatory, partly to the abundant use of gilt and also to the fiery glint of glass pinnings between the marble chips in Byzantine mosaic portraiture. Saints would be standing in light not in fire, but possibly sages (in the sense of pre-Christian philo-sophers, who had a vision of truth, like Yeats's favourite Plotinus) might be there. Yeats asks these saints or sages to teach his soul, which always means for him the eternal and simple part of his being, to sing, that is, to teach it harmony and wisdom. He longs also for their fire to burn his heart away, and by his heart in antithesis to his soul he means all his human and worldly passions, including the passion of love. The heart is 'sick with desire/And fastened to a dying animal/It knows not what it is' : it should be noticed that the stress on the heart's pain here is, whether intentionally or not, far more incisive and moving than the stress on the soul's aspirations. Though the country of the body may not be a country for old men, we cannot be sure that Yeats is yet free of it. It is perhaps more to escape from the 'sick heart' than to teach the soul to sing that he wishes to escape into 'the artifice of eternity'.

That last phrase is very puzzling, and is a key phrase in the poem. One thing to note is that Yeats believed it to be literally true that when we die, the next world we find ourselves living in (not the permanent next world, for he also believed that we are sooner or later born again) is furnished out of our imaginations with the beautiful things, or images of them, that we have most admired in this world. As he had written in 'The Tower' :

> *I have prepared my peace*
> *With learned Italian things*
> *And the proud stones of Greece,*

But another thing to note is that it is of course a very ancient commonplace in poetry (at least as old as Horace's *aere perennius*, his claim that his poetry was 'more lasting than brass') for a poet to claim that though he dies his poems will be immortal, and that he will have at least a vicarious immor-tality in his poetry.

In the last stanza, certainly, Yeats seems to be thinking of poems when he says he wants in the next world, or once he is dead, to take his 'bodily form' not from any 'natural thing' but from such a form as the golden clockwork singing nightingale which craftsmen made for one of the Emperors of Byzantium. (I feel also, however, that he may have had obscurely at the back of his mind the clockwork nightingale in Hans Andersen's story about the Emperor of China; this bird proved in the end a very poor substitute for a real nightingale.) If he has a kind of eternity like that of a clockwork bird singing the same song over and over again, this is not unlike the eternity of a dead poet who, whenever we open his book at the same page, will sing the same song to us. It is perhaps for the sick heart, fastened to a dying animal, not a wholly satisfactory eternity : there seems, at least to me, to be a great deal of irony in the last four lines :

> ... To keep a drowsy Emperor awake:
> Or set upon a golden bough to sing
> To lords and ladies of Byzantium
> Of what is past, or passing, or to come.

Alfred Alvarez has noted how effectively the line in the last stanza,

> Of what is past, or passing, or to come,

echoes in structure as well as sense the line in the first stanza,

> Whatever is begotten, born, and dies.

The aged poet, in fact, seeks to escape from the Transience of Life to the Permanence of Art, but finds that all Art can celebrate is the Transience, and of course the Joy and Pain, of Life. A similar pattern of escape from Life to Art, and return to Life, can be found in 'Byzantium'. I do not find this weak; it is rather that Yeats's greatness was such that, even when pursuing fantasy quite deliberately he found himself in the end, through fantasy, heroically re-encountering reality.

(4)

The Irish poet and story-teller, Frank O'Connor, gave a lecture on Yeats at Trinity College, Dublin in 1965, Yeats's centenary year, which was broadcast on BBC television. (O'Connor, sadly, died very shortly after paying this tribute to his great friend.) One of O'Connor's main points was that it is wrong to think of Yeats, in his lyrical mode, as primarily a great love-poet. In Yeats's poems to Maud Gonne there is an element of strained idealism, of bitterness, of hurt self-regard. His long hopeless devotion made him look a little absurd, and he could not help seeing this. Yeats has written no love poems with the naked desolate tenderness and the absolute honesty of feeling of the poems which Thomas Hardy, at the age of 70, wrote about his memories of his early happiness with his estranged dead wife.

On the other hand, O'Connor thought that Yeats was probably the greatest poet of friendship in the English language. As a friend, Yeats had very great gifts of affection, admiration for noble qualities combined with humorous perception of a friend's endearing weaknesses, understanding, and forgiveness. These two poems, 'In Memory of Major Robert Gregory' and 'The Municipal Gallery Revisited', the first of which belongs to Yeats's early fifties, having been published in the *English Review* in August 1918, the other to his last years, having come out in a small pamphlet, *A Speech and Two Poems*, in 1937, two years before Yeats's death, are both essentially celebrations of friendship. Both have the easy, relaxed, informal tone, a conversational note, but one capable of modulating to formal rhetoric or lyrical intensity, which always marks those poems of Yeats's springing from a mood of affectionate reminiscence.

Robert Gregory was the son of Yeats's great friend and patroness, Lady Gregory. He was a young man of great charm and talent, a typical Irish country gentleman in his love for horses and hunting, but also a water-colour painter of some talent, and interested in all the arts. For Yeats, he represented one type of ideal man, the Renaissance courtier who excels in everything he sets his hand to, but at the same time does everything with a certain ease and indifference, with what Castiglione, in his book *Il Cortigiano*, calls *sprezzatura* (a certain gentlemanly disdain for mere professionalism). Yeats, very much a professional himself, had almost a wistful admiration for this kind of all-roundedness. Gregory had been killed in the First World War, as an airman, driven to his death, Yeats suggests in another poem, not by any passionate belief in the rightness of the Allied cause or hatred of the Central Powers, but by the impulse of the cavalier, the knight, to risk life gallantly : by 'a lonely impulse of delight'. Yeats wrote the poem mainly to console Lady Gregory, but the thought of Gregory's death brought to mind other dead friends, more intimate ones, of Yeats's own youth in the 1890s and his struggle for the Abbey Theatre in the 1900s : Lionel Johnson and John Synge. Also, because he is newly married, has almost settled in the half-ruined tower, Thoor Ballylee, which Lady Gregory had given him, and is becoming a family man, he thinks of his own family, his old uncle George Pollexfen, who was, in youth, like Robert Gregory, a sportsman, a lover of horses, but in old age became a mystical astrologer, 'sluggish and contemplative'.

The stanza form of this poem, Professor Frank Kermode has pointed out in his important book, *The Romantic Image*, is borrowed from that of a poem by the late metaphysical poet, Abraham Cowley, on the death of his friend, William Harvey. The stanza lends itself to a quiet and natural movement of feeling, and an effective use of short, plain words. The poem begins very quietly. Now that he and Mrs Yeats are almost settled in their new house, and are talking late by the fire, Yeats feels an impulse to name 'the friends that cannot sup with us'. He is aware of the danger of introducing new friends to old; they often do not like each other, but there is no danger of quarrels when all the friends one brings together are dead.

He thinks first of his early friend Lionel Johnson, the type, for him, of a fastidious devotion at once to learning and to religion. He then thinks of John Synge for his loneliness, his dedication to the lively art of the theatre, even in mortal sickness, his love of the Aran islanders, his 'passionate and simple' heart. The picture of old George Pollexfen, the racing man turned astrologer, has a touch of humour, of affectionate mockery, not found in the other two. The thought of these earlier deaths leads to the thought of Gregory's death: and the tone here grows more deliberately formal and celebratory:

> I am accustomed to their lack of breath,
> But not that my dear friend's dear son,
> Our Sidney and our perfect man,
> Could share in that discourtesy of death.

In turn, Yeats then celebrates Gregory's love of his native countryside: his daring as a horseman,

> ... and where was it
> He rode a horse without a bit?
> And yet his mind outran the horses' feet.

Gregory could have been a great painter; he was an expert in architecture and interior decoration, and could have advised the Yeatses about their new house. But he was one of these Renaissance men who must die young. Yeats had begun at this time to show a great interest in Donne, and this extravagant but exact metaphor is very much in Donne's manner:

> Some burn damp faggots, others may consume
> The entire combustible world in one small room
> As though dried straw, and if we turn about
> The bare chimney is gone black out ...

In the last stanza, Yeats says that he had thought 'seeing how bitter is that wind' (and he is thinking of the dark storm of violence gathering over Ireland, not merely of the outer physical weather) to call to mind all the friends he had loved but

> ... the thought
> Of that late death took all my heart for speech.

In fact, he has already said, and nobly, all that can be said of Gregory, but the gesture of modest inadequacy is appropriately in tone. Yeats in a sense withdraws himself, withholds any proud statement of his own achievement, so that we do not reflect that the men he commemorates so splendidly interest us now mainly (except for Synge, a minor genius in his own right) through their relationship to Yeats. The homely language, typified by the ten monosyllables of the last line, just quoted, somehow enhances one's sense of Yeats's generous humility.

'The Municipal Gallery Revisited', though written nearly 20 years later, is remarkably similar in tone and diction; but where 'In Memory of Major

Robert Gregory' has a remarkably firm logical construction, disguised by the ease of its manner, some critics have found the later poem a little rambling in construction, and even careless in detail. One stanza, the fifth, has seven lines instead of eight, and begins with a line which seems a little out of character,

> *My medieval knees lack health until they bend.*

Here and there in the poem a feeling is stated, rather than expressed :

> *Heart-smitten with emotion I sink down.*

Yet, even more miraculously than in the earlier poem, Yeats in his early seventies seems to have mastered the art of turning the manner of swift, casual, lively talk, a moment of reminiscence,

> *Before a woman's portrait suddenly I stand,*
> *Beautiful and gentle in her Venetian way.*
> *I met her all but fifty years ago*
> *For twenty minutes in some studio,*

or a condensed piece of art-criticism :

> *Mancini's portrait of Augusta Gregory,*
> *'Greatest since Rembrandt', according to John Synge:*
> *A great ebullient portrait certainly ...*

into high poetry. The 'fifty years', the 'twenty minutes' in the first quotation give strange and exact precision to the old topic of the passing of the glory of the world, the triumph of time. The phrase 'in her Venetian way' suggests the fastidious and exact connoisseurship of the wonderful old man both in the beauty of paintings and the beauty of women. In the second quotation the adjective 'ebullient' is a splendidly courteous correction of Synge's extravagant praise. The style of the great old poet, like that of many great artists (though one thinks of painters' rather than poets) in old age, has become a kind of masterly shorthand. And the last stanza is wonderful, again, in its proud humility :

> *Think where man's glory most begins and ends,*
> *And say my glory was I had such friends.*

(5)

'The Second Coming' was first published in the American magazine, *The Dial*, in November 1920. It reflects some of Yeats's most esoteric ideas, the ideas which he was to develop in his book of occult philosophy, *A Vision*, yet strangely enough it has been one of Yeats's most popular poems. Readers not at all interested in Yeats's 'system' have seen it as a vivid prophecy of the advent of Fascist and other totalitarian systems and of the growing destructiveness of war and dehumanization of political activity in our time. It may well be that Yeats's reaction, less against the First World War, which did not deeply engage his emotions, than against the growing violence of rebellion, repression, and finally Civil War in Ireland, was the deep emotional spring of the poem.

The poem is in blank verse, though its texture is enriched by typical Yeatsian half-rhymes, or Anglo-Irish rhymes, like 'gyre' and 'falconer', 'hold' and 'world', 'man' and 'sun'. The first section is notable, and rather unusual in Yeats, for its deliberate use of a kind of high rhetoric rather than images: 'Mere anarchy' ... 'The blood-dimmed tide' ... 'The ceremony of innocence' ... He is making, with passion, a great abstract statement, that our civilization has lost its inner coherence, its sense of direction and control :

> The best lack all conviction, while the worst
> Are full of passionate intensity.

The first section is a prelude to a second section which, by contrast, is deliberately pictorial, in, for Yeats, a rather hard and Parnassian way. The disorder of the world is a prelude, surely, to some revelation. He repeats, twice, the phrase, 'The Second Coming', but with mounting irony. For the image which appears before him, out of the *Spiritus Mundi* (in Yeats's system, roughly the equivalent of Jung's 'collective unconscious') is certainly not Christ come again to judge the world. More directly, in fact, than out of the *Spiritus Mundi* it is out of the British Museum, which Yeats frequented a great deal when he was in London. It is one of these frightening Assyrian lions with bird's wings and bearded human faces, which make us think how utterly alien to us some early civilizations are. It represents an unpitying mindless fierceness :

> ... somewhere in the sands of the desert
> A shape with lion body and the head of a man,
> A gaze blank and pitiless as the sun,
> Is moving its slow thighs, while all about it
> Reel shadows of the indignant desert birds.

It is this 'rough beast', not Christ, which 'slouches' towards Bethlehem to be born. It is the emblem of some primeval savagery which 20 centuries of Christianity have put under a spell but not killed :

> The darkness drops again; but now I know
> That twenty centuries of stony sleep
> Were vexed to nightmare by a rocking cradle ...

The 'rocking cradle' is that, of course, of the baby Jesus, the Christian birth-story. The primeval Assyrian creature has been frozen as it were by the Christian miracle into a stony sleep but also 'vexed to nightmare' by the new gospel of gentleness and is now being born to bring in a new dispensation of incredible horror and terror.

It is difficult to say either that Yeats believed, or disbelieved, in Christianity. He believed in it as one of a number of successive revelations, each of which dominated Western culture for about two thousand years, and each of which seems to contradict, or state the antithesis of, the previous dispensation, to make nonsense of a whole accepted set of values. As the Assyrian beast denies everything that is at the heart of Christianity, so Christianity, he believed, denied everything that was at the heart of the Greek and Roman pagan world.

In his play *Resurrection*, for which 'Two Songs from a Play' were written, this view is stated clearly. To a Jew in the play, Jesus is not the Messiah, and this in a way is a relief. To a Greek, Jesus was divine but not human; he did not really suffer on the cross, for he was merely an apparition, a phantasm. The cult of the resurrected Jesus is also connected with the cult of the slain Dionysus, one of the newer developments of late classical religion, with a strong emotional element, an appeal to slaves and women, and with Eastern roots. The climax of the play is the moment when the Greek touches the body of the resurrected Christ and cries out, in awe and horror: 'The heart of a phantom is beating!' A sudden violent miracle has made nonsense, once more, of all the assumptions of a culture. In the new Christian dispensation, God comes down to earth and shares man's most humiliating sufferings; at the same time, unlike the Greek gods, who kept their distance, and kept man at his distance, Christ wants man to turn away from love of the beauty of the world and to make him aspire to the imitation of Christ himself. The two songs in *Resurrection* celebrate this new revelation with a mixture of awe, triumph, and horror.

The first song is hard to understand unless one can see that for Yeats the death of Dionysus was a type of Christ's death and resurrection, or, more accurately, another form of the same archetypal revelation. (Christianity and classical mythology were both, for Yeats, 'true' and he meant something more than 'poetically true'.) Both Christ and Dionysus died and were resurrected 'at the spring'. Both died under the astrological signs of Virgo, the virgin holding in her hand the star Spica, and when Dionysus was torn to pieces Athena ('the staring Virgin') rescued his heart. (The bleeding heart of Jesus is, of course, a special object of Roman Catholic devotion.) The deaths and resurrections of both Christ and Dionysus usher in a new cycle of civilization, Plato's 'Magnus Annus', or great year: for Yeats, as has been said, this was an historical cycle of about two thousand years. Yeats is not eccentric, or not so eccentric as he seems, in accepting a cyclical theory of history: his predecessors include Vico and Nietzsche, and Yeats himself noted the uncanny resemblance between his own cyclical theories in *A Vision* and Spengler's in his almost exactly contemporary *Decline of the West*.

Yeats does not, however, seem to accept his own theory of eternal recur-

rence happily, with a Nietzschean *amor fati*. A miraculous death and resurrection should usher in a new Golden Age, but the sardonic and desperate
tone of the beginning of the second stanza suggests a horror of endless meaningless repetition of human folly and violence. I emphasize words and phrases
which suggest this disgust and contempt:

> *Another Troy must rise and set,*
> *Another lineage feed the* crow,
> *Another Argo's* painted *prow*
> *Drive to a* flashier bauble *yet.*

The adjective 'painted' need not have this flavour, need not suggest, say,
rouge on a raddled complexion, or gilt on rotting wood, but it clearly acquires this tone from its context. And the effect of the Christian revelation
is, in fact, to bring things to a stop:

> *The Roman Empire stood appalled:*
> *It dropped the reins of peace and war*
> *When that fierce Virgin and her Star*
> *Out of the fabulous darkness called.*

I think the meaning of the stanza as a whole may be deeper than Yeats's conscious intention. We do not, as it were, *want* the endless flashy repetition of
classical violence. One perhaps thinks of the fierce Virgin and her Star as
breaking the endless circling of history rather than reinforcing it.

The second song is less difficult, though the phrase 'the fabulous, formless
darkness' has important connotations, which most readers would not immediately grasp. A neo-Platonist philosopher, Proclus, thought of Christianity
as a 'fabulous, formless darkness' that had come in from the East and destroyed both the balance and harmony of the classical culture and the fair
images of the classical gods. Like most late Hellenistic neo-Platonists, Proclus
was willing to accept the classical gods, if he might put a moralizing or metaphysical interpretation on them. It is this 'Platonic tolerance' which the brute
violence of miracle, the irruption of the actual Divine, its acceptance of
suffering, 'odour of blood when Christ was slain', had dissolved. The 'Doric
discipline', the simple and athletic harmony of early Greek culture, is destroyed too. Readers who have not been brought up in a Christian tradition
might be referred to St Paul's account of how the Christian gospel offended
the two main groups to whom he preached. The gospel of Christ crucified
was 'to the Jews a stumbling-block, to the Greeks foolishness'. It was a
stumbling-block to the Jews that their Messiah should, instead of triumph-
ing, die like a common criminal, and for all men, not just for them: that
Love should triumph over the Law; it was to the Greeks foolishness that any
God could suffer, or care enough for men to suffer for them.

The second stanza of the second song has no difficult mythological, philosophical, or theological references; it triumphs, paradoxically, in the triumph

of time, in the way in which man's most splendid energies consume and destroy themselves, so that there may be space for renewal. As Yeats said in another poem,

> *Man is in love and loves what vanishes.*
> *What more is there to say?*

The last two lines of this stanza are like a variation on these lines:

> *Whatever flames upon the night*
> *Man's own resinous heart has fed.*

Resinous wood, like the wood of pine trees, burns of course brightly and aromatically: the paradoxical image of accepted disaster as the final triumph, of destruction as the guarantee of the perpetuity of human energies, is re-current in Yeats. His meaning might almost be a neo-Voltairean one: the greatness and nobility of man's religious images and his sacred myths may merely reflect man's own needs, but then how sublime these needs are! As a poet dealing with religious themes (I think he was never, by temperament, something quite different, a 'religious poet'), Yeats shows an imaginative sym-pathy for contradictory attitudes, is largely and splendidly human. He has something to offer devout Christians and he has something to offer to atheis-tic humanists, if they share his own vivid and intuitive historical imagination. Even in poems like 'Two Songs from a Play' and 'The Second Coming', which are in a sense doctrinal, doctrine, or special knowledge or learning, is only an element in a total composition: Yeats is a great poet because he shares, and appeals to, the whole rich contradictory flux of human experience; because he puts down no shutters, puts on no blinkers, and is, in the end, however rich and strangely embroidered his singing robes, a 'poet of reality'.

3 · YEATS AND THE BALLAD STYLE

Shenandoah: The Washington and Lee University Review (Lexington, Virginia, XXI no. 3 (Spring 1970).

One of the most obvious elements of continuity in Yeats's poetry is the regular recurrence, among poems of complex thought and of subtle and difficult modulation of feeling, among poems also of ornate diction and of rhythm delicately modulated to changes of feeling, of poems of a quiet different sort: poems simple in thought, sweeping and obvious in their rhythmical appeal, broad and popular in their emotional impact, sometimes violent and coarse in their invective or their sensuality. Such poems in their style often remind us either of genuine traditional ballads or folk-songs or of broadsheet ballads and popular songs, of the kind which generally do not claim to be literature; though Yeats can also write literary ballads, like 'The Cap and Bells', deriving ultimately through the pre-Raphaelites from the tradition established by Keats's brilliant use of the objective ballad technique to express a subjective romantic agony, 'La Belle Dame sans Merci'.

Yeats's more important sources, however, are of a non-literary or sub-literary kind. In one of his most complex poems, 'Easter 1916', he alludes at the end to a very popular song of very little poetic or literary merit, 'The Wearing of the Green': in another difficult poem, 'Lapis Lazuli', he brings in a quotation from the crude Orange ballad, 'The Battle of the Boyne'. The main important tradition of popular song and balladry in Ireland was, of course, in Irish Gaelic, which Yeats never learned to speak or read currently. But throughout the nineteenth century, various Irish poets, of whom the most famous was James Clarence Mangan and the most accomplished was Sir Samuel Ferguson, had been translating such popular Irish poetry, and bringing across, at least, a spirit, a rhythm, and various recurrent images, which Yeats would be able to use. One might quote one of Ferguson's finest translations, 'Cashel of Munster', which in rhythm, diction, and mood looks forward very much to early Yeats:

> *I'd wed you without herds, without money, or rich array,*
> *And I'd wed you on a dewy morning, at day-dawn grey;*
> *My bitter woe it is, love, that we are not far away*
> *In Cashel town, though the bare deal boards were our*
> > *marriage-bed this day!*

> *Oh, fair maid, remember the green hill-side,*
> *Remember how I haunted about the valleys wide;*
> *Time now has worn me; my locks are turned to grey,*
> *The year is scarce, and I am poor, but send me not, love, away.*

Compare the rhythms and indeed the rhymes of the last stanza of 'The Lake Isle of Innisfree' :

> *I will arise and go now, for always night and day*
> *I hear lake water lapping with low sounds by the shore;*
> *While I stand on the roadway, or on the pavements grey,*
> *I hear it in the deep heart's core.*

I do not mean that there is any direct derivation, or that the rhythmical pattern is identical, or, indeed, that 'Cashel of Munster' is not a very much better poem than 'The Lake Isle of Innisfree'. But the family resemblance is obvious, and Yeats's debt to these earlier nineteenth-century poets and translators, whose patriotic spirit he admired, but whose often slapdash technique he on the whole deplored, could bear a good deal of looking into.

My subject now, however, is a rather wider one. I am interested not so much in Yeats's exercises in pure ballad style, as in his incorporation of elements of ballad style into poems of quite a different sort, and in just what, poetically, the ballad style meant to him. In a famous late poem, 'The Municipal Gallery Revisited', Yeats writes :

> *My permanent or impermanent images:*
> *Augusta Gregory's son: her sister's son,*
> *Hugh Lane, 'only begetter' of all these:*
> *Hazel Lavery living and dying, that tale*
> *As though some ballad-singer had sung it all.*

Why does the mention of a ballad-singer seem so apt there, not only in the context of the poem as a whole, but in the setting also of these few lines taken by themselves? Simply, I think, because in true ballad style, the naming of a name, of a relationship, is, for the assumed closely-knit tribal audience, sufficient shorthand for what, in an art poem, would demand elaborate description. Compare 'The Battle of Otterbourne' :

> *He chose the Gordons and the Graemes,*
> *With them the Lindsays, light and gay:*
> *But the Jardines wald not with them ride*
> *And they rue it to this day.*

Or compare, and the resemblance is much closer, another of these Victorian translators of old Irish Gaelic popular poetry, George Fox, in his version of 'The County of Mayo' :

'Tis my grief that Patrick Loughlin is not Earl in Irrul still,
And that Brian Duff no longer rules as Lord upon the Hill;
And that Colonel Hugh McGrady should be lying dead and low,
And I sailing, sailing swiftly from the County of Mayo.

Such lines move even readers who are not of the tribe, readers in whom the proper names awaken no echo, or the faintest of echoes, because they convey the proud assurance of a tribal cohesion we have lost. But, in a sense, Yeats, by the time he came to write 'The Municipal Gallery Revisited', had created his own tribe, to whom he could communicate in his own balladic shorthand: we know that Augusta Gregory was the great patron and support of Yeats and of the Abbey Theatre, the translator and popularizer also of the old Irish epics; that Robert Gregory was in Yeats's eyes 'our Sidney and our perfect man', the one all-round Renaissance man that the Irish Renaissance produced; we know about Hugh Lane and all the row about his pictures; Sir John Lavery is a painter almost forgotten, but if we are sufficiently thorough Yeatsians it is somewhere at the back or corner of our minds that his wife was a great beauty, who died painfully, as Mabel Beardsley had, but preserving like Mabel Beardsley her poise and gaiety to the last. These people were also all Protestant Irish gentlefolk, but nationalists without being democrats:

The people of Burke and Grattan,
Who gave though free to refuse ...

This habit of shorthand is to be seen everywhere in Yeats's later poems. Maud Gonne, in the early poems and even up to 'Responsibilities', is not presented directly, but in metaphor: twice, significantly, the metaphor of a cloud, or one treading on a cloud:

For she had fiery blood
When I was young,
And trod so sweetly proud
As 'twere upon a cloud ...

A crowd
Will gather, and not know it walks the very street
Whereon a thing once walked that seemed a burning cloud ...

And once she is a sun obscured by clouds:

These are the clouds about the fallen sun,
The majesty that shuts his burning eye ...

But in 'Beautiful Lofty Things' from Last Poems we get again, and in a sense how much more humanly vivid it is, the uncloudy presentation of a character, again in what I would call balladic shorthand:

... Maud Gonne at Howth station waiting a train,
Pallas Athene in that straight back and arrogant head ...

The kind of influence I have been talking about so far, from Gaelic Irish poetry in translation, are 'literary' both in the sense that some of the translations, those I have quoted from George Fox and Samuel Ferguson, for instance, are of high literary quality, and in the sense that Yeats got them from books. There was another, a different influence, from Irish political poems in English, full of passionate feeling, but with a broadsheet ballad crudeness in their technique. I think that Yeats as a young man, admiring the passion, revolted against the crudity, but as an old man began to find a kind of earthy savour in it. Here are some stanzas from a typical good–bad poem of this sort, William Drennan's 'The Wake of William Orr'. The poem opens thus:

There our murdered brother lies;
Wake him not with women's cries;
Mourn the way that manhood ought –
Sit in silent trance of thought.

Write his merits on your mind;
Morals pure and manners kind;
In his head, as on a hill,
Virtue placed her citadel.

Why cut off in palmy youth?
Truth he spoke, and acted truth.
'Countrymen, UNITE', he cried
And died for what our Saviour died.

One feels in this a directness, a strong emotion, but one may be worried by the eighteenth-century *clichés*, and by the queer truncated syntax: 'Mourn the way that manhood ought': 'And died for what his Saviour died'. But it gets much better:

Hunted thro' thy native grounds,
Or flung rewards to human hounds,
Each one pulled and tore his share,
Heedless of thy deep despair.

Hapless Nation! Hapless Land!
Heap of uncementing sand!
Crumbled by a foreign weight:
And by worse, domestic hate.

God of Mercy! God of peace!
Make this mad confusion cease!
O'er the mental chaos move,
Through it speak the light of love.

What does it remind you of? It reminds me very much, in the beat of the rhythm, of Blake's 'The Tiger'. Compare:

> *Hapless Nation! Hapless Land!*
> *Heap of uncementing sand!*
> *Crumpled by a foreign weight:*
> *And by worse, domestic hate,*

with

> *What the hammer? what the chain?*
> *In what furnace was thy brain?*
> *What the anvil? What dread grasp*
> *Dare its deadly terrors clasp?*

Much of Blake's style in his lyrical poems does, of course, come out of popular poetry of this kind, hymns, broadsheet ballads, poems for children. But a poet very different from Blake, one of Yeats's favourite poets, Shelley, when moved by direct political indignation, could adopt this same broadsheet ballad style:

> *Men of England, wherefore plough*
> *For the lords that lay you low?*

or:

> *I met murder on my way.*
> *He had a mask like Castlereagh.*
> *Very smooth he looked yet grim.*
> *Seven bloodhounds followed him.*

It seems to me that Yeats, in later life, may have become reconciled to this popular broadsheet ballad style when he realized that two poets whom he specially admired, one of whom, Shelley, was a poet of a very wide learning and very fastidious literary taste, were able to use this tradition and somehow hammer great poetry out of it. The two poems in *Last Poems* on Roger Casement seem to me to come out of this tradition, though I have not found a poem in the ballad style written in the hammering form, quatrains made out of two octosyllabic couplets, that appealed to Drennan, Blake, and Shelley:

> *I say that Roger Casement*
> *Did what he had to do.*
> *He died upon the gallows,*
> *But that is nothing new.*

Afraid they might be beaten
Before the bench of Time,
They turned a trick by forgery
And blackened this good name ...

The second Casement poem, 'The Ghost of Roger Casement' is more complex, with a use of ballad refrain, and a mocking use of popular tags of speech and false rhyme. It is a very powerful poem in its way, but less genuinely like a ballad than the first. The ballad style cannot carry very much irony nor can it carry the mixed feelings about England, which I think are here as deep in Yeats as they are in 'Easter 1916', and force him, here, a little towards stridency :

John Bull has stood for Parliament,
A dog must have its day,
The country thinks no end of him,
For he knows how to say,
At a beanfeast or a banquet,
That all must put their trust
Upon the British Empire,
Upon the Church of Christ:
The ghost of Roger Casement
Is beating on the door.

John Bull has gone to India
And all must pay him heed,
For histories are there to prove
That none of another breed
Has had a like inheritance,
Or sucked such milk as he,
And there's no luck about a house
If it lack honesty.
The ghost of Roger Casement
Is beating on the door.

'For there's no luck aboot the hoose/When oor guid man's awa'.' The sudden turn at the end of the last stanza, and the allusion to Mickle's song, are very effective: but the beanfeast, the no end, the rhyme of 'trust' and 'Christ' suggests a forced animus, a willed picture of John Bull as an overfed vulgarian. Yeats, after all, was a great English as well as a great Irish poet, London of the 1890s has half the credit of his formation, many of his dearest friends were English to the end of his life. The last stanza brings out the real pain and contradiction of Yeats's feelings about England and is, therefore, I think, less ballad-like but also more poetical :

I poked about a village church
And found his family tomb

And copied out what I could read
In that religious gloom;
Found many a famous man there;
But fame and virtue rot.
Draw round, beloved and bitter men,
Draw round and raise a shout:
The ghost of Roger Casement
Is beating on the door.

Yeats, in his youth, would have thought a style like that of the Roger Casement poems incredibly vulgar, and I am not sure that he would have been entirely wrong. What he wanted to do at first was to keep the passion of popular Irish poetry and political oratory of the late-eighteenth and nineteenth centuries, but to purge that passion of a taste for coarse and easy rhetoric. Perhaps he realized that this kind of passion needs this kind of rhetoric, and can on occasion ennoble it. But I do not think, for instance, that he can ever have had much real taste or admiration for 'The Wearing of the Green':

I met with Napper Tandy and he tuk me by the hand,
And he said, how's poor old Ireland and how does she stand?
She's the most distressful country that ever you have seen,
They're hanging men and women now for wearing of the green.

It is partly that the ballad has a jaunty, jigging rhythm which makes one feel inappropriately jolly; it is partly that Napper Tandy has a comical name and that, if one knows anything about him, this eloquent old drunk was a singularly absurd and unheroic though in a way sympathetic personage. And the song, too, has a flavour about it of the stage Irishman, a flavour which Yeats, like Shaw, rightly hated. Yet Yeats, in the greatest of all his political poems, 'Easter 1916', brings in a reference to this ballad, which he must have detested. 'Easter 1916' is a poem beautifully balanced in its sympathies, seeing every side of the question with the kind of ironic yet sympathetic impartiality which practical politicians detest. It says that the Easter Rebellion is an act of extraordinary heroism, which Yeats had not expected, led by people whom Yeats either thoroughly disliked, as he disliked Maud Gonne's estranged husband, Major MacBride; or by people whom he loved, but thought destroyed by fanaticism, like Con Markiewicz, Constance Gore-Booth: or by schoolmasters, minor poets, about whom he cannot help being even in the context of heroic elegy faintly patronizing. They have shown a heroism which, in an earlier poem, 'September 1913' he had said they were incapable of: the similar title of Yeats's 'Easter 1916' indicates that it is partly a retraction of the scorn he had flung on the Dublin lower middle classes in the earlier poem. Yet, saluting heroism, he also points out the stony fanaticism which heroism can breed – 'The stone's in the midst of all': 'Too long a sacrifice/Can make a stone of the heart'. And he wonders whether the whole heroic episode is, as a matter of practical policies, foolhardy and unnecessary :

> *For England may keep faith*
> *For all that is done and said.*

Like all really great poems, this, in fact, was one in the width and suppleness of its appreciation of a complex situation not calculated to flatter or appease the rage of faction : Cromwell, similarly, cannot have really enjoyed Marvell's 'Horatian Ode', if he ever read or understood it. I have been told by Ian Fletcher and Donald Gordon of Reading University (Reading has the best Yeats library in England) that Yeats put in his reference to 'The Wearing of the Green' on the advice of a friend who told him that the great poem must somewhere make a gesture towards the most popular, if you like the most vulgar, kind of Irish national mythology. He did so :

> *I write it out in a verse –*
> *MacDonagh and MacBride*
> *And Connolly and Pearse*
> *Now and in time to be,*
> *Wherever green is worn,*
> *Are changed, changed utterly:*
> *A terrible beauty is born.*

There is a balladic use of proper names there, as well as the allusion to 'The Wearing of the Green'. And a year of two ago I made the interesting discovery that the phrase, 'changed, changed utterly', which occurs twice in the poem, and at the end of another section is verbally varied as 'transformed utterly', was not Yeats's own invention, but was lifted, consciously or unconsciously, from a children's book of retold medieval legends and romances, which included a prose retelling of Yeats's own play 'The Countess Cathleen'. The book, like all books retelling heroic stories for children, or indeed like some novels for grown-ups, for instance Sir Walter Scott's *Old Mortality*, was written in what, in a broad but I hope not a meaningless sense, I would call a prose version of the ballad style: set phrases, repetitions, and what Willa Muir in her fine book, *Living with Ballads*, calls 'token characters'.

A number of important ballad poems, and one very moving lyrical non-balladic poem, about Constance Gore-Booth, were written by Yeats around 'Easter 1916'. But before I get on to that, I would like to deal briefly with some interesting instances of Yeats's picking up balladic phrases, like 'changed, changed utterly' in new contexts, and also of his introducing submerged balladic quotations into definitely non-balladic poems. I quoted, at the beginning of this talk, George Fox's very beautiful version of 'The County of Mayo'. In another stanza of that version, there are these lines :

They're altered girls in Irrul now; 'tis proud they're grown and high,
With their hair-bags and their top-knots – for I pass their buckles
by ...

'For I pass their buckles by' : because I do not think their buckles worth men-
tioning : I imagine this is, or was, an Anglo-Irish idiom, since I do not remember hearing it in current English speech, or finding it in English writing,
though its meaning, of course, is quite clear. In a late, great poem of Yeats's,
'The Curse of Cromwell', from *Last Poems*, there are these lines :

They have schooling of their own, but I pass their schooling by,
What can they know that we know that know the time to die?

That particular odd idiomatic phrase, the rhythm of the two couplets, and,
clinchingly, the rhyme, are identical : I would think this is a case of conscious
or unconscious reminiscence of one specific poem in ballad style. And this, I
would think, is how what we call tradition in poetry generally works. The
style of the poetry of a past period does not exist, for a practising poet, as a
set of historical or critical generalizations about itself. It exists as a number of
specific poems, read passionately, and perhaps without much historical or
critical understanding, in youth; in the poet's later years lines, phrases, images
from that early reading may suddenly ask to have themselves rewritten, the
same but different.

Another example of this kind of recurrence of a ballad read in early youth,
or heard in early youth, is odder. 'The Battle of the Boyne', the great Orange
marching song, is a poem of historical importance but ludicrously inept in
its diction :

King James he pitched his tents between
    The lines for to retire:
But King William threw his bomb-balls in,
    And set them all on fire.

In 1938, Yeats published one of the finest of his last poems, 'Lapis Lazuli'. It
opens with a first stanza, in which the poet dissociates himself mockingly
from those who, like most of us in the 1930s, felt that it was the duty of the
poet at that time to warn, to alert us all to do something, even if it seemed
too late, to halt Hitler, to avert the danger of a Second World War. Probably
it was too late, but we honour in retrospect those writers, from Auden to
Orwell, who did warn us. The first short section of Yeats's poem reads :

I have heard hysterical women say
They are sick of the palette and fiddle-bow,
Of poets that are always gay,
For everyone knows or else should know

> *That if nothing drastic is done*
> *Aeroplane and Zeppelin will come out,*
> *Pitch like King Billy bomb-balls in*
> *Until the town is beaten flat.*

The mention of Zeppelins, of course, makes King Billy suggest not only William of Orange but Kaiser Bill of the First World War and these Zeppelin raids which aroused a disproportionate, perhaps hysterical fear. He may also have been remembering King Lear's: 'Down, down *hysterica passio*!' He may have also had in mind his own remark, in his preface to *The Oxford Book of Modern Verse*, that poetry cannot be made out of 'the passive suffering' of war, but only out of war's heroic actions, or out of the kind of cruel farce of ballads like 'O Johnny, I hardly knew ye'. He goes on to say that all tragedy is essentially gay. If 'worthy their prominent parts in the play', tragic heroes and heroines 'do not break up their lines to weep'. He then moves from tragedy to epic, saying that civilizations are always being put to the sword, but that (one might say, like Shiva or Kali, these Hindu deities) destruction is the midwife of creation :

> *All things fall and are built again,*
> *And those that build them again are gay.*

Finally, he moves from the tragic and epic art of the West to the lyrical and contemplative art of the Far East :

> *Two Chinamen, behind them a third,*
> *Are carved in lapis lazuli,*
> *Over them flies a long-legged bird,*
> *A symbol of longevity ...*

He imagines the Chinamen sitting at a little half-way house on a mountain side, no longer contemplating individual tragic agony or epic stories of the destruction of civilizations, but merely the lovely mountain landscape. Yet they are aware, also, however remotely, of human suffering, on the calm beauty of nature as a background for that :

> *There, on the mountain and the sky,*
> *In all the tragic scene they stare.*
> *One asks for mournful melodies;*
> *Accomplished fingers begin to play,*
> *Their eyes 'mid many wrinkles, their eyes,*
> *Their ancient, glittering eyes, are gay.*

This is one of Yeats's most profound and beautiful later poems, and yet most of us probably feel that the basic attitudes it expresses, however right as art or about art, are wrong and dangerous as attitudes to life and society. Looking back on Belsen and Auschwitz and Hiroshima, looking at the world around us today, an attitude of fatalistic gaiety seems callous and inept. The world is neither an art-work or the raw material for one. As Auden says:

> Art is not life, and cannot be
> A midwife to society.

And yet, of course, one remembers that, in war-time, one found this poem more calming and bracing than many poems full of practical counsel and humanitarian good sense. The ballad attitude enabled Yeats to retain a poise, as a poet, which men more immediately, perhaps more humanely involved with the horrors of our time were to lose. Auden has never recommended gaiety: 'How madly ungay when the goldfish die.' The word 'gay' is a ballad word, but also one of these words of Yeats's which to the last have a smack of the 1890s:

> We who are old, old and gay,*
> O so old!
> Thousands of years, thousands of years,
> If all were told . . .

The gaiety in these early lines from 'A Faery Song', first published in 1891, has an oddly doleful cadence or ring about it, as I have remarked elsewhere. Auden, with his basically Christian attitude, very different from Yeats's, does at least now get as near to the moral of 'Lapis Lazuli' as to say that one of our duties to God, however grim the world or our lives may seem, is to be happy; and that an apparent frivolity, in our terrible time, is one of the marks by which we recognize a serious person.

I want now to get on to the ballad poems written around 'Easter 1916'. That poem, as I have said already, is a beautifully fair and just poem, comparable as a heroic meditation on politics only to Marvell's 'Horatian Ode'. It fuses admiration and horror, as Marvell's poem does, or fuses, let us say, the sense of loss and gain. The sense of loss comes out in the lovely poem, 'On a Political Prisoner', about Con Marciewicz:

> She that but little patience knew
> From childhood on, had now so much
> A grey gull lost its fear and flew
> Down to her cell and there alit,
> And there endured her fingers' touch
> And from her fingers ate its bit.
>
> Did she in touching that lone wing
> Recall the years before her mind
> Became a bitter, an abstract thing,
> Her thought some popular enmity:
> Blind and leader of the blind
> Drinking the foul ditch where they lie?

This is the element, in 'Easter 1916', of pure revulsion against the stone in the midst of all: against the hardening of the heart, the fanatical dogmatism, that goes with all popular rebellions. And yet, he seems to say, she is that wild bird, and she has needed her fanaticism, her desertion of her class, to bring out the full beauty of her wildness:

> When long ago I saw her ride
> Under Ben Bulben to the meet,
> The beauty of her countryside
> With all youth's lonely wildness stirred,
> She seemed to have grown clean and sweet
> Like any rock-bred, sea-borne bird:
>
> Sea-borne, or balanced on the air
> When first it sprang out of the nest
> Upon some lofty rock to stare
> Upon the cloudy canopy,
> While under its storm-beaten breast
> Cried out the hollows of the sea.

The point about that poem is that, though excellently plain in its diction, it is *not* a poem in the ballad style, but a poem embodying a subtle modulation of feeling, a complexity of poetical argument, a presentation of character far deeper than the presentation of the token character, things of which the ballad style is incapable. We are presented first with the always restless but always beautiful spirit taming, in her prison cell, with unexpected gentleness and patience a wild bird. Taming that bird, does she recall the early days before she became fanatical and full of hate, riding by the sea where the bird comes from, herself with the beauty and courage of the bird? Is she not, in fact, herself the bird? And was the tragic political destiny, with all its harshness, its coarsening effect, which Yeats deplores for her in the second stanza, not in fact just the other face of her self-fulfilment, in wild-bird-like courage, above the stormy waves, which he applauds in the last stanza?

In the American magazine *The Dial*, Yeats, however, published in November 1920 not only this poem, but a number of others, two of them ballads treating the 'popular enmity', the 'bitter ... abstract thing', and the 'blind and leader of the blind' in a ballad-heroic vein. One of these poems, 'Sixteen Dead Men', is a kind of recantation of these magnificently generous lines in 'Easter 1916':

> What is it but nightfall?
> No, no, not night but death:
> Was it needless death after all?
> For England may keep faith
> For all that is done and said.

In the ballad, Yeats writes :

> O but we talked at large before
> The sixteen men were shot,
> But who can talk of give and take,
> What should be and should not
> While those dead men are loitering here
> To stir the boiling pot?

This is not a poem in pure ballad style, however : ballad style in feeling and diction, rather than thought. 'The Rose Tree' is in pure ballad style, one of the few genuinely purely popular poems that Yeats ever wrote, and in that mode I think magnificently successful. He takes the mystic image of the rose, which was so important in his symbolist love poems of the 1890s, and uses it as a straightforward political emblem. He was not a Christian, though generous towards Christianity, as towards all great manifestations of the human spirit; but the heroes of the 1916 rebellion were, many of them, devout, simple, and sincere Christians, and implictly he equates the Rose Tree with the Cross, and the self-sacrifice of the Irish leaders with Christ's sacrifice on the Cross :

> 'O words are lightly spoken,'
> Said Pearse to Connolly,
> 'Maybe a breath of politic words
> Has withered our Rose Tree;
> Or maybe but a wind that blows
> Across the bitter sea.'

> 'It needs but to be watered,'
> James Connolly replied,
> 'To make the green come out again
> And spread on every side,
> And shake the blossom from the bud
> To be the garden's pride.'

> 'But where can we draw water,'
> Said Pearse to Connolly,
> 'When all the wells are parched away?
> O plain as plain can be
> There's nothing but our own red blood
> Can make a right Rose Tree.'

And yet strangely, in *The Dial* in 1920, along with these two magnificent popular political poems, Yeats published a short poem, 'The Leaders of the Crowd', sharply and savagely dissociating the poet from political commitment :

They must to keep their certainty accuse
All that are different of a base intent;
Pull down established honour; hawk for news
Whatever their loose fantasy invent
And murmur it with bated breath, as though
The abounding gutter had been Helicon
Or calumny a song. How can they know
Truth flourishes where the student's lamp has shone,
And there alone, that have no solitude?
So the crowd come they care not what may come.
They have loud music, hope every day renewed,
And heartier loves; that lamp is from the tomb.

Yeats's great gift as a political thinker was the ability to make high poetry out of the most bitter divisions in the self, or in the culture out of which he grew, without falsifying, through dull compromise, opposing loyalties. I have given enough examples of his ballad style, of some of his sources, and of the uses to which he put the ballad style, to occupy your minds in an hour. If I were writing a short book, instead of a lecture, I would have much also to say about the use of the ballad style or folk-song style in love poetry. From 'Down by the Salley Gardens' through 'Brown Penny' and the Crazy Jane poems to a late poem like 'John Kinsella's Lament for Mrs Mary Moore', the ballad style serves Yeats as a counterpoint to the love poetry of hopeless and worshipping adoration, the poetry in 'the old high way of love', for which he is more famous. The ballad style, all through, helped him to touch earth, to feel rooted, at times when he was baffled by his own complexities :

In a field by the river my love and I did stand,
And on my leaning shoulder she laid her snow-white hand.
She bid me take life easy, as the grass grows on the weirs:
But I was young and foolish, and now am full of tears ...

O love is the crooked thing,
There is nobody wise enough
To find out all that is in it,
For he would be thinking of love
Till the stars had run away
And the shadows eaten the moon.
Ah, penny, brown penny, brown penny,
One cannot begin too soon.

A bloody and a sudden end,
  Gunshot or noose,
For Death who takes what man would keep,
  Leaves what man would lose,

He might have had my sister,
My cousins by the score,
But nothing satisfied the fool
But my dear Mary Moore,
None other knows what pleasures man
At table or in bed.
What shall I do for pretty girls
Now my old bawd is dead?

And one might quote, finally, the street-singer's song at the end of Yeats's last play, pure ballad style, but made dramatic, summarizing, also, all his great images:

The harlot sang to the beggar-man.
I meet them face to face,
Connall, Cuchulain, Usna's boys,
All that most ancient race;
Maeve had three in an hour, they say,
I adore those clever eyes,
Those muscular bodies, but can get
No grip upon their thighs.
I meet those long pale faces,
Hear their great horses, then
Recall what centuries have passed
Since they were living men.
That there are still some living
That do my limbs unclothe,
But that the flesh my flesh has gripped,
I both adore and loathe.

(Pipe and drum music)

Are those things that men adore and loathe
Their sole reality?
What stood in the Post Office
With Pearse and Connolly?
What comes out of the mountain
Where men first shed their blood?
Who thought Cuchulain till it seemed
He stood where they had stood?

No body like his body
Has modern borne,
But an old man looking on life
Imagines it in scorn.

A statue's there to mark the place,
By Oliver Shephard done.
So ends the tale that the harlot
Sang to the beggar-man.

(Music from pipe and drum)

And so ends, with these haunting reverberations, from the edge of the grave, the tale I have to tell you. It is worth noticing, in conclusion, that in Yeats's posthumous volume, *Last Poems and Plays*, there are more poems in ballad style than in any other volume. Was he growing nearer, in old age and illness, to a rooted reality? Or was the late obsession with the ballad style partly an evasion of the complex and tormenting sense of the antinomies of reality which, in *The Tower* and *The Winding Stair*, he had so heroically faced? I find myself at least going back to the last volume, the last exercises in the ballad style, more often and with more affection than I once thought I would.

4·YEATS: TWO DREAM POEMS

This is the most interesting item, purely bibliographically. It was a contribution to the symposium in which the University of Dacca in East Pakistan intended to commemorate the hundredth anniversary of Yeats's birth in 1864. It was set but funds were lacking to bind and distribute the volume. In the late 1960s a Ph.D pupil of mine, Professor Chowdhury, on returning to Dacca was kind enough to track down and send me a proof. He then disappeared for several years in the turmoil of the invasion by West Pakistan, Mrs Ghandi's liberating war, and the birth-pangs of Bangladesh. I doubt whether the commemorative volume, of which the proofs remain, will ever now be published.

Yeats wrote two poems directly on dreams, about both of which he wrote notes, expressing a certain puzzlement or doubt, or a relinquishing of personal responsibility, about their ultimate meaning. Both poems were written before Yeats could have become aware, as he was aware when he wrote his great late poem, 'The Circus Animals' Desertion', of the Freudian theory of dreams, but both lend themselves to a broadly Freudian interpretation. With both poems (though perhaps more especially with the second, 'His Dream') we can relate the poem to stresses and worries in Yeats's life at the time of their composition. Neither is a major poem. The first, 'The Cap and Bells', is, in a minor, rather pre-Raphaelite way, a success; the second, 'His Dream', though it has a queerly teasing and haunting quality, is, I think, a failure. But both have considerable biographical and psychological interest, and the notes about them throw considerable light on Yeats's theory of symbolism. I am less interested in this study in the purely literary qualities of these poems than in some clues which, as it seems to me, they give us to the deepest psychic drives, the most intense hopes and frustrations, underlying Yeats's poetry up to his final relinquishment of a hope or desire to marry, or physically to make love to, Maud Gonne.

Yeats's early poems are like Petrarch's sonnets or like Sidney's *Astrophel and Stella*, in that the emotional drive behind them is an intense and frustrated passion, a sexual passion combined with what the Jungians would call *anima-projection* for a beautiful woman. Joyce described Yeats's earlier poems, up to about 1900, as 'onanistic'; and their soft, Keatsian sensuousness, their richly decorative imagery (there is an almost obsessive recurrence of images of hair and flowers), a certain melancholy self-indulgence in their plangency, and a fine sense of almost too carefully controlled climax make the harsh adjective not wholly unjust. Between about 1903, when Maud Gonne's marriage to MacBride struck him (he got the news in a telegram when he was delivering a lecture, delivered a brilliant lecture, but never afterwards remembered a word he had said) like a thunderbolt, and about 1909, when she had parted from her husband and there was a kind of reconciliation between her and Yeats, Yeats wrote fewer non-dramatic poems than at any other time in his life. It is, also, in these years between 1900 and 1910 (not later, not after 1914, as many critics have suggested) that the main switch in Yeats's poetic style takes place.

These two dream poems, comparatively unimportant in themselves, are very important indeed as clues to motivations behind the stylistic switch. I would like, however, before examining the two dream-poems in some detail, to make an examination of that stylistic switch itself. It has often enough been described by critics, in a rather impressionistic way. The early poetry has been described, for instance, as lyrical, passive, sensuous, Keatsian : the later poetry has been described as dramatic, active, emotional, Yeatsian. It has often been said that Yeats's drastic late revisions (which turn a poem like 'The Old Pensioner' about an old melancholy wandering tramp with 'the fret' on him, to a poem like 'The Lament of the Old Pensioner', about an aged rebel, conspirator, Don Juan, who spits into the face of Time that has transfigured him) are a deliberate remaking, and disguising, by the mature Yeats of the embarrassingly soft and gentle early Yeatsian *persona* in the image, as far as possible, of the later tragic, ironic, mocking, and above all dominating *persona*.

There is biographical and pictorial evidence of a very strange alteration in Yeats's character and aspect between his thirty-fifth year, at the turn of the century, and his forty-fifth year around 1910. Max Beerbohm's cartoons show a weedy, gangling, toothy figure with long thin wrists pushing out of a too tight and too short jacket, like an overgrown schoolboy. There is a portrait by Yeats's father, who was a psychologically very acute portrait painter, if not a great technician, painted around 1900 : it shows a slim, shrinking figure, a face rather like that of a pretty and intelligent spinster schoolmistress, beginning to wither in her early thirties, an impression strengthened by a velvet jacket, floppy shirt, and pince-nez stuck uneasily on the short aquiline nose. There are drawings, on the other hand, by Augustus John, around 1910, that make Yeats, with strong shoulders, a blue jowl, a look of aggressiveness and strength, seem something like a burly tinker.

The years between 1900 and 1910 were years of extreme emotional and sexual frustration (though Yeats was now willing to seek sexual satisfaction without being romantically in love), and years also of masterful but also often frustrating and exasperating practical activity, connected especially with the Abbey Theatre. They were the years in which Yeats began to become unpopular with the younger poets in Dublin, and with the more radical and revolutionary Irish nationalists, acquiring a reputation for arrogance, for a bitingly contemptuous manner, and for frankly reactionary, though not pro-English, social attitudes. His love both for Maud Gonne and for Ireland turned into what, in the useful current stereotype, is called 'love–hate'. He became aware of the extraordinary nature of his gift and of the extent to which he, and it, were perpetually exploited by those whom he began sharply and consciously to think of as his inferiors. He began also to assert his personality in verse, to use the pronoun 'I' frequently. He began to wonder if he had been tempted away from the proper use of his great gift by a foolish passion, an infatuation, both for Ireland and for Maud Gonne: a key poem, perhaps the best and most important poem of this period, is 'Adam's Curse'.

'Adam's Curse', first published in December 1902 (Maud Gonne was to marry MacBride two or three monthse later), has been noted by many critics, including Ellmann, as the most important early 'transitional' poem in Yeats's opus. It is a conversation piece. At the end of summer, Yeats is talking with Maud Gonne and a close friend of hers, 'a beautiful mild woman' (Maud was anything but mild) about poetry. He talks about the sheer hard work involved in writing a good poem, with a familiar, harsh, and earthy imagery that is quite new in his work:

> Better go down upon your marrow-bones
> And scrub a kitchen-pavement, or break stones
> Like an old pauper, in all kinds of weather;
> For to articulate sweet sounds together
> Is to work harder than all these, and yet
> Be thought an idler by the noisy set
> Of bankers, schoolmasters, and clergymen
> The martyrs call the world.

There is this earthiness, there is an aggressiveness. There is a new ability to express complicated 'prose' ideas, the ideas of a literary critic, say, in verse:

> I said 'A line will take us hours may be;
> Yet if it does not seem a moment's thought,
> Our stitching and unstitching has been naught ...'

The beautiful mild woman consoles Yeats by saying that women must work just as hard to be beautiful (and, the implication is, the result must not seem 'laboured') as the poet of his poetry. Yeats then turns the conversation to love, to romantic, courtly love, in the tradition of Petrarch and Sidney, a love

> So much compounded of high courtesy
> That they would sigh and quote with learned looks
> Precedents out of beautiful old books;
> Yet now it seems an idle trade enough.

He uses, for the romantic and courtly love to which he has devoted his best human energies and his finest poetic gifts, the same adjective which the 'noisy set' of philistine intellectuals, the complacent educated *bourgeoisie* who are always the poet's glibbest false friends and, secretly, his most determined enemies, use about poetry. One should think of the implications or connotations of the English adjective 'idle' : they are quite different from the implications or connotations of 'lazy'. An idle person is not lazy or slothful, he is active in an unprofitable or purposeless or dangerous way; in Elizabethan English, the word could occasionally be almost a synonym of 'wicked' : the devil findeth work for idle hands to do. An idler is somebody who has talents and gifts he should use profitably, but out of a kind of pride chooses not to. The two ladies in the poem, naturally enough, fall silent, for what Yeats is really saying is that romantic or courtly love, love in the tradition of Castiglione, brings no profit, no fruit with it. He is still polite, for in his hearers' ears there must be lingering the use of the word 'idler' about poets by the dull clerks. And yet have the dull clerks a case? The poem ends with something Yeats might have said, but did not. The three friends watch a beautiful but melancholy sunset and moonrise :

> *I had a thought for no one's but your ears:*
> *That you were beautiful, and that I strove*
> *To love you in the old high way of love;*
> *That it had all seemed happy, and yet we'd grown*
> *As weary-hearted as that hollow moon.*

Between 1900 and 1910, in fact, a certain way of feeling, writing, thinking, loving is, in the idiomatic phrase, 'going dead' on Yeats. He has the courage to say so. Let us compare two poems, one of which shows his style in the later 1890s at its most masterly, the other of which, written a few years later, shows the new style crystallizing. The first is all images and patterning of rhythms and images, makes (in a complex sense) no statements, but makes instead a gesture of pure adoring submission and idealization. The second has no images, has a complex syntax which drives through to a clinching statement of a very bitter and resentful sort. Both are famous, and among the great successes of Yeats's shorter and slighter poems. They bring into play almost totally opposite, or clashing, aspects of his gift. The first, first printed in 1899 towards the end of *The Wind Among the Reeds*, is 'The Cloths of Heaven' :

> *Had I the heavens' embroidered cloths,*
> *Enwrought with golden and silver light,*
> *The blue and the dim and the dark cloths*
> *Of night and light and the half-light,*
> *I would spread the cloths under your feet:*
> *But I, being poor, have only my dreams;*
> *I have spread my dreams under your feet;*
> *Tread softly because you tread on my dreams.*

The second, first published in (of all places) the popular Canadian journal *McClure's Magazine* in 1905, is 'Never Give All The Heart':

> *Never give all the heart, for love*
> *Will hardly seem worth thinking of*
> *To passionate women if it seem*
> *Certain, and they never dream*
> *That it fades out from kiss to kiss?*
> *For everything that's lovely is*
> *But a brief, dreamy, kind delight.*
> *O never give the heart outright,*
> *For they, for all smooth lips can say,*
> *Have given their hearts up to the play*
> *And who could play it well enough*
> *If deaf and dumb and blind with love?*
> *He that made this knows all the cost,*
> *For he gave all his heart and lost.*

It is interesting to note that two of the key words, 'embroidered' and 'enwrought', in 'The Cloths of Heaven' are picked up in the famous dismissal of the early style, 'A Coat', first published in *Poetry* (Chicago) in 1914:

> *I made my song a coat*
> *Covered with embroideries*
> *Out of old mythologies*
> *From heel to throat;*
> *But the fools caught it,*
> *Wore it in the world's eyes*
> *As though they'd wrought it.*
> *Song, let them take it,*
> *For there's more enterprise*
> *In walking naked.*

Let us compare and contrast 'The Cloths of Heaven' and 'Never Give All the Heart'. Syntactically, the first poem is a gapped hypothesis, 'Had I ...I would', followed by two simple sentences, 'But I ... have ... I have spread ...' and ending with an imperative, 'Tread softly ...' The syntax is merely a framework, however, and the poetic 'work' (so to call it) is done by a dreamlike repetition, repetition of end-words substituting for rhyme, cloths, light : cloths, light : feet, dreams : feet, dreams. The lack of real rhyme is compensated for by the internal chime of the fourth line,

> *Of* night *and* light *and the half*-light,

where, it should be noted, the Anglo-Irish, as distinct from the English pronunciation, is '*half-light*', a spondee, rather than *half*-light', a trochee. The

rhythm is also enriched by frequent use of the connective 'and', a charac-
teristic of lyrical as against discursive poetry,

> ... *golden* and *silver light*,
> *The blue* and *the dim* and *the dark cloths*
> *Of night* and *light* and *the half-light*,

It should be noted, also, how the definite articles there ('the blue', 'the dim',
'the dark', 'the half-light') have a specifying effect where the dropping of
them ('night', 'light',) has a generalizing effect. Fairly specific colour adjectives 'golden' and 'silver' similarly lead up to the more generalizing 'dim'
and 'dark'. The contrast of 'cloths' with 'light' (the material with the
ethereal, mysterious, or immaterial) works in parallelism with the contrast of
'feet' and 'dreams'. The two active verbs in the last two lines, 'spread' and
'tread' (twice repeated) are linked by rhyme like 'night' and 'light' and
'half-light'. The whole effect of the poem is, in fact, one of intricate em-
broidery, of a patterning of sense-sounds within a given formal framework.
The mood could be called lulling and incantatory. This was the sort of poem,
no doubt, that Joyce had in mind when he described Yeats's early poems as
'onanistic'. It is nevertheless a memorably beautiful poem, creating an
extraordinarily precise total pattern out of repeated elements of feeling and
imagery that, taken in isolation, might seem to have a certain intrinsic remoteness, unreality, or vagueness. Yeats's metaphor about 'stitching and un-
stitching' from 'Adam's Curse' applies very well to the whole sampler-like or
tapestry-like effect. Perhaps the whole effect of the intricate, vague, romance
forest, of Brocelyande, has never been caught so effectively in eight lines.

By comparison, 'Never Give All the Heart' in its nakedness and through-
thrusting syntax seems almost like one of the bitter poems of Catullus to
Lesbia. The syntax is that of complex exposition : 'Never give ...' (imperative
main clause), 'for love ...' (adverbial clause of explanation or reason qualifying 'never give'), 'if it seem ...' (adverbial conditional clause, the subordinate clause of a subordinate clause, qualifying 'will hardly seem'), 'and
they never dream' (this could be a co-ordinate clause with 'for love/Will
hardly seem' but more probably, for sense, it is co-ordinate with 'if it seem/
Certain ...') : 'For everything that's lovely is' goes back in co-ordination to
'for love/Will hardly seem worth thinking of', though, like all 'for' clauses,
it feels like a main clause, and could stand as a sentence on its own. (For 'for'
substitute some such periphrasis as 'to explain all this'.) Then there is another new start with an imperative, 'O never give', followed by two subordinate clauses enclosed one within the other, Chinese-box fashion, with
two quite different senses of 'for' :

> *For they, for all smooth lips can say*,
> *Have given their heart up to the play*.

('*Because they*, *in spite of* all that smooth lips can say, have given their

heart up to the performance, the game, the unhampered movement' –
Matthew Arnold's 'free play of mind' – free swing of mind.) There is then
a question-sentence with an elliptical conditional clause:

> And who could play it well enough
> If deaf and dumb and blind with love?

('For who could act the part, play the game, let the free swing through well
enough, if he were ...') The reader has the sense of having been led in a
masterfully abrupt way through a small but baffling maze. The key conjunction 'for' comes in again in the last line, the *explanatory* conjunction
(where 'and', in the other poem, is the *expressive* conjunction):

> He that made this knows all the cost
> For he gave all his heart and lost.

It would sound frivolous to say that Yeat's great technical discovery between
1900 and 1910 was his discovery of the complex as opposed to the compound sentence, a discovery of the uses of the subordinate clause, but if
one said that he discovered the use of syntax as opposed to imagery the statement (which can be backed by all sorts of evidence, of the kind I am educing
here) one's statement would probably seem to have a correct academic
portentousness. One might also say that where, in the 1890s, he exploited a
quality of individual words that can be called vagueness or suggestiveness
(in 'The Cloths of Heaven', the effect of the sequence, golden, silver, blue,
dim, dark), by the early 1900s he was learning to exploit the kind of conceptual tension, or emotional polarity, in individual words which Empson
has taught us to call ambiguity.

I think that, with his preoccupation with the theatre, Yeats almost certainly intended by the noun 'the play' and by the verb 'to play' in this poem
the theatrical sense – 'a drama', and 'to perform'. But the senses of 'play' as
'a game, something frivolous', and of 'free play', as 'natural unconstrained
movement', and of a 'game' as 'something to be won or lost', cannot possibly
be excluded. One's rapid sense-scanning, for expository purposes, of the last
couplet, gives: 'He that made this (poem) knows all the cost (of giving all
your heart) for he gave all his heart and (therefore, he) lost (his heart, the
game, you, his leading part in the play).'

The movement in the style, in the short gap of five or six years between
these two poems, is from the expressive to the exploratory; the movement in
feeling is from the submissive and celebratory to the bitterly and ironically
questioning. One should not speak of a movement from preoccupation with
detail to preoccupation with structure, for 'The Cloths of Heaven' is beautifully structured. But there is a movement from a grasp of structure as, in a
sense, timeless, a patterning of words and rhythms around a single unchang-
ing mood or feeling, or around some simple contrast of moods and feelings,
towards something more like what Charles Olson calls 'field composition':

an exploring and an attempting to define some complex of feelings whose puzzling nature (rather than whose continuing similarity or identity) is what sparks the poem off.

Of the two dream poems, which are (though I am slow in engaging with them) the main subject of this essay, the first belongs to the period of what I would call vague, suggestive, timeless poetry, the second to what I have called the early period of exploratory poetry. One reflects a mood of lyrical acceptance, a mood in which sadness, frustration, loss are worked, as it were, into a total texture of lyrical pleasure; the second reflects a mood of existential doubt about the whole function of the lyrical poet, a doubt about the life-pattern and the vocation : a doubt again reflected in many of Yeats's poems between 1900 and 1910 :

> ... since you were gone,
> My barren thoughts have chilled me to the bone ...
>
> > (Reconciliation – 1910)

> The fascination of what's difficult
> Has dried the sap out of my veins, and rent
> Spontaneous joy and natural content
> Out of my heart.
>
> > (The Fascination of What's Difficult – 1910)

> All things can tempt me from this craft of verse:
> One time it was a woman's face, or worse –
> The seeming needs of my fool-driven land ...

> ... When I was young,
> I had not given a penny for a song
> Did not the poet sing it with such airs
> That one believed he had a sword upstairs;
> Yet would be now, could I but have my wish,
> Colder and dumber and deafer than a fish.
>
> > (All Things Can Tempt Me – 1910)

Both of the dream poems are also, in a sense, about desire, sublimation through idealization, and a kind of frustration or death-wish that comes through that sublimation. They are comments on what I will call, to use a loose but comprehensible term, Yeats's Petrarchanism. And relevant to them are a number of short folk-song style, anti-Petrarchan poems, of which the burden is that love is a perfectly natural youthful physical and emotional impulse, which will work out all right, if one does not take it too seriously. The peasantry have a more instinctive natural sense about this than the would-be Castiglione-style courtiers, the lovers who

> ... would sigh and quote with learned looks
> Precedents out of beautiful old books.

The little ballad pleas for natural, spontaneous, uncourtly, unromantic, unself-tormenting love have never, so far as I know, been set together in order, and I will do this here:

DOWN BY THE SALLEY GARDENS

Down by the salley gardens my love and I did meet;
She passed the salley gardens with little snow-white feet.
She bid me take love easy, as the leaves grow on the tree;
But I, being young and foolish, with her would not agree.

In a field by the river my love and I did stand,
And on my leaning shoulder she laid her snow-white hand.
She bid me take life easy, as the grass grows on the weirs;
But I was young and foolish, and now am full of tears.

(1886)

O DO NOT LOVE TOO LONG

Sweetheart, do not love too long:
I loved long and long,
And grew to be out of fashion
Like an old song.

All through the years of our youth
Neither could have known
Their own thought from the other's,
We were so much at one.

But O, in a minute she changed –
O do not love too long,
Or you will grow out of fashion
Like an old song.

(1905)

BROWN PENNY

I whispered 'I am too young',
And then, 'I am old enough';
Wherefore I threw a penny
To find out if I might love.
'Go and love, go and love, young man,
If the lady be young and fair.'
Ah, penny, brown penny, brown penny,
I am looped in the loops of her hair.

O love is the crooked thing,
There is nobody wise enough
To find out all that is in it,

For he would be thinking of love
Till the stars had run away
And the shadows had eaten the moon.
Ah, penny, brown penny, brown penny,
One cannot begin it too soon.

(1910)

Take love easy. Do not love too long. Love, in the third poem, is not something to be thought about, but simply to be engaged in, as early as possible.
One cannot begin it too soon. All these three poems are slight enough in
themselves but they mark a continuing undertow in the tides of Yeats's mind,
against the main tide of idealizing, spiritual, complex love, forever post-
poning crude physical gratification. It was perhaps the very closeness in
spiritual sympathy between Maud Gonne and Yeats that made her continually hold him at a distance; it was perhaps MacBride's very crudity and
vulgarity that made him able to possess and conquer her at once. Slight as
they are, these three poems by Yeats carry a bitter echo of a great and
bitter poem by Blake:

Never seek to tell thy love
Love that never told can be;
For the gentle wind does move
Silently, invisibly.

I told my love, I told my love,
I told her all my heart,
Trembling, cold, in ghastly fears –
Ah, she doth depart.

Soon as she was gone from me
A traveller came by
Silently, invisibly –
O, was no deny.

Rossetti, for the last line there, preferred to print the more obviously euphon-
ious but less startling and exact deleted line:

He took her with a sigh.

MacBride might have been the traveller in Blake's poem. Yeats had told her
too much, not to make her 'trembling, or cold, or in ghastly fears', but simply
to make her (simple-minded, fanatical, and in many ways rather stupid
woman as she was) weary and distrustful of him; he never shared her passionate social pity or her revolutionary fierceness. She, the aristocrat by
birth, style in her bones, was able to dispense with all aristocratic ideas; he,
the middle-class man, just counting in Ireland as of the gentry though not

of the landed gentry, counting in England as merely another member of the professional middle-classes (writing is a profession in England, and a middle-class one) desperately needed aristocratic ideas, contacts, and vague or scattered pretences to aristocratic ancestry. She, also, had no great interest in the arts as such, and, becoming a Roman Catholic, became so in a dogmatic–objective way which was at the opposite pole from Yeats's own poetic and subjective sense of religion. What was physical in her Yeats was too delicate and indirect to stir, though it was, in the end, very stirrable. MacBride, the traveller, a soldier of fortune, a heavy drinker, a man without subtlety or culture, though not without courage and passion, took her – though not with a sigh on her side, though the marriage soon foundered. 'O, was no deny.' The two dream poems are, in a crude sense, about Yeats's sense of a fundamental mistake, blunder, *harmartia* in his approach to Maud Gonne – about the sense that quite early on he should have stopped sighing and gazing and writing poems, but instead wooed her with physical directness; about the sense, later, that, however intense and noble a devotion, physically unfulfilled, of this sort may have been, it will in retrospect seem like a devotion to death, and the memory of it may breed a sort of death-wish. I have taken a long time setting up the machinery for the explication of these two dream poems, 'The Cap and Bells' and 'His Dream'. But the machinery I have been setting up should make the task of actual explication, of confrontation with the texts, comparatively brief. I shall take the two poems in date-order.

I shall give first Yeats's note on 'The Cap and Bells' and then the earliest text of the poem, with its pre-Raphaelite quaintnesses of diction which Yeats later smoothed away. In a poem coming directly from a dream one wants, if one is investigating personal sources and meanings, the earliest, crudest texts, not the latest and most sophisticated: not, in this case, that Yeats's revisions fundamentally altered the tone or structure of the poem. This is the note:

> I dreamed this poem exactly as I have written it, and dreamed another long dream after it, trying to make out its meaning, and whether I was to write it in prose or verse. The first dream was more a vision than a dream, for it was beautiful and coherent, and gave me the sense of illumination and explanation that one gets from visions, while the second dream was confused and meaningless. The poem has always meant a great deal to me, though, as is the way with symbolic poems, it has not always meant quite the same thing. Blake would have said 'The authors are in eternity', and I am quite sure they can only be questioned in dreams.

This is the poem, in the earliest printed version:

A Queen was loved by a jester,
And once, when the owls grew still,
He made his soul go upward
And stand on her window sill.

In a long and straight blue garment
It talked, ere the morn grew white.
It had grown most wise with thinking
On a foot-fall hushed and light.

But the young Queen would not listen:
She rose in her pale night-gown,
She drew in the brightening casement,
She snicked the brass bolts down.

He bade his heart go to her,
When the bats cried out no more:
In a garment red and quivering
It sang to her through the door.

The tongue of it sweet with dreaming
Of a flutter of flower-like hair;
But she took her fan from the table
And waved it out on the air.

'I've Cap and Bells' (he pondered),
'I will send them to her and die.'
And as soon as the morn had whitened
He left them where she went by.

She took them into her bosom,
In her heart she found a tune,
Her red lips sang them a love-song,
The night smelled rich with June.

She opened her door and her window,
The heart and the soul came through,
To her right hand came the red one,
To her left hand came the blue.

They set up a noise like crickets,
A chattering wise and sweet;
And her hair was like a folded flower,
And the quiet of love in her feet.

One should note, first of all, some obvious literary sources: Jack Point, for instance, in Gilbert and Sullivan's *The Yeoman of the Guard*, with his melancholy, haunting death-song. 'He died for the love of a lady': and the medieval legend, turned into a prose story by Anatole France (but, I think, after the composition of this poem) about Our Lady's Juggler, the juggler who has no way of expressing his devotion to the Virgin Mary except by performing a difficult juggling feat, juggling and tumbling, in front of her image in a church. A priest comes in and wants to interrupt what he thinks this strange buffoonery, but suddenly, as the juggler is standing in front of the image of Our Lady, sweating with his exertions, she bends forward and uses a hand-kerchief which she is holding in her right hand to mop, gently, the sweat off his brow. If one thinks of the poem along these lines, interpreting it in terms of what Eliot called 'the high dream' as opposed to the 'low dream' (the high dream being concerned with the spiritual life, with supernatural vision, the low dream being concerned with the revelation of suppressed sexual desires) it is easy enough to interpret this poem in an 'idealistic' rather than a 'realis-tic' way. The idealistic interpretation depends on a dualistic, the realistic interpretation on a tripartite division, schematically, of the human psyche; or rather the division, in the case of the idealistic interpretation, is also tri-partite, but in a different way.

Some of the symbolism is traditional. The colour blue, the colour of the sky, in European medieval painting and poetry stands for chastity, purity ('blue of Mary's colour'). The colour red stands for blood, for flesh, for un-satisfied passion ('red and quivering'). The window obviously stands for the eyes (it is through the eyes that the soul speaks) and the door for the mouth (but the mouth under the nose, or both?). The soul has to soar to enter, the heart enters at a door level with itself. The soul is in some sense maladroit (at the climax of the poem, it lies down by the lady's left hand), the heart adroit (it lies down, at the climax, by her right hand). The soul has been dreaming of the lady's gentle approach to it (her 'foot-fall hushed and light'); she appears to it and rejects it and shuts it out dressed in a colour which symbolizes purity even more definitely than the colour blue does – in her 'pale night-gown'. (But Yeats does not say 'white night-gown'; and the pallor could be the pallor of a certain preliminary excitement, the withdrawal in sudden fear of the suddenly excited blood.) The riddle of the poem is what the cap and bells, the jester's cap which is also the badge of his trade, stands for. If soul, in the sense of spiritual affinity, and heart, in the sense of passion-ate desire, have already been rejected, what exactly does the cap and bells stand for? Why is its removal death to the poet? And why does its discovery lead to an intimate acceptance of it, and, with it, of heart and soul, and a final delight and harmony?

The cap and bells is the mark of the jester's trade (and the trade of the jester stands for the trade of the poet, an 'idle trade enough'). To please his lady, on this interpretation, the jester sacrifices, offers to her, the badge of his pro-fession, though without this badge he is nothing, has no human function. Yeats, as it were, offers his poetic gifts to Maud Gonne's purposes (he might have won her if he had become a straight nationalist propagandist poet, thus 'dying' as a real poet; he might have won her if he had said, 'My poetry does not matter, only my desire for you' : she could have clutched the sacrifice, as many women married to men who have sacrificed for them a central creative potentiality do, as a sort of trophy). Out of the death coming from this sort of sacrifice there would have been a kind of resurrection, in acceptance, in love.

This interpretation certainly cannot be ignored. But there is a harsher, more obviously Freudian interpretation which cannot be ignored either. The cap and bells are not a very apt phallic symbol, but the human head on which they are worn is one, and cap, as a word, is related, or might well be, to the Latin *caput-capitis*. The twin bells hanging downwards from the jester's cap have an affinity with the testicles. Throwing off the cap and bells, leaving them in the Queen's way, is like an act of self-exposure. On the lady's side, 'the flutter of flower-like hair' has sexual associations (there is pubic hair, as well as the hair of the head; somebody in Proust remarks how odd it is to think that a flower is the sexual organ of a plant; the 'hair like a folded flower' in the last stanza might well be the hair round the vagina; and both the feet and the bosom, earlier in the poem, might be stand-ins for that, too).

The broad meaning of the poem then would be that it is no good offering a woman spiritual or emotional love unless you also offer her sexual love, something in comparison with these, in its specificity, low and ridiculous. There might be an Attis-element: the shedding of the cap and bells might be like a sort of self-castration in honour of the White Goddess. Her purring satisfaction in the last stanza might be genuinely loving, or sadistic. (There is a long tradition, which Empson has looked into, of using the word 'die' in English poetry – Empson's example is from Dryden, but many other examples could be found – as a metaphor for the climax of the sexual act.) The interest of this poem, therefore, I would suggest is that it allows itself to be interpreted in two quite opposite ways, which I will try to indicate schematically:

i: 1 Rejection of the soul.
   2 Rejection of the heart-cum-body.
   3 Acceptance of some kind of sacrifice or offering, or both, of the poet's specific gift.

ii: 1 Rejection of the merely spiritual.
   2 Rejection of the merely emotional.
   3 Acceptance of the grossly and absurdly physical (either lovingly or sadistically) and, with this, harmonious acceptance of the lover's total being.

Maud Gonne, in fact, never accepted Yeats's cap and bells in either sense. Jon Stallworthy has a touching poem about a volume of poems which he has, dedicated in Yeats's hand-writing to her, of which she had never cut the leaves; she may have let him kiss her sometimes, and she wanted to keep him on a string, but she never let him make love to her,* and when MacBride's execution, after the 1916 Easter Rebellion, left her free to marry him, and he asked her to do so (more out of a sense of duty than anything else, since he was now in love with her illegitimate daughter, Yseult, who considered the possibility, but in the end refused him) she again said no. He had met her in 1889, the attachment had been painful but constant, and the final relinquishment of any idea of fulfilment was after a relationship of 27 years. Yeats's poems are a long life-commentary and in relation to that, not in itself, this poem is of primary importance: a kind of dream-seeing, 'beautiful and coherent', understood and not understood by Yeats himself.

The other dream poem, 'His Dream', is shorter and not even a minor success, but as evidence about some of the deep disturbances under Yeats's development even more interesting. Again, I shall give first the note, and then the poem. Here is the note:

> A few days ago I dreamed that I was steering a very gay and elaborate ship upon some narrow water with many people upon its banks, and that there was a figure upon a bed in the middle of the ship. The people were pointing to the figure and questioning and in my dream I sang verses which faded as I awoke, all but this fragmentary thought, 'We call it, it has such dignity of limb, by the sweet name of Death'. I have made my poem out of my dream and the sentiment of my dream, and can almost say, as Blake did, 'The Authors are in Eternity'.

The poem was considerably revised but here, reconstituted from the Variorum Edition, is the text first published in *The Nation* on 11 July 1908.

There on the high and painted stern
I held a painted steering oar,
And everywhere that I could turn
Men ran upon the shore.

And though I would have hushed the crowd
There was no mother's son, but said,
'What is the figure in a shroud
Upon a painted bed?'

And fishes, bubbling to the brim,
Cried out upon that thing beneath,
It had such dignity of limb,
By the sweet name of Death.

Though I'd my finger on my lip,
What could I but take up the song?
And fish and crowd and painted ship
Cried out the whole night long.

Crying, amid the glittering sea,
Naming it with ecstatic breath,
Because it had such dignity
By the sweet name of Death.

It should be noticed that the fish, whose behaviour offends even dream-logic, do not figure in the prose account of the dream. It looks as if the phrase 'bubbling to the brim' was suggested by a reminiscence of Keats's 'beaded bubbles winking at the brim', but, allowing that fishes in a dream can sing, the figure in the shroud could not be 'beneath' them, as they stuck their heads out of the surface of the water – unless they were flying fish, flying above the boat. Yeats did not, however, get rid of them till the *Later Poems* of 1922. By the first book-printing however of the poem he had substituted for the comparatively neutral or even favourable adjective 'painted' of the *Nation* printing, in its three occurrences in the poem, the emotively hostile adjective 'gaudy', with its connotations of vulgarly over-ornate. It is worth printing the final as well as the first version, for this is a case which, by revision, Yeats seems to have been working close towards some original implications of the dream which, in his first version, he was perhaps unconsciously resisting:

> *I swayed upon the gaudy stern*
> *The butt-end of a steering-oar,*
> *And saw wherever I could turn*
> *A crowd upon a shore.*
>
> *And though I would have hushed the crowd,*
> *There was no mother's son but said,*
> *'What is the figure in a shroud*
> *Upon a gaudy bed?'*
>
> *And after running at the brim*
> *Cried out upon that thing beneath*
> *– It had such dignity of limb –*
> *By the sweet name of Death.*
>
> *Though I'd my finger on my lip,*
> *What could I but take up the song?*
> *And running crowd and gaudy ship*
> *Cried out the whole night long,*
>
> *Crying amid the glittering sea,*
> *Naming it with ecstatic breath,*
> *Because it had such dignity,*
> *By the sweet name of Death.*

In the first book-printing of the poem and in quite a number of subsequent reprintings, the last two lines read:

> *Because it had such dignity*
> *By the sweet name of Death.*

where the omission of a comma can convey a quite opposite sense. Without the comma the lines mean that the ship and the crowd cried out the whole night long, because the form in the shroud had such dignity *when called* by the sweet name of Death. The comma implies that the figure in the shroud had, in itself, such dignity that the sweet name of Death was the only appropriate title for it.

The prose account of the dream is very useful. Roughly, I would say (though there are deeper, more purely sexual meanings which I shall go into later) that the painted or gaudy ship is Yeats's poems, that he is the steersman, that the figure in the shroud is Maud Gonne (now 'dead to him', since her marriage), that the narrow water (not specified in the poem, but implied by there being crowds on both banks, crowds 'wherever I could turn') is the Irish Channel, and that the crowds on either bank are Yeats's admirers in England and Ireland. They are cheering something that he feels embarrassed about ('. . . I'd my finger to my lip') and since he is steering at night he might have expected privacy. Joyce's phrase about the early poetry being 'onanistic' seems here to take on an almost literal application. The change from the first,

> There on the high and painted stern
> I held a painted steering-oar,

to the much more vivid and physical

> I swayed upon the gaudy stern
> The butt-end of a steering-oar,

suggests, much more vividly, sexual self-manipulation; and, standing at the stern, not at the prow, Yeats is looking backwards to the past, rather than forward to the future, and this is typical of masturbatory fantasies. He is embarrassed by the cheering, as he well might be, but joins in it. The strange phrase about 'dignity of limb' is, I think, an unconscious reminiscence, like the phrase about the fishes 'bubbling to the brim'. The reminiscence is from Wordsworth's 'We are Seven':

> A simple child, dear brother Jim,
> That lightly draws its breath,
> And feels its life in every limb,
> What should it know of death?

Wordsworth's poem is about a child so fully alive that she cannot imagine or conceive that her little brothers and sisters are really dead. The crowds here on the bank are her opposites; they are so impressed by the 'dignity of limb' of the figure under the shroud upon her gaudy bed that they think Death must be finer than life. Yeats takes up their cry, but with a certain hysteria. The phrase 'the sweet name of Death' is a kind of oxymoron:

physically death is corruption, putrescence, the opposite of the 'sweet', the fresh (one should think of 'sweet water', as opposed to brackish or muddy water). I think these funny fish may have got into the first version of the poem from some obscure sense that the only thing to do with the shrouded figure, in the end, would be to throw it overboard and feed it to them.

Neither of these two poems is, as I have said, great; the first is a minor success, the second, even after Yeats's worried revisions, a failure. But they do throw a great deal of light on the tension, in Yeats's earlier development, between an idealistic and a realistic view of sexual love, and on the intense bitterness and frustration that accompanied his devotion to an idealistic love. The best comments on both poems are, perhaps, to be found in the great volume of 1914, *Responsibilities*. In the opening poem of that volume, an invocation to his forefathers to sustain him in a rootedness in Irish history, rather than in a cloudy devotion to Irish legend, thinking that all rootedness is based in family tradition he says:

> *Pardon that for a barren passion's sake,*
> *Although I have come close on forty-nine,*
> *I have no child, I have nothing but a book,*
> *Nothing but that to prove your blood and mine.*

There is another poem in this volume, 'The Dolls', on which Yeats writes a note intended to direct the reader to a very abstract interpretation of what reads, in fact, like a bitterly personal poem: 'The fable for this poem came into my head while I was giving some lectures in Dublin. I had noticed once again how all thought among us is frozen into "something other than human life ..."'

And he goes on to say that 'The Magi', a poem as powerfully beautiful as 'The Dolls' is powerfully ugly, came out of the same inspiration. But it is a poem, really, about how the woman who has been idealized, set on a pedestal, turned into an icon, by a 'barren passion' will resent her adorer's sudden interest in life and fruitfulness. The doll-maker's wife has had a baby, and the oldest of all the dolls, the Maud Gonne doll, screams in rage that the serenity of the doll-images should be disturbed by this 'noisy and filthy thing'. The doll-maker's wife apologizes:

> *'She murmurs into his ear,*
> *Head upon shoulder leant:*
> *"My dear, my dear, O dear,*
> *It was an accident".'*

It is like one of Hardy's little fables. These dream poems and their wider context show us that Yeats's journey to rootedness and life lay through a gradual growing into consciousness of a sense of something stifling, deathly, unnatural, indecent, and frustrating in the romantic, idealized, Petrarchan love to which he had devoted all his younger days. But a doll is a less fundamentally hateful and unmanageable image than a corpse; it can be put back on the shelf, and does not need to be fed to the fishes. The 'noisy and filthy thing', new life, is here, through irony, accepted. Yeats was ripe, though he did not know it, for the final breaking off of any amorous obsession with Maud Gonne, for marriage, for happiness, and for the rich fruitage of the autumn tree.

5 · POUND:
MASKS, MYTH, MAN

Vision and Rhetoric, Faber and Faber, London, 1959; *Ezra Pound: A Collection of Essays edited by Peter Russell to be presented to Ezra Pound on his 65th birthday*, Peter Nevill, London and New York, 1950.

(1)

This will not be the kind of essay that Ezra Pound himself would approve of. I am writing on the passenger deck of a vessel bound for Japan, the books I want to quote from are in the hold, and so I shall have to talk around him, digging up what illustrative tags I can from my memory. That is not his own way of criticizing. It is perhaps not quite true of him, as John Crowe Ransom says it is of Eliot, that he 'never lifts his nose from the page'; he has forcible opinions on a hundred subjects, and his critical essays are full of all sorts of pungent 'asides'; but on the whole he is at his best as a critic when he opens a book, thrusts it at you, and says 'See for yourself'. What you have to *see*, generally, is not an illustration of some favourite thesis but a poem on a page, worth looking at for its own sake. He exposes you to impacts. Some of his best critical essays – that on French poetry, for instance – are not so much even close examinations of texts as little anthologies, with just enough commentary to let the reader get to grips on his own. And in the essays illustrated by translations, those on Provençal poets or on Cavalcanti's *Donna mi prega*, the prose setting of the translations has often the air of acute, but disconnected, note-book jottings. And Pound's best criticism, no doubt, *is* in his translations. He makes ghosts walk again, in their habit, as they lived; yet his ghosts, paradoxically enough, have a common aspect; we know them by their gait, and the gait is Pound's. *Homage to Sextus Propertius*, for instance, will send you (if you have the kind of schoolboy smattering of Latin I have) to Propertius, looking for a wry humour, which is perhaps only Pound's, or which anyway no one would have seen in Propertius until Pound had read it into him. He gives things his own flavour; but I am not, in this essay, attempting to give him *my* flavour. I am trying to arrive at a tentative judgment of him as he is in himself.

Such versions, or such handlings, rather, as *Homage to Sextus Propertius*, are what Pound calls *personae*, as he might say masks or maybe roles. But the puzzle for his readers is, of, say Pound and Propertius, which is the actor and which is the part: is it a question of Garrick as Hamlet, or Hamlet as Garrick? Perhaps we should think of neither of these simple alternatives; Pound's Propertius is more an antique Roman than a Yank, but just sufficiently a Yank

to be not too stuffily an antique Roman. This is perhaps Pound's great gift as
a poet of roles – his power of forcefully combining partial inadequacies into
an almost adequate whole. Propertius, for instance, needs re-interpretation,
even distortion, to bring him within our own framework; but we must also
re-interpret and distort that framework (we must correlate two variables, in
fact) to come to terms with *him*. This is why both Pound's rage against
academic scholars, and the rage of academic scholars against Pound, are
largely critically irrelevant. Academic scholars are able to get an objective
view of a text by dissociating it as far as possible from their own contemporary sensibility, which is what the poetic critic and translater – who for that
very reason can never get a wholly objective view – dare not do. The scholar
must not, and the poet must, project himself into the text. A kind of amateur
scholarship has, perhaps, been a stumbling-block to Pound. It is right for a
poet, making the first draft of a translation, to guess, guess all the way – to
use his intuition about how a poem of a certain kind *must* be built up – but
I think he should then check his guesses with a good dictionary or a reliable
crib. His guesses will be brilliant but not necessarily accurate. Pound, I feel,
has too often omitted this checking; he has more of the spirit of scholarship
than many scholars, but, after all, the letter counts too. On the other hand,
it is this schoolboy eagerness that has kept him for so many years, so wonderfully fresh as a man and a poet.

The sensibility, then, of Propertius, or Li Po, or Bertrans de Born, is one
variable that Pound has had to adjust in shaping his masks; another variable
has been his own raw, quick, exceedingly American sensibility. That, in isolation, has its inadequacies too. Pound's emphasis, for instance, on the notion of
'culture' is very American, and there is that little early poem (not one of his
best) where he imagines American life strangely transformed by a general
study of 'the Classics'. I think that for the intelligent American reader today –
for the intelligent reader almost everywhere, for that matter – one trouble
is that there are too many 'Classics' altogether. The point about somebody
like Jefferson was not that he had read a great deal (the eighteenth-century
novel, for instance, which for us is a 'classic', for him was an unwholesome
distraction), but that what he had read was what most educated gentlemen of
his time, in England and France as well as Virginia, would have read too. That
age demanded of a gentleman a wide, clear, and superficial range of knowledge over a known range of subjects; Lord Chesterfield, for instance, told his
son that a young man should know about architectural styles, but not about
building materials, for the latter kind of knowledge was not 'liberal' but
'mechanical'.

A great deal of what was once liberal knowledge has today become
mechanical in that sense; even literary criticism has today its quite elaborate
technical jargon. But our liberal knowledge, the part of our knowledge that
is still genuinely liberal, has no longer the cohesion that it had in Jefferson's
day. There are more books worth reading than we shall ever read, and more
arguable points of view than we shall ever come to terms with. Let us
imagine that Pound could dictate a course of reading in 'general literature'

for the leading American universities; it would be a drop in the bucket, it would leave the general cultural confusion richer, perhaps, but also more thick and sticky than ever. Our reading today is rather, in fact, like an American salad – cheese, gherkins, nuts, lettuces, pears, endives, perhaps a slice of pineapple and a rub of garlic – and one needs a bottle of thick mayonnaise to mask the contrasting flavours, and the name of the mayonnaise, in the United States, is 'culture'.

'Culture', as most Americans use the word, covers anything that is not obviously practical or pleasurable; like visiting, for instance, Stratford-on-Avon. In this sense, the notion of culture can become a blanket smothering individual taste and discrimination – and this, of course, is not, one would never dare hint it, exactly Pound's sense of culture. But his sense has something, at least, in common with what the American humanists, Irving Babbitt and Paul Elmer More, understood by culture; and what they understood was in a sense the opposite of what an anthropologist understands by *a* culture; they understood not something that could be encouraged to grow out of the habits and perceptions of daily American life, but something that had to be protected from these. Their humanism was an admirable notion, but it had no roots in the American soil, and so produced no flowers or fruits there. On the contrary, one would be tempted to say that some of the best and most racy American writing (*Huckleberry Finn, Fiesta, Soldiers' Pay, The Thin Man*) springs from the soil of a sensitive philistinism; poetry, too, William Carlos William's poetry of red brick houses, suburban wives, cheerful standardized interiors. It was a weakness, an amiable and typically American weakness in Pound, that he was too eager to make everybody else read his own favourite authors and too hopeful about the changes that would spring from such a reading. It is not so much *what* people read, as *how* they read, that can make them startlingly and pleasantly different.

Our point, however, is the poetry. In these masks or roles of Pound's, the inadequacies of an eager American eclecticism, and of various primitive or archaic attitudes, not easily revivable in contemporary terms, do seem to combine, after all, as something poetically adequate. This whole question of the triumphant combination of inadequacies becomes peculiarly fascinating in the unique case, before *The Cantos – Hugh Selwyn Mauberley –* where the *persona*, the mask, the role, is not the old empty armour that begins to shape, and clank, and move as if it had life in it, as Pound's swan passes on the stream – I am making an allusion, there, to the opening of one of the early Cantos – but, on the contrary, a role, a contemporary role, rather like Pound's own. I say 'rather like' for *Mauberley* is not *exactly* Pound. He is, one gathers, a minor poet of genuine talent, high, frail ambition, and classical tastes : a sort of Landor *de ses jours*, but with a wistfulness and an irony that are more like Laforgue. The poem has the smell of its time. When we read, for instance, of Mr Nixon advising the poet to 'take a column', and 'butter reviewers', warning him that the 'nineties tried your game, but died of it', we cannot help thinking of Arnold Bennett, playing the part of the Card in life as in literature.

In such a discouraging atmosphere, Mauberley can only drift, collect fugitive impressions, remember the 'nineties and the pre-Raphaelites, bitterly note decay.

> In that thoroughfare
> The sale of half-hose has
> Long since superseded the cultivation
> Of Pierian roses.

In the end he vanishes to a euphoric death in the South Seas:

> I was
> And I no more exist;
> Here drifted
> An Hedonist.

Mauberley, in his passivity, is in some degree inadequate as a person, though not in the least so as a *persona* (F. R. Leavis, if I remember rightly, though a passionate admirer of this poem, has something sniffy to say about the 'merely aesthetic' attitude implied in it). Pound himself was made of tougher stuff. He did not drift to the South Seas, but instead started to study economics and to write the longest readable poem of our time, *The Cantos*. This was a move from the lyrical scale to the epical; and it implied, at the same time, a move from the lyric mask to the epic myth.

(2)

The nature of the underlying myth in *The Cantos* begins to become really clear about half-way through, in the two long sections where the anecdotes, of which the poem is largely composed, are no longer broken off in the middle to be taken up, in a different setting, several Cantos further on. Of these two large monolithic chunks, intruding so strangely into a kaleidoscopic poem, one is about John Adams, the second President of the United States; it consists largely of extracts from letters by him or about him, of documentation. For most readers, just as poetry, it is one of the least successful sections; it presupposes, for the English reader at least, a grounding in the early history of the United States which few English readers are likely to have. The other section is a condensed version of the history of China; and on the whole most readers, I imagine, will find this one of the most wonderful sections of the poem – it is, perhaps more than any other part, properly epical.* But, failures or successes, these two sections give the key to the myth.

It is the myth of the noble leader and the stable community, of the good society which has been, and can be again, and which wicked men seek to destroy. The good society, for Pound, is stable rather than changing; the only natural kind of change is deterioration, and therefore to preserve the stability of society a constant, daily effort of *renewal* is required. Certain sacred exemplars of stability must be kept in mind, figures like Confucius and Adams, documents like the Confucian writings and the American Constitution. The noble leader, like Adams, and the stable society, like China, have qualities in common. Their stability is preserved by the exercise of an acute but severely practical intelligence. They both respect tradition, but by that they mean the cultural inheritance of skills and insights and wisdom; not merely anything at all that has come down from the past. There are times when a break must be made,[1] but when the break has been made, it has something of finality about it – just as for Burke, for instance, the 'Glorious Revolution' of 1688 was, among other things, a kind of sacred barrier against any subsequent revolutions whatever. Stability has two enemies besides its own natural tendency to decay. One is the activity of the moneylender, the tax-gatherer, the banker, the great financial combine; the other is otherworldliness – like Taoism in China – which treats life as a vain dream.

Pound thus thinks of certain purposes as valid throughout history, but as constantly thwarted. He thinks it possible to separate the wheat of history from the chaff; and this distinguishes him from historicists in the strict sense like Hegel, Marx, Croce, or Collingwood, for whom such a distinction is untenable, for whom everything that happens in history is necessary, and reasonable, and therefore right. To separate the wheat from the chaff, Pound must feel sure that he has a stance *outside* history; or access to certain permanent values.

What set? Partly those of the artist who keeps his eyes open. 'By their fruits ye shall know them.' There must be something right about the society that produces Chartres and something wrong about the society that produces, say, London south of the river. Men like Adams and Jefferson respect the arts, but they are not in Mauberley's sense 'aesthetes', and indeed throughout *The Cantos* Pound seems to be moving away from Mauberley's still faintly 'ninetyish attitude towards one more like Ruskin's in *Unto This Last*; it must be good men, in a good society, who build a good cathedral.

The odd thing is that in religion Pound is a kind of eighteenth-century deist (one of his literary heroes, and an oddly assorted set they are, is Voltaire), and there must be a sense in which the cathedral, and the whole outer fabric of medieval life that he loves so passionately, is nothing for him but an adorable mockery or a beautiful empty shell. Critics have noted, and very rightly, the new and very moving note of religious humility in the 'Pull down thy vanity' passage in *The Pisan Cantos*; but none of them have noted that the divinity not exactly invoked but hinted at there – the deity that sheathes a blade of grass more elegantly than a Parisian dressmaker sheathes a beautiful woman – is just the divinity of the Deists: 'Nature', or 'Nature's God', it hardly matters which one calls it, for it is just enough of a God to keep Nature running smoothly. The *feeling* of the passage is anything but Vol-

---

[1] But those making the break – Confucius, the Whigs of 1688, the American Founding Fathers, Pound himself as a poetic innovator – will claim always to be going back to an earlier and sounder tradition.

tairean, but the *notion* is quite Voltaire's: the God envisaged is wholly immanent. There is a good deal of disquiet and horror at odd moments in *The Cantos*, but so far as I can see there is no sense of the transcendental, no awareness of the great gulf that separates finite existence from the mystery of nothing or the mystery of being. These ultimate questions are for Pound, as for Confucius or William James, vain distractions from the immediate business of living. There is work to be done, danger to be met; do not let us, Pound seems to be saying, vainly sit and brood, in solitary uselessness.

The anguish that Pound feels most acutely is not about eternity, but about time. 'Time is evil. Evil.' That couple of tiny sentences comes in a passage where Pound is describing how Ignez da Castro, who has been murdered because the old King of Portugal did not want her to be the wife of the young Crown Prince, was dug up from her grave when the Prince ascended the throne, how she sat crowned with 'the King still young beside her', and how 'a day, and a day, all the Lords of Lisboa' filed past her to kiss her hand. Time is evil that has corrupted her beauty in the grave, that has left of the young King's love only pride and bitterness and a dry ache for revenge. Such are among the most moving moments in *The Cantos* and they break through the sturdy and enclosed optimism which is (surprisingly, when one considers the violence and cruelty of so many of the incidents related) the prevailing mood of the myth. The *myth* of *The Cantos* which comes out very often, for instance, in *The Pisan Cantos*, is that of a total waste, bitterness, and loss, which it is not really within human power to compensate or repair. It is something other than man himself that gives him strength to recognize, and to outface, the worst. 'It was not man/Made courage, or made order, or made grace.' Who was it then? This question, in *The Cantos* that are still to come, seems to demand a more positive answer. There is something in the whole pattern of the poem that demands an encounter with the transcendental at a culminating point.

The Cantos started off with a Homeric sea voyage (significantly enough from Circe's island, where Mauberley perhaps, like poor Elpenor, might have been glad enough to linger), and with a visit to hell-mouth, the sacrifice of a sheep, and a raising of the spirits of the mighty dead; while another sort of hell, the hell, as some critic has acutely said, of *others* – of newspaper proprietors, war profiteers, puritan bishops, and those who think of sex in terms of rubber goods, but certainly not of 'ole Ez' himself – plays a prominent, if jarring, part in the earlier Cantos. There are glimpses, too, of a kind of earthly paradise, sea and sun dazzle, nymphs, Bacchus transforming pirates into furry animals, masts into trees, of troubadours, of Renaissance soldiers, of American pioneers, of the Cid – a great froth and flurry of everything that is lively in Pound's memory or imagination; a great invocation, with sidelong snarling glances at the present, of everything that seems splendid in the real or legendary past. The effect is wonderful, but would be bewildering if the pattern – of interweaving stories started, dropped, taken up again at random – were continued indefinitely. The first 30 or so Cantos state a 'matter' one might say, in the medieval sense, the 'matter of Europe'. The American episodes there come in with a strange, disquieting gritty effect, more 'realistic' but less 'poetic'; the Chinese allusions with an effect of remote, grave, and not immediately relevant wisdom.*

Then came, soberly, the great exemplars: the poem touches, if sometimes a little leadenly, the ground of China and America. We know where we are, we have a clearer sense of direction. After all, against brilliant and unstable Europe – and the European ghosts have all been called up from Hell, after all – some more stolid but safer concept of society is to be justified. Then, with *The Pisan Cantos*, there is a change again; we have left hell, and the heavenly phantasmagorias that a classic hell affords, the

> ... *hero's iron shade*
> *Glittering through the gloomy glade*,

and we have ascended from the broad plains of earth, of America and China, to the mountain of purgatory.

The poet moves for the first time mainly through his *own* past, recalling dead or distant or estranged friends – Yeats, Hueffer, Jepson, Newbolt, Nancy Cunard – with a new tenderness; expressing his personal feelings more frankly and on the whole with less toughness than in the past – there are no just wars in spring or autumn (ancient Chinese wisdom, but he feels it personally, the sacredness of sowing and harvest), and, however unpractical and sentimental such a view is, he has learned, from his own sad experience, that he does not like the idea of either animals or men being in cages. Things have not worked out either as he had hoped or as he had calculated. His poem itself, which was to be an impersonal epic, is taking an unexpected direction. He must cast down his vanity.

There are, I believe, about 18 Cantos still to come. It would be rash to make any predictions about them, but we have had a long sea journey and we must have a return to Ithaca; we have had a raising of many ghosts, and they must be ceremoniously laid; we have had the gods of Greece, and the sacred human wisdom of Confucius and Adams, and the *Deus sive Natura* of Spinoza or Voltaire; it is time, as I have already suggested, for us to confront the Transcendent. We have had hell, and earth, and the earthly paradise, and a personal purgatory; of a truly supernatural paradise (not necessarily or very probably a Christian one) we must also have a glimpse.

But these are abstract formal demands, and about abstract form in this sense, a preconceived form into which whatever matter immediately available must be moulded, Pound has never cared much. All these prophecies may be wrong. What does seem certain is that, in *The Pisan Cantos*, he has been forced for the first time to come to grips in poetry with *himself*; to recognize to what great extent the whole pattern of his long poem is, as it were, not objectively read off from history, but projected from his own inner being. If one takes them as an objective statement about history, *The Cantos* are, one must recognize, a failure; a great deal of evidence is presented but in the nature of the case it is not, and cannot be, exhaustive; and even if one accepts it as tendentiously selected, it is not certain that it will prove what Pound wants it to prove. Even as a special pleader, he does not quite make out his case.

He will be forced, I think, in the Cantos that are to come, to recognize that *The Cantos* are an objective failure (that flattened and smothered into prose, so to say, they would not make a convincing thesis about history), but at another level, which one cannot call a merely subjective level, this recognition might set the seal on the poem's success. Pound might recognize that, like Langland, he has written a *vision*. And it is a much more personal vision than Langland's. Pound is free, certainly, of the shadows of Freud and Proust, but we are none of us free of the shadow of Rousseau. The structure of *The Cantos* has in fact no exact analogy in previous literature, but if it is in some sense epical, it is also in some sense confessional. Pound is quite without *introspective* interest in himself, yet perhaps the clearest impression *The Cantos* leave with us, after we have rejected their myth, and accepted their truth, is one of Pound the man. It is perhaps Pound the man at the centre of *The Cantos* that prevents them falling apart into mere fragmentary chaos.

(3)

Yet about the man himself, apart from his poetry, it is perhaps not critically proper to say very much. I shall merely say one word about what I think is the main error in his thinking; an error responsible for flaws in his work and also, of course, for his personal misfortunes. It is a very common error, especially among loyal, active, passionate, and courageous men. It has to do with his ideal of stability. I am not writing as an irresponsible advocate of change for its own sake. We are creatures of habit and, though some changes are always necessary, change in itself is always disagreeable to us. Like Ezra Pound, I too think we should aim at stability in society. But I do not really think that we shall get it, ever, in any permanent sense. We are aiming at something ideal: we have no models of a really stable society in history (certainly neither China nor medieval Christendom is such a model, if one looks into its history in any detail, since the one society stagnated and rendered itself vulnerable to outer pressure and inner upheaval, and the other, a society of perpetual war and debate, was shaken to pieces by its own inner strife). We have only models of more or less striking and ambitious failures to achieve stability.

We seek society's stability, by a kind of instinct, as we seek our own health; though we know that in the long run we shall fall ill and die. It is this instinct, or this impulse, to stabilize that seems permanent in history. There are probably also permanent *elements* of human behaviour; but there are no permanent stable social forms. Every social form is at the best showily, and imperfectly, stable; it will be broken down in time, and a new form (still imperfect, but more suited to new times and circumstances) will take its place. Politics is a heroic activity just because, almost by definition, it is bound to fail.

It is Pound's error, it seems to me, not to recognize this; to believe in stable forms that have been destroyed by malice, and to believe in the possibility of reinstating them, and of curbing the malice that would destroy them. Malice, certainly I would agree, is something that works permanently for the destruction of stability. But whose malice? That, for instance, as Pound sometimes suggests, of those who sell armaments? What about the malice of those who buy? We are *all*, in fact, malicious, and must curb our malice (or pray or think hard for help to curb it) as well as we can. The human race cannot be divided into the many simple, innocent good and the few cunning wicked. That way lie persecution and death-camps. It is Pound's weakness, as a man and a poet, to be able to spot evil in his enemies and not in himself and his friends. The problem of evil, or of innate human self-centredness and aggressiveness, is the one problem with which his life, his poetry, and his politics, have never come to grips. He has been right to stand up, indeed, for human dignity in an age in which there has been an almost hysterical cult of guilt.[1] But there is a sense, and perhaps he has failed to recognize this, in which human dignity is itself a *persona*, a mask, a role. I would rather read Pound any day than Kafka; but there is a sense, after all, in which Kafka goes more deep.

We should think not of this error and these misfortunes but of the man himself, as his works and his friends present him to us, the most generous and impulsive and unworldly of men; devoting two or three hours every day to his poetry and the rest to helping and encouraging younger friends. The evocation of comradeship in *The Pisan Cantos* has a peculiarly touching and genuine quality, and my own feeling, for what it is worth, is that there is more natural goodness in Pound than in half a dozen of his distinguished contemporaries who have had enough common sense – Pound has no common sense at all, I would say, he is a kind of eternal schoolboy, or magnificent *naïf* – never to put a foot wrong. Where he yields himself to blind and stupid hate, or to harsh, uncharitable, destructive anger, I shudder; but whether or not we can hold him fully responsible for such outbursts (and it seems clear that he is the victim of certain compulsive obsessions), it is clear also that they are not *central* to what he has to say. In the perspective of history, his errors will seem incidental; his epic, his vision, his confession, his discovery of himself through his exploration of history, of humility through the assertion of pride, of truth through persistence in error, these will seem typically and broadly human, and in their pathos noble and profound.*

[1] By talking loudly about *universal* guilt one intends, generally, to assuage an uneasy sense of *individual* guilt. 'You are, at least potentially, as bad as me.' True, but not *actually* so bad, and this is resented.

6 · 'THE WASTE LAND' REVISITED

Vision and Rhetoric, Faber and Faber, London, 1959; *The Times Literary Supplement*, no. 2691, 28 August 1953.

Thirty years after its first appearance, three facts about *The Waste Land*, two of which could not be foreseen, and one of which was not known, by contemporary critics, are of peculiar interest. The first fact is that, though perhaps no contemporary poem has had through its mood, its imagery, and its diction – and through some but not all of its technical devices – a more striking influence on a subsequent generation of poets, no subsequent poet has written a successful poem which imitates or adapts the *form* of *The Waste Land*. It might be said that even the influence of the mood and imagery of the poem has been though a powerful, a rather oblique one. A younger poet like Louis MacNeice found, as he has told us, in his university days a romantic excitement in Eliot's metropolitan imagery which Eliot did not consciously intend to put there. When he read such lines as

> *On a winter evening round behind the gashouse*
> *Musing upon the king my brother's wreck*
> *And on the king my father's death before him*

his youthful reaction was not so much a perception of ironic contrast as a feeling that it would be rather fun to play Hamlet beside the gasworks. (Eliot might have murmured like Mr Prufrock, 'That is not what I meant at all. That is not it, at all.') The history of literary influences is full of such paradoxes. 'Prufrock' has similarly given a glamour for many of us to the idea of 'one-night cheap hotels' and, by the play he makes with the idea of 'seediness', Graham Greene has given us a romantic interest in dim and flavourless interiors, and the Tottenham Court Road. Any good writer injects by his skill a positive quality even into scenes and episodes of which he may consciously merely intend to emphasize the negative value. There is no doubt that one of Eliot's purposes in *The Waste Land* was to point a contrast, as in the lines quoted above, between the splendour and dignity of some aspects of the past and the sordidness of some aspects of the present. What younger poets learned from him, however, was that the sordidness could have its own tang. They had enough sense, in the early 1930s, to see that a complexity and elaboration of form like that of *The Waste Land* were beyond their youthful scope. They could, however, appropriate the gashouse, and note, as Eliot did, the run of the contemporary speaking voice. It is rather as if young admirers of Braque had decided that fish on a kitchen table make a first-rate subject for a painting, but that the way to paint them is not as Braque does, but in a traditional naturalistic manner.

The second fact has some relation to the first. No contemporary poem has been subjected to more detailed and laborious analysis than *The Waste Land*, yet no critic has either confidently assigned it to one of the traditional kinds of poetry or, if he considers it as the invention of a quite new kind of poem, has invented a new name for that kind. In conversation, indeed, such names may be sometimes thrown out. An enthusiastic young man may describe *The Waste Land* as a condensed epic; a stubborn traditionalist may call it a cento.[1] But obviously neither of these names fits. The third fact has perhaps again some connection with the second. Eliot very largely left the final decisions about the form of *The Waste Land* to his friend, Ezra Pound. The fact that he sought and welcomed such advice (it might even be correct to say, such instructions) suggests that there must have been a stage in the composition of the poem when he found its matter so disturbing that he could not take a detached view of its form. He had been exploring, as an early reviewer of *The Waste Land* shrewdly noticed, 'the limits of coherency'. On Pound's advice, he very drastically cut and rearranged his first version. For a generation that has grown up with *The Waste Land*, it is hard to imagine the poem as having any other shape. Eliot was obviously right to trust Pound's technical judgment. But at the same time, if we consider the history of the poem's composition, it is clear that its form falls between two stools. It is not a traditional form, imposed on poetic matter, planned in advance. Neither, on the other hand, is it Sir Herbert Read's 'organic form' which naturally grows out of poetic matter – though the form of the first, uncut version of the poem may have been so. It is to some degree at least an *ad hoc* contrivance – a deliberately devised scheme for holding together in a coherent shape an already existing body of poetry.

The existence of Pound's own *Cantos* may seem to some readers to contradict the statement made above that no other living poet has written a successful poem which imitates or adapts the *form* of *The Waste Land*. But *The Cantos* were begun earlier. Full though they are of magnificent poetry, few critics would be willing to say that as a whole they *are* a formal success. The difference in scale in any case makes any very general comparison unprofitable. And the similarity of technical devices is rather superficial. Blackmur has described the main narrative device of *The Cantos* as that of the interrupted anecdote. A story is begun, broken off, and taken up in a new setting later on. The main narrative device of *The Waste Land*, on the other hand, is that of cinematic cutting between various more or less self-enclosed scenes and episodes. Again, a simple implicit theme – that of drifting barrenness in a world incapable of self-sacrificing devotion and no longer held to-

[1] A cento is a poem made up of lines and phrases appropriated from other poems.

gether by the bonds of love and faith – unifies *The Waste Land. The Cantos* have several themes, economic, political, artistic, and personal; they are a panorama of one man's view, at once more scrappy and more various than Eliot's, of the significance of history; and the themes, or the moral lessons which Pound deduces from them, are often stated with didactic explicitness. If we were to compare these poems with two important works of a former age, we might see *The Cantos* as having something of the wide, rambling range of *The Ring and the Book*, and *The Waste Land* as having something of the unified tone and concentration on a single problem of *In Memoriam*.

Is it possible, in fact, now that we have lived with it for 31 years, to say what sort of a poem *The Waste Land* is? It is not in any plain traditional sense a lyrical, a meditative, a descriptive, a didactic, a satirical, a narrative, or a dramatic poem, though there are elements in it that link it with all these broad kinds. Lawrence Durrell has noted that it would be easy to arrange it as a radio feature with the voice of a male commentator taking the narrative and meditative portions of the poem and actors and actresses the various 'speaking parts'.[1] Eliot, in his own reading of the poem, suggests magnificently the variations of pace, but does not very strikingly dramatize the separate voices. Robert Speaight, on the other hand, in a recent recording, not only effectively mimics these voices but actually sings both the fragment of an Australian ballad about Mrs Porter and her daughter and the line or two of 1920-ish jazz : *

> O O O O that Shakespeherian Rag –
> It's so elegant
> So intelligent ...

It is clear from any hearing of the poem that the narrative and dramatic elements in it are of primary importance; but it is clear from any reading of it that what may be called a covert didacticism is an element of primary importance, too. It is tempting, in fact, to think of *The Waste Land* as a narrative poem of covert didacticism, introducing speaking characters who represent virtues and vices, like the medieval allegory. It is not, of course, an allegory in any strict sense, but it has much in common with a vision-poem like *Piers Plowman* in which the abstract framework of all allegory tends to crumple under the weight of the poet's concrete apprehension of contemporary life.

The human figures in *The Waste* Land do not, to be sure, to any notable extent, represent virtues. But they do represent vices, and like the figures in *Piers Plowman* they also represent different estates of the realm (the rich couple, the clerk and the typist, the false friend of Lil and Albert in the public bar, the humble people with dirty hands and broken finger-nails on Margate Sands). They also represent the sterile constriction or the pointless loosening of traditional social bonds in a society whose order is being under-

[1] It *was* broadcast as a wireless 'feature' before the 1939–45 war.

mined. The scale of the two poems is, of course, quite different, and where the author of *Piers Plowman* can deal with social bonds of every sort Eliot has to concentrate on those of love and marriage. And there is a broader and more significant general resemblance. Both poems make an immediate appeal to the radical temperament; they both vividly call attention to breakdowns of various sorts in a contemporary society. They both take a rather desperate view of the seriousness of these breakdowns. Nevertheless, neither Eliot nor the author of *Piers Plowman* is what Marxists call a progressive. Both are what Marxists call reactionaries. The author of *Piers Plowman* criticized a rapidly changing late medieval society by the rigid standards of an early feudalism, which retrospectively he somewhat idealized. Similarly, Eliot was a man of his age in illustrating what he regarded as the failure of society by examples of the failure of love between men and women. This was a favourite theme both of good and bad novels in the 1920s. But the progressive solution for the problem was more emancipation, not less; it was hygiene, broad-mindedness, and common sense, the gospel according to Havelock Ellis. *The Waste Land* does not in any explicit way put forward a solution for this problem; but the reader of today, in the light of Eliot's subsequent development, is likely to see the failure of all the levels of human love that are evoked in the poem as arising from a failure of the typical modern metropolitan man to consider chastity a virtue, compunction a necessary persistent check in all human relationships, and marriage a sacramental bond.

But this comparison should not be pushed too far. The characters in *The Waste Land* are perhaps not more real than those in *Piers Plowman*, but for a modern reader they are more actual. They adorn a possible tale (some of Eliot's earlier poems, 'Prufrock' and 'Portrait of a Lady', had resembled more than anything else poetic condensations of themes for a Henry James short story); they do not merely point a moral. They have the ambiguity of actual human existence; and this, moreover, is combined with a fluid vagueness, a shifting of outlines, which allows us to recognize in them also the indefinable human essence – or, in other words, our own deeper self. All the men in the poem, as Eliot has told us, are really one man, all the women really one woman; and the figure of Tiresias stands for the terrifying plastic poetic imagination, the imagination for which even that barrier between the sexes is a vague one. Tiresias (who is the poet and the reader) can identify himself with all levels of human experience. He has been male and female. He has argued with the gods and paid for it, but he has also 'slept among the lowest of the dead'. Thus the human essence with which the poem puts us in touch is not that merely of archetypal maleness and femaleness, in various social disguises. It is not even some permanent image of man as a wanderer in a desert, a knight on a quest, a dry soul looking for living waters, a prisoner in a tower. Each of these images may be here and there relevant, but the essence we are put in touch with is something more concrete, less describable, above all more intimate. It is our own terrible plasticity, which is also at the root of our deepest *rapport* with others – a *rapport* that can exist without conscious sympathy, approval or even understanding. We not only know Madame Sosostris, we know what it is to be she. We not only watch the crowd flow over London Bridge, we are part of it.

The abrupt transitions of the poem give it, in fact, the effect not only of a vision but a dream. One of the most alarming aspects of dreams is the ability of the dreamer to identify himself in turn with everybody he is dreaming about. He dreams about the pursuit of a criminal. He perhaps dreams that he joins the chase. He is even the great detective leading it. Then, suddenly, it is he himself who is being pursued. And has he not known obscurely from the beginning of the dream that the great detective and the criminal were two alternating disguises for the same inescapable identity? A kind of phantasmagoric shifting of roles and merging of sympathies of this sort accompanies every really sensitive and absorbed reading of *The Waste Land*. A reader has not really become soaked in the poem until he knows even what it was like to be the carbuncular young man on whom assurance sat like a silk hat on a Bradford millionaire. There is a contrary sense, of course, in which the isolation of the individual – the 'horrible tower' – is a main theme of the poem. But there is another, everyday isolation, in which we are comfortable enough; that of our habits, our hobbies, our routine. *The Waste Land* awakens us from that. It makes us intimately aware of a general human condition in which we participate.

If we are to think of *The Waste Land* in this way, however, as not only a vision-poem but a dream-poem, it is well to bear in mind a remark of Pascal's: 'Life is a slightly less inconsistent dream.' For the subject-matter of *The Waste Land* is life, not fantasy; paradoxically, it seeks to awaken us to, and to awaken us from, life's actual dreamlike quality – life's inconsistency, to which religion and philosophy and high poetry all in their different ways seek to call our attention – by presenting waking perceptions to us in a dream pattern. Thus the London of the opening section of the poem is an 'unreal city' at several levels. It is unreal precisely as a dream is unreal. It is unreal also in the more noble sense in which a poetic vision is unreal – in the sense in which Wordsworth glimpsed a London from Westminster Bridge in the early morning, which few of the rest of us are likely to glimpse except at highly privileged moments. But though these implications are there for us now, and must have been there for sensitive readers from the beginning, they cannot have been consciously uppermost in Eliot's own mind. London, at that level, for Eliot, must have been unreal though actual; unreal like the top-story of Dante's Hell, the place of the drifters, whose lives had been without coherence, without tension or purpose, without noble endeavour or tragic failure, 'without infamy or glory'. It is of Dante's Hell, the weak scum floating on the top of it, that he is thinking when he presents to us the London crowd:

> *A crowd flowed over London Bridge, so many*
> *I had not thought death had undone so many,*
> *Sighs, short and infrequent, were exhaled,*

And each man fixed his eyes before his feet.
Flowed up the hill and down King William Street,
To where Saint Mary Woolnoth kept the hours
With a dead sound on the final stroke of nine.

The bell with its dead sound has begun to toll in the first lines there,

...so many,
I had not thought death had undone so many,

and the words themselves, 'dead sound' (with the thick dentals and the long
dark diphthong) actualize what they allude to. The church bell, with its
dulled note, is like a warning bell not heard by ships drifting at sea. The
dead-and-alive crowd, not looking up, or around, or very far ahead, will
flow on, not seeking a safe harbour, nor feeling any need for prayer. Yet
there is something else. The melancholy clangour of the lines gives the dead-
and-alive the dignity of real death. They are not the lost, but the allusion
to Dante compares them to the lost, and the lost have their own very terrible
dignity. The crowd has suddenly, when we feel this, the black grandeur of
some great funeral procession. If we remember Langland, once more, the
crowd also takes on yet another significance. Langland started off with 'a
field full of folk'. When we think of his world we think of town and country
growing into each other, booths and apprentices, open stalls, varieties of
bright costume, chattering groups, rich merchants, poor scholars, priests and
friars, women going to market, strong men on horseback. The amorphous,
undifferentiated, well-disciplined 'crowd' is a quite modern conception. It
does not divide easily into 'folk'. It typifies the sameness-in-diversity of our
world, its organization and loneliness, its patient law-abidingness and its in-
human unawareness of its neighbour. It stands for drift, incoherence, merging. Yet by seeing how good a symbol it is for death, for the acquiescent and
patient flowing, the failure to notice and protest, that are as near as we can
get in life to the feeling of death, we lend it a kind of life, the compelling life
and the power over the imagination that the idea of death has.

The Waste Land has been examined in detail by several sensitive and
thorough critics. A conducted tour of the whole poem, on the scale of these
prolix remarks on a single short passage, would obviously at this stage be
wearisome. Yet it is worth making the general point that the kind of
ambiguity that pervades both the idea of unreality and the idea of death in
the first passage tends to pervade the whole poem. Negative ideas accrete a
positive glamour round them, through the poet's phantasmagoric art; and
positive ideas tend to have their basis undermined through his abrupt irony.
Thus the main human episodes of the poem, those in the second and third
sections, are concerned, as we have noticed, with various kinds of failure in
human love. Eliot is dealing in these sections with what happens to romantic
love, to sexual urgency and passion and to marriage as an institution, outside
the Christian sacramental tradition. The element of covert didacticism is very

important here. For, if we were reading *The Waste Land* not as a poem but as a tract or sermon we might be inclined to accuse him of rigging his evidence.

Thus, the neurotic upper-middle-class couple who appear at the beginning of 'A Game of Chess' are not really at all centrally typical of either legal or irregular relationships between wealthy and cultivated people, even in our own troubled times. They belong to a very special Eliotic world that echoes the tones of Jacobean drama:

> '*My nerves are bad to-night. Yes, bad. Stay with me.*
> '*Speak to me. Why do you never speak? Speak.*
> '*What are you thinking of? What thinking? What?*
> '*I never know what you are thinking. Think.*'
>
> *I think we are in rats' alley*
> *Where the dead men lost their bones . . .*

The episode is so magnificently put over that we do not pause to criticize it. But in 'real life' he would stay, he would speak, or there would be a divorce or a separation or, if the relation was an irregular one, the woman would find a slightly less unnerving lover. However rich, bored, sophisticated, and unhappy our friends may be, few of us really know a couple like this. We do, on the other hand, accept without question the social reality, and the reasonably central social significance, of the disloyal friend of Lil and Albert in the pub, of the typist who smooths her hair and puts a record on the gramophone, of the girl who raised her knees supine on the floor of a narrow canoe, and of the weeping young man who promised a 'new start'. Yet we may still feel that the instances have been rather carefully chosen to buttress a rather doubtful case. People do certainly pay for their pleasures and suffer for their passions, but in these two central sections of *The Waste Land* we may feel that the poet has not made it sufficiently clear – and perhaps does not himself imaginatively realize – that pleasure and passion may be, to the ordinary human creature at most times, worth paying and suffering for. Do sexual relationships, even in a period of fundamental social crisis, consist *essentially* of nervous exasperation, coveting your neighbour's husband, pawing, disgusted acquiescence, and a humble making-do with second – or third – bests?

> *He wept. He promised a 'new start'.*
> *I made no comment. What should I resent?*

Eliot is a great and profound poet, but it might be suggested – on the evidence not only of these sections of *The Waste Land* but of the rather glum and limited, though common-sensical and moral, view of the possibilities of marriage put forward in *The Cocktail Party* – that there is a range of human experience he has never adequately explored. What it is can be perhaps best suggested by a quotation from Yeats:

> *That there are still some living*
> *That do my limbs unclothe.*
> *But that the flesh my flesh has gripped*
> *I both adore and loathe.*

(Pipe and drum music)

> *Are those things that men adore and loathe*
> *Their sole reality?*
> *What stood in the Post Office*
> *With Pearse and Connolly?*

It might be said that the sexual episodes in *The Waste Land* make it clear enough that lovers can loathe each other and the act of love, but not that they can alternately or even almost simultaneously adore each other and it. 'Pipe and drum' music, moreover, would be appropriate at no moment in *The Waste Land*; nor, in spite of all the poem's abrupt transitions, is there room in it for a transition so very abrupt and yet so very natural as that from the harlot's loathing and adoration of her trade to Pearse's and Connolly's loathing and adoration of the violent death they heroically faced in 1916 in the Dublin Post Office. For all Eliot's devotion to the seventeenth century, there is one trite comparison of that age which he has never appreciated – the thought that love is like war, as terrifying and exciting.

Thus in these two sections of *The Waste Land* there is something that may strike us at first as a captious and arbitrary destructiveness, as an analysis of a polar experience ('We hate what we love, we are disgusted with what we desire') too much in terms of the secondary and uncreative pole. Yet in the end, in the total pattern, this is not as a flaw. The reader out of his own experience can make actual these positive values of human passion which Eliot himself does not choose to actualize; and, resolving his negative responses in a higher complex of feelings, Eliot does actualize for us humility, compassion, and compunction :

> '*On Margate Sands,*
> *I can connect*
> *Nothing with nothing.*
> *The broken fingernails of dirty hands.*
> *My people humble people who expect*
> *Nothing.*'

'Nothing with nothing' there, is a 'breakdown', a final analysis of human existence in terms of the meaningless. 'The broken fingernails of dirty hands' begins, however, to mingle compassion with distaste. And if the 'humble people who expect/Nothing' are at one level still being destructively analysed – if the statement that they 'expect nothing' means at that level that they lack culture, faith, hope, purpose, and money – at another level to be humble and expect nothing is a condition at which saints might aim. The

people on Margate Sands are the wretched debris of an industrial civilization, but they are also the meek who shall inherit the earth.

About the splendid fifth section of *The Waste Land* there is, at this stage,
nothing new to say. But one observation about the fourth and shortest
section of the poem, 'Death by Water', may be new. This section has sometimes a very odd effect on the listener when the poem is read aloud. It can,
like nothing else in *The Waste Land*, directly induce tears. This effect of
pathos is partly from contrast. The other sections of the poem are, or seem,
long: and they are complex. Their images come home to us with a familiar
but sometimes shocking immediacy. Their techique is partly impressionistic
and partly dramatic. Their cinematic cutting from episode to episode keeps us
anxiously alert. We may be anxious also to spot allusions to the Grail story
and to the sacrificed gods in *The Golden Bough*. 'Death by Water' is short,
simple, unallusive – except in so far as Madame Sosostris had told us to fear
death by water, and death by water is the polar opposite of death by hanging,
and death by hanging stands for crucifixion, and taking up one's cross means
following in the footsteps of Christ, and offering up one's life and witness as
a sacrifice, so that death by water would mean the dissolution of the natural
once-born man into the eternal flux – and classical, and remote. But it moves
us also because it states more directly than any other part of the poem the
essential pathos of the human condition. We are mortal. We are young and
grow old. When we hear that somebody else has died, we remember that we
shall die. The differences of class, of culture, of creed, of historical period,
with which the rest of the poem makes so much play, do not after all
affect the general and fundamental pathos of our lot:

> *Gentile or Jew*
> *O you who turn the wheel and look to windward,*
> *Consider Phlebas, who was once handsome and tall as you.*

Such a cursory re-exploration of some selected aspects of *The Waste Land*
will have added little, if anything, to the ordinary sensitive reader's understanding of the poem. Yet it may help us to answer some of the questions
with which we started off. It seems clear that *The Waste Land* will remain
a unique successful example of its form, whatever that form may be called.
It was a form specially suited to an exploration of the 'limits of coherency'
(both in the poet's inner responses, and in his outer world) and it performed
that task of exploration in a final fashion, not only for Eliot's contemporaries
in the 1920s, but for his successors in the 1930s, and for ourselves today. Eliot
himself, with his usual scrupulous and ironical self-criticism, described it as
expressing not a generation's disillusionment, but its illusion of being disillusioned. Another very fine critic described it, when it was new in the
world, as a 'music of ideas', divorced from any kind of belief. Still another
fine critic thought that it exhibited no progression, that it ended, morally,
where it began. Time makes so many things clearer, even to minor com-
mentators. Far from being a 'music of ideas' – in the abstract sense in which

some of Paul Valéry's poems might be thus described – *The Waste Land*
seems to a modern reader to be, quite apart from its poetic value, an extremely significant document about London life in the 1920s. Far from being
divorced from any kind of belief, it seems to express what might be called
a radical and reactionary, as opposed to a liberal and progressive, attitude
towards the disorders of modern society. Far from exhibiting no progression,
it seems to progress towards the expression, in the fifth section, of very
definite moral and religious aspirations. If it ends on a subdued and ironical
note, it is because the poet is sanely aware that there is a difference between
aspirations and having them realized. And the reason why the poem's form
has still no exact parallels is fairly clear. Eliot was immersing himself in 'the
destructive element'. He managed to express perfectly, for his own generation and for all its successors till now, a sense of the disintegration of modern
society, of our world's being, in a phrase of Gabriel Marcel's, 'a broken
world'. The natural human response to a vivid awareness of 'a broken world'
is an attempt to mend it. That was Eliot's response in his own later prose and
poetry, and it was certainly the response of the young poets of the 1930s.

7·A LANGUAGE BY ITSELF

Vision and Rhetoric, Faber and Faber, London, 1959; *T. S. Eliot:
A Symposium edited by R. Marsh and Tambimuttu*, Editions
Poetry London, London, 1948. This was an anthology of tributes for
T. S. Eliot's sixtieth birthday.

I would like to express the gratitude which, like every poet of my generation, I feel towards Eliot in language worthy of himself. I feel, of course, that
this is beyond me: as Lord Herbert of Cherbury, struggling to express a
similar gratitude towards John Donne, said, I could do it

> *...did I not need*
> *A language by itself, which would exceed*
> *All those which are in use; for while I take*
> *These common words which men may even rake*
> *From dunghill-wits, I find them so defiled,*
> *Slubber'd, and false, as if they had exiled*
> *Truth and propriety, such as do tell*
> *So little other things, they hardly spell*
> *Their proper meaning, and therefore unfit*
> *To blazon forth thy merits, or thy wit.*

That quotation, besides expressing one's sense of embarrassed inadequacy
on an occasion like this, suggests something else: Eliot resembles Donne in
having given the more sensitive spirits of his time a new, a critical awareness
of language. That is what Lord Herbert intends to suggest, and that also is
what Thomas Carew suggests in his more famous, more brilliant elegy, which
is, indeed, perhaps the best piece of criticism in verse in the English language:

> *The Muses' garden, with pedantic weeds*
> *O'erspread, was purged by thee; the lazy seeds*
> *Of servile imitation thrown away,*
> *And fresh invention planted ...*

That is as true of Eliot in his time, as of Donne in his. Donne, like Eliot,
had refreshed the language, and in every innovator and renovator there is a

certain quality of harshness; the classics of an age of experiment may be thrown somewhat into the shade in a succeeding age of established convention. They are likely, however, to reassert themselves as soon as convention has exhausted itself. Such, as Carew foresaw, was to be the fate of Donne; such perhaps may be the fate of Eliot.

> *Thou shalt yield no precedence, but of time,*
> *And the blind fate of language whose tun'd chime*
> *More charms the outward sense; yet thou mayst claim*
> *From so great disadvantage greater fame,*
> *Since to the awe of thy imperious wit*
> *Our stubborn language bends, made only fit*
> *With her tough thick-ribbed hoops to gird about*
> *Thy giant fancy, which had proved too stout*
> *For their soft melting phrases.*

Their soft melting phrases: there was a difficulty, as Carew saw, in keeping up along 'the line of masculine expression' opened up by Donne – there was a counter-attraction, against his harsh genius, of the mild, the gentle, the soothing cadence; against his precise and passionate thought, of a noble and vague eloquence. Therefore, Carew thought,

> *...thy strict laws will be*
> *Too hard for libertines in poetry.*
> *They will repeal the goodly exil'd train*
> *Of gods and goddesses, which in thy just reign*
> *Were banished nobler poems; now, with these,*
> *The silenced tales o' th' Metamorphoses*
> *Shall stuff their lines, and swell the windy page,*
> *Till verse, refi'd by thee, in this last age*
> *Turn ballad-rhyme, or those old idols be*
> *Adored again with new apostacy.*

These passages have a certain relevance, also, to Eliot's position today. They cannot, of course, be applied to him literally. Unlike Donne, he is not a writer who is ever likely, in any age, to seem metrically harsh to any educated ear. Unlike Donne, he cannot be said exactly to have banished 'the silenced tales o' th' *Metamorphoses*' from his verse; classical mythology, but understood with a historical breadth of view and a religious depth of feeling, is one of his main sources of allusions. But, like Donne, he came on his age with a peculiar shock of immediacy. Extremely learned, as Donne was extremely learned, he nevertheless, like Donne, was to bring poetry almost uncomfortably close to the language and the feelings of common life. For our age, like Donne for his, he has been a salutary disturbing factor. He is also, like Donne, an eminently masculine writer and a writer who sets

standards both of aim and execution which are hard for weaklings to follow.
We have only to open, today, the latest anthology of work by young Oxford
or Cambridge poets, we have only to look, even, at the accomplished but,
in comparison to Eliot, quite academic diction of such a promising and regretted young poet as Sidney Keyes, to realize that Eliot's laws are, indeed,
'too hard for libertines in poetry': and we have only to read the critical
attack by a contemporary of Eliot's, like Herbert Read, on the 'line of wit' in
poetry – on the tradition, that is, which Eliot has drawn onwards to fresh
triumphs – to realize that wit, like Eliot's or Donne's, is not at every man's
fingertips, and that for those who lack it, it is hard to admit that it is an
essential ingredient of the highest poetry. Why is it, for instance, that in spite
of the enormous talent, the enormous industry, of Browning and Tennyson,
a faintly musty odour still hangs about their work? Dr Johnson's answer, in
another connection, will tell us. It had not enough vitality to preserve it from
putrefaction. It had not enough wit to keep it sweet.

I am talking, then, of Eliot especially as a poet (not as a critic, as a teacher,
or as a representative of any particular beliefs) and from the point of view,
especially, of what other poets of his time have got from him. He has, I am
suggesting, for all of us, refreshed the language of poetry. I first read him
myself when I was about 15 or 16. Much of what he was talking about was
beyond my experience or above my head. I found myself, nevertheless, reading him with tingling excitement, and pausing, with absorbed delight, on,
for instance, such lines as these:

> In the mountains, there you feel free.
> I read, much of the night, and go south in winter

or these:

> ...turning
> Wearily, as one would turn to nod good-bye to Rochefoucauld
> If the street were time and he at the end of the street

or these:

> Would she not have the advantage, after all?
> This music is successful with a 'dying fall'
> Now that we talk of dying.

lines which, for the ordinary reader, may well seem not among his most
absorbing or most exciting. They are transitional not climatic passages. For
the reader, on the other hand, who is beginning to write poems, such lines
are absorbing and exciting; he thinks he knows how to manage climaxes,
but transitions are what stump him.

A struggling young poet, coming for the first time on Eliot's work, is struck
by such transitional passages because they reveal to him the possibility of

conveying in verse, with exactness, an equivalent of his passing moods and of the tone, and even of the shades of tone, of his individual speaking voice. Such lines reveal to such a young man a new possibility in verse as an instrument. Donne, of course, reveals the same possibility; but still, his voice, though still a living and individual one, is the voice of another age; and his metric meets the demands not only, one might say, of a special rhetoric but of a special physique. It is the metric of a preacher, who has learnt to cast his voice to the back of the hall; the metric is successful, but behind the success there is strain, and the voice, loud, slow, harsh, resonating – with what Saintsbury called its 'sad clangor' – is not a voice for most young poets to imitate. Eliot's voice in verse, in spite of a certain dryness, is much nearer to the common tone, the common cadence of poetry. It is an easy and graceful voice, and it could have revealed to us, if his interests had been other than they were, the possibility of combining that 'natural, easy' manner with a highly wrought artificial form. The poem which, as a boy, I knew by heart of Eliot's was 'La Figlia che Piange'. It is one of his slightest poems; perhaps his only strictly conventional one; and certainly one of his most purely beautiful :

> So would I have had him leave,
> So would I have had her stand and grieve,
> So he would have left
> As the soul leaves the body torn and bruised,
> As the mind deserts the body it has used.
> I should find
> Some way incomparably light and deft,
> Some way we both should understand,
> Simple and faithless as a smile and shake of the hand.

Such a passage is not typical of Eliot, and yet I felt it to be typical of something. In its simplicity, its transparency, its lack of larger implications, it has its equivalent in a famous passage in Donne, where he, too, for the moment lays aside his usual apparatus of scorn and irony :

> Sweetest love, I do not goe
> For weariness of thee,
> Nor in hopes the world can show
> A fitter love for mee . . .

> Yesternight the Sunne went hence,
> And yet is here to-day,
> He hath no desire nor sense
> Nor halfe so short a way . . .

It is a mark of some very fine poets that, even in slight, occasional pieces, outside the main line of their development, they can suggest new lines of development to others. In an essay of Ezra Pound's, I was to discover what 'La Figlia che Piange' is typical of. Pound was comparing *Provençal lyrics*, which had specially influenced his own lyrical writing, with early Italian lyrics. Provençal is for singing; its metric is elaborate, but its sentences are short and abrupt, like Pound's sentences in many of his own poems. Early Italian verse, the verse of the *dolce stil nuovo*, is to be read, and to be read on the page; the sentences are longer, the words more weighted with thought, the connections of thought more carefully worked out. The type of poetry which I divined through 'Le Figlia che Piange' was, I think, that of the *dolce stil nuovo*. Similarly, what one feels about 'Sweetest love, I do not goe' is that Donne, if he had not had other work in hand, might have developed the conventional Elizabethan lyric towards a new deep and sober intimacy of tone. I am not a very original writer myself; I am lost, on the whole, without a convention of some sort, and so, I suppose, I may have been among the few to notice that, if Eliot had not had more important things to do, he could have become a poet of restrained and sad lyric grace in a quite conventional tradition. That possibility would naturally not be of much general interest. What must, however, have interested every young poet who read him was that immediacy of language to which I have already drawn attention : what has been called, too vaguely, his conversational tone.

What do we mean, in fact, by his conversational tone? As his work progresses, that description becomes less apt; the language of *Ash Wednesday*, of some of the Ariel Poems, of the *Four Quartets*, is, indeed, 'a language by itself'. It can hardly influence anybody, for it has exhausted its own possibilities. For the ordinary reader, admiring Eliot's later poetry, the first impulse must be, not to go and do likewise, but to go and do something else; and such contemporary writing as has modelled itself on that later manner (some of Henry Reed's poems, for instance) strikes me as more accomplished cold pastiche. 'Prufrock', on the other hand, the first poem of Eliot's that we all read – for we all open the book at the beginning, and we all find it impossible to dip or skip – is another cup of tea. As the first thing of Eliot's that we read, and are absorbed by, it has a great practical influence on our own work. And 'Prufrock' is very largely an exercise in Eliot's peculiar conversational tone, and may help us to define that.

Eliot's conversational tone in 'Prufrock' is not, for instance, that of Pope, even when Pope is most direct and least mannered :

> *Nothing so true as what you once let fall:*
> *'Most women have no characters at all.'*

It is not that of Byron in *Don Juan*, a garrulous, loquacious tone. It is not the buttonholing, breathing-down-your-neck tone that Browning has sometimes. It may, however, have something in common with all these three writers; like Pope, Eliot gives an effect of frequenting always the best company, who can quickly pick up a hint or an allusion; like Byron, he can be apparently inconsequent and flippant; like Browning he can conceive a poem most effectively as a sort of dramatic soliloquy. Yet it is more illuminating to go back, once more, to Donne. Compare these two passages of verse in a conversational tone, one by Donne, the other by Pope, rewriting him:

(Donne)

Sir, though (I thank God for it) I do hate
Perfectly all this town; yet there's one state
In all things so excellently best,
That hate towards them breeds pity towards the rest.
Though poetry, indeed, be such a sin,
As I think, that brings dearth and Spaniards in:
Though, like the pestilence and old-fashioned love,
Riddingly it catch men, and doth remove
Never, till it be starved out; yet their state
Is poor, disarm'd, like Papists, not worth hate.

(Pope)

Yes, thank my stars! as early as I knew
This town, I had the sense to hate it too:
Yet here, as e'en in Hell, there must be still
One giant vice, so excellently ill,
That all beside, one pities, not abhors:
As who knows Sappho, smiles at other whores.
I grant that poetry's a crying sin:
It brought (no doubt) the Excise and Army in:
Catched like the plague, or love, the Lord knows how,
But that the cure is starving, all allow.
Yet like the Papist's is the poet's state,
Poor and disarmed, and hardly worth your hate.

Pope, in correcting Donne's 'rugged and most unmusical versification', has missed his point. Donne's stretch and contortion are deliberate, they have a rhetorical purpose, as in the blank verse of another of Eliot's models, Cyril Tourneur. What Pope has lost, rhetorically, by a metrical regularity may be seen by comparing

Is poor, disarm'd, like Papists, not worth hate.

where the asyndeton accumulates the climax (and the phrase 'like Papists', where the climax piles up, looks both back and forward in the line) with the flat amenity of

Poor and disarm'd and hardly worth your hate.

Donne adapts his language and his metrical framework to his thought: Pope adapts his thought to a conventional language (how weak, for instance, is the polite, pert 'Thank my stars!' compared to the fierce, 'I thank God for it!') and to a strict metre. His passage seems smart and vapid, at the most mildly facetious: Donne's, on the other hand, has sinister force. That comes out in things that Pope just leaves out – the adverb 'riddingly', and the phrase 'old-fashioned love' – which might mean normal love, as opposed to homosexual love, in which one ran less risk of the pox; or even love itself, the romantic and chivalrous love of the Petrarchan tradition, as opposed to fashionable lust ... Eliot has a perpetual elegance of language, a conscious refinement, which makes him in one sense more like Pope than Donne; but like Donne he dramatizes (and we should remember, in justice to Pope, that the background of Donne's passage is Elizabethan tragedy; the background of Pope's merely the Addisonian polite essay, gentlemanly chatter about literature); and like Donne he is always adapting his language to his thought, never his thought to a fixed convention of language.

What shall we say, then? The language of 'Prufrock' *feels* like conversation, but it is rather a dramatic imitation of conversational language: heightened, condensed, contorted, with an uncanny precision which ordinary conversation could never have. 'Prufrock', for all its settings at a fashionable party, for all its air of being a Henry James short story, drastically boiled down (the 'story' left out, and the moral, the atmosphere left in) is really a tragi-comic soliloquy. It makes remarks which one does not, in fact, make at parties, though one may think afterwards that one has made them; but one is remembering odd thoughts and perceptions that flashed, unbidden, to one's mind,

> *And I have known the arms already, known them all –*
> *Arms that are braceleted and white and bare*
> *(But in the lamplight, downed with light brown hair!)*

What it creates rather (and memories of a party create this too, for if one arrives at a party late, sober, one finds that very trite and disconnected things are being said) is the *illusion* of conversation: the illusion that, in a quiet corner near a noisy group, one is being talked to quietly, or is quietly talking to oneself. That illusion creates a lull, a soothingness: against the lull, the images flash out, like lightning against a dark sky, with all the more startling effect, the famous evening

> *... spread out against the sky*
> *Like a patient etherized upon a table;*

the paragraph in which the fog prowls like a great cat, the crustacean velleity,

> *I should have been a pair of ragged claws*
> *Scuttling across the floors of silent seas.*

and then at the end in a passage, after so much petulance, wit, and triviality, after such a deliberate excess of the 'personal touch', suddenly purely formal, utterly impersonal, drained of all these polite hesitations of the voice, the mermaids :

I have seen them riding seaward on the waves
Combing the white hair of the waves blown back
When the wind blows the water white and black.

We have lingered in the chambers of the sea
By sea-girls wreathed with seaweed red and brown
Till human voices wake us, and we drown.

As the Russians all came out of Gogol's *Overcoat*, we might say that we all came out of Prufrock's drawing-room. Nearly every important innovation in the English verse of the last 30 years is implicit in this poem. If some of the younger poets, at least, know when to be easy and when to be formal; if they know how to lead up quietly to a startling image; if they know that the point of highest concentrated feeling in a poem must be the most objectively, the most impersonally expressed – they could have learned these things, and to a large extent they *have* learned these things, from 'Prufrock' and from Eliot's other early poems. Our gratitude for the later poems is, as I have already suggested, of another sort; it is a gratitude which we share with the general reading public, for these later poems mark out a path which only Eliot himself could have trodden – there is everything in them to admire, but from the point of view of a young poet who is just beginning, there is nothing in them to imitate. It would be as fatal for him to imitate the language of *Samson Agonistes* or *The Tempest*. But 'Prufrock' is a beginner's poem, and it has lessons for all of us in the art of how to begin. It refreshed, as I have already suggested, the whole language of poetry in our time. Thinking of Eliot's work, poets must share the general admiration of the public for enormous talent, for enormous learning, and for a steady, sad, and noble vision of the world; but they have also, as I have been trying to suggest, this special gratitude to him, as a craftsman who has provided them with new, sharp tools, and as a teacher from whom they have learned how to use these tools and how to keep them clean. Our time has been a terrible one, and for poets that terror has expressed itself as a struggle to say anything at all, to find any resource in language. Yet, like the 'girl of Tereus' in the *Pervigilium Veneris*, Eliot, by his example, has helped us to transform the grief of the time to art :

iam loquaces ore rauco stagna cycni perstrepunt;
adsonat Terei puella subter umbram populi
ut putes amoris ore dici musicos,
et neges queri sororem de marito barbaro.

illa cantat, nos tacemus: quando ver venit meum?
quando fiam uti chelidon ut tacere desinam?
perdidi musam tacendo, nec me Apollo respicit:
sic Amyclas, cum tacerent, perdidit silentium.

Noisy, with harsh cries, swans now thrash the pools.
The girl of Tereus sings in the poplar shadow
So you would think a love song coming from her
And not a sister's complaint of a cruel spouse.

She is singing, we are silent: when will my spring come?
When may I be as the swallow that I may cease to be silent?
I lost my Muse by silence, Apollo does not look at me:
So Amyclae, through being silent, silence lost it all.

Silence will not lose *us* all, though we may lose much : but we too have heard (in Eliot's poems, as well as in other places) the voices under the poplar shade of Philomela and Procne :

The change of Philomel, by the barbarous king
So rudely forced; yet there the nightingale
Filled all the desert with inviolable voice
And still she cried, and still the world pursues,
    'Jug Jug' to dirty ears.

Not all the ears have been dirty, and, in the desert of our time, Eliot's voice has been inviolable; seeking, as I have been seeking all through this essay, for some final adequate compliment to pay to him, I am driven back, as I feared I would be driven back, on that 'language by itself' that I was seeking for – I pay him back, as we are all forced to pay him back in the end, in his own coin : his own incomparable words.

8 · T.S. ELIOT: A REAPPRAISAL

Revue des Langues Vivantes, Tijdschrift voor Levende Talen (Liège, Belgium), xxxxiv no. 6. My special thanks are due to Professor Irène Simon, who immediately asked for this lecture script for publication after hearing me delivering it to the Association Belgo-Brittanique in Liège in March 1968.

It very commonly happens after the death of a great writer that a certain silence falls around his name, that a period of 10 to 20 years elapses in which little is heard of him : his contemporaries, old and young, have already had their say in his lifetime; after 10 or 20 years, a new generation of critics begin to see him not as part of their own lives, but as part of history. After 10 or 20 years, also, biographies and letters are published. It becomes possible to relate what is known of the author's life to one's appreciation of his work. I did not know Eliot well; as a very young man, just after the Second World War, I had the honour of a long conversation with him in his office at Faber and Faber's, and at intervals I used to see him at various literary gatherings. I think the most piquant of such occasions was a party which the publishers Jonathan Cape were giving for another great American poet, Robert Frost. Frost was wearing a loose informal suit of rough tweed, a soft shirt, and a loose tie, he was leaning as if casually against a bookcase which happened to be full of volumes of his own poetry; he had grey untidy hair and a face like a great granitic landslide, wrinkled, grey, and craggy, but interrupted by a most delightful smile. I asked Frost to read me one of my favourite poems, and in return he asked me to read it to him. Frost immediately conquered my heart, where Eliot, for all my admiration, had always a little awed and chilled me. Into this gathering Eliot suddenly made a royal entrance. He was wearing full evening dress, and round his neck was wearing the ribbon of the Order of Merit. He was accompanied by his new young wife and was on his way with her to some important reception and dance. He was wearing patent leather shoes and I noticed how lightly he moved on the balls of his feet, like a cat. He and Frost, I remember, just touched the tips of each other's fingers, Eliot bowing a little, Frost with his warm grin. It was like the meeting of two rival kings, courteous but cautious. But then some irresistible current seemed to sweep the two great men apart, and Eliot was moving like a dancer from one group to another, while Frost still leaned shyly against his bookcase, waiting for his admirers to come to him. It seemed a contrast between urban sophistication and rustic simplicity; yet to read Frost's letters or to study his poems carefully is to realize how deliberate and calculated that role of simplicity, of the rustic sage was; and what appeared a certain worldly polish in Eliot's social manner was, no doubt, the reserve of a very shy man, a shy man who was, of course, also proud.

Eliot's pride and shyness both came, I think, from the sense that in his poems he had exposed himself nakedly, had exposed intimate areas of suffering. He had made a great deal in early essays of the impersonality of poetry, of the Flaubertian distinction between the man who suffers and the artist who creates; yet I have heard F. R. Leavis, in a fine lecture on Eliot, say that the great quality of Eliot's poetry is what Leavis called 'a heroic sincerity', that its great quality is the identity in it of the man who suffers and the artist who creates. Of the precise nature of that suffering we still know, biographically, very little. His earliest important poems, 'Prufrock' and 'Portrait of a Lady', were written when he was still an undergraduate at Harvard, and in 'Prufrock' he disguises the social awkwardness of a young man of genius, his raw immediacy of sensibility, behind the half-comic mask of a man who would like to be Hamlet and suspects that he may be Polonius; and in 'Portrait of a Lady', again, in the young man in that poem taken up by the tiresome middle-aged lady, who in the end proves to have more psychological insight than he has, we have a picture of the social blunders, the emotional imbroglios, into which youthful genius can lead one. There may be poets of our time who are as great or even greater than Eliot, but no one else has that raw immediacy, nobody else presents us with a world, a climate, into which we immediately, willingly or not, enter.

It is a world with a peculiarly intense atmosphere, a dense world, and yet there is an odd sense in which it is sparsely furnished. I have lately been working with a research student who has almost completed an exhaustive study of the vocabulary of Eliot's early poems. He has tabulated things which a good reader would pick up intuitively : the subdued range, for instance, of Eliot's colour adjectives, brown, grey, yellow, black, and white, never for instance scarlet or azure; the frequent mention of streets and corners, the emphasis in the early poems on the sordid and dingy : the constant association of flowers, particularly hyacinths and lilacs, spring flowers, with a feeling of intense but frustrated romantic passion – Eliot's 'hyacinth girl', in *The Waste Land*, he got, I discovered recently, from Strindberg's *Dream Play*. I think this is a source for Eliot that might well be explored; he resembles Strindberg, at least, in his sense of the female image as either the prostitute or the madonna, and in his equation of the sexual relationship with suffering. His vocabulary seems a large and unusual one because of its occasional ostentatious use of unusual words like 'anfractuous' or 'juvescent' or 'polyphiloprogenitive'. In fact, compared with Hardy's vocabulary, full of coinages, or Yeats's, it is rather small, partly because certain kinds of images, of brown fogs, of streets and street lamps, of hyacinth girls, of cats and creatures of the cat tribe like jaguars and tigers, recur so often. It is the vocabulary also in the early poems if not of an imagist, at least of an impressionist, closely tied to outward things. In an early poem like 'Preludes' the poet lets scenes and objects speak for him, only at the very end speaks for himself, and then ambiguously or self-contradictorily, two aspects of the self clashing with each other:

> *I am moved by the fancies that are curled*
> *Around these images, and cling:*
> *The notion of some infinitely gentle,*
> *Infinitely suffering thing.*

> *Wipe your hands across your mouth, and laugh:*
> *The worlds revolve like ancient women*
> *Gathering fuel in vacant lots.*

The *I* who is moved and the *you* who wipes his hand across his mouth and laughs are both aspects of the one person, the suffering *persona* of the poet, who earlier in the same section of 'Preludes' is a *he*, a soul crucified against the drab urban skies:

> *His soul stretched tight across the skies*
> *That fade behind a city block,*
> *Or trampled by insistent feet*
> *At four and five and six o'clock:*
> *And short square fingers stuffing pipes,*
> *And evening newspapers, and eyes*
> *Assured of certain certainties,*
> *The conscience of a blackened street*
> *Impatient to assume the world.*

One should notice in passing how important eyes are in the early poems:

> *And I have known the eyes already, known them all –*
> *The eyes that fix you in a formulated phrase ...'*

> *The street-lamp said, 'Regard that woman*
> *Who hesitates toward you in the light of the door*
> *Which opens on her like a grin.*
> *You see the border of her dress*
> *Is torn and stained with sand,*
> *And you see the corner of her eye*
> *Twists like a crooked pin.'*

> *Clasp your flowers to you with a pained surprise –*
> *Fling them to the ground and turn*
> *With a fugitive resentment in your eyes ...*

Eyes I dare not meet in dreams
In death's dream kingdom
These do not appear:
There, the eyes are
Sunlight on a broken column

— Yet when we came back, late, from the Hyacinth garden,
Your arms full, and your hair wet, I could not
Speak, and my eyes failed, I was neither
Living nor dead, and I knew nothing.
Looking into the heart of light, the silence.

... Here, said she,
Is your card, the drowned Phoenician Sailor
(Those are pearls that were his eyes. Look!)

In the world of isolation, almost of solipsism, which is the world of the early poems, it is in the eyes of others, expressionless, or aggressive, or full of fugitive resentment, the eyes that in a sense judge him, that the poet becomes aware of the otherness of others: of his own loneliness and vulnerability, shut in his horrible tower, his *orrible torre*. The note from Bradley's *Appearance and Reality* is very important, at the end of *The Waste Land*: 'My external sensations are no less private to myself than are my thoughts or feelings. In either case my experience falls within my own circle, a circle closed on the outside; and, with all its elements alike, every sphere is opaque to the others which surround it ... In brief, regarded as an existence which appears in a soul, the whole world for each is peculiar and private to that soul.' The early poems, it appears to me, up to *The Waste Land*, explore this double sense of isolation and vulnerability, and explore a feeling of spiritual paralysis which accompanies this sense:

Between the idea
And the reality
Between the motion
And the act
Falls the Shadow

For Thine is the Kingdom

Between the conception
And the creation
Between the emotion
And the response
Falls the Shadow

Life is very long

But these negative qualities, however brilliantly expressed, would not of themselves make great poetry. Poetry is not made, as Yeats said (though not in connection with Eliot) out of passive suffering. But it can be made out of compassionate suffering, the ability to identify with, to praise, to see something holy or sacrificial in the passive sufferings of others. The young Eliot saw suffering as something essentially feminine, as something evoking the notion

> ... of some infinitely gentle,
> Infinitely suffering thing.

With that economy in the use of his few leading images which I have noted, he evokes this feeling again and again in *The Waste Land*:

> Trams and dusty trees.
> Highbury bore me. Richmond and Kew
> Undid me. By Richmond I raised my knees
> Supine on the floor of a narrow canoe.

> My feet are at Moorgate, and my heart
> Under my feet. After the event
> He wept. He promised a 'new start'.
> I made no comment. What should I resent?

> On Margate Sands.
> I can connect
> Nothing with nothing.
> The broken fingernails of dirty hands.
> My people humble who expect
> Nothing.

Caring little for the idea of beauty – the statement in Keats's 'Grecian Urn',

> 'Beauty is truth, truth beauty.' That is all
> Ye know on Earth, and all ye need to know.

seemed to him a flaw in a fine poem – Eliot thought that the true and deep poet is concerned with the boredom, the horror, the glory of life: the glory seems to me to come out in the early poems chiefly as a profound compassion, as what one could almost call a desperate charity.

Ash Wednesday, his religious poem of 1930, seems to me a turning point. The feeling of this poem moves from a total renunciation, combined with a submission of the will to God,

> Because I know that time is always time
> And place is always and only place
> And what is actual is actual only for one time

And only for one place
I rejoice that things are as they are and
I renounce the blessèd face
And renounce the voice
Because I cannot hope to turn again
Consequently I rejoice, having to construct something
Upon which to rejoice

It moves from that renunciation, as I say, to what I can only call a rechristening, a rebaptism of nature, of the senses, in the wonderful sixth section of the poem:

Although I do not hope to turn again
Although I do not hope
Although I do not hope to turn

Wavering between the profit and the loss
In the brief transit where the dreams cross
The dreamcrossed twilight between birth and dying
(Bless me father) though I do not wish to wish these things
From the wide window towards the granite shore
The white sails still fly seaward, seaward flying
Unbroken wings

And the lost heart stiffens and rejoices
In the lost lilac and the lost sea voices
And the weak spirit quickens to rebel
For the bent golden-rod and the lost sea smell
Quickens to recover
The cry of quail and the whirling plover
And the blind eye creates
And empty forms between the ivory gates
And smell renews the salt savour of the sandy earth

The granite shore, the white sails seaward flying: these are the great granite boulders of Cape Ann, the white sails of the yachts (or perhaps also the white wings of the gulls) at Gloucester, to the north of Massachusetts, boyish memories of nature as beautiful, thrilling, and sacramental, that had not emerged so far in Eliot's poetry: for the scene of the early poetry is the city,

. . . certain half-deserted streets,
The muttering retreats
Of restless nights in one-night cheap hotels
And sawdust restaurants with oyster shells:

and the *persona* of the earlier poems is the suffering persona, haunted by the fear of death and damnation, the victim of a profound insecurity, masking despair with irony :

> The lamp said,
> 'Four o'clock,
> Here is the number on the door.
> Memory!
> You have the key,
> The little lamp spreads a ring on the stair.
> Mount!
> The bed is open; the tooth-brush hangs on the wall,
> Put your shoes at the door, sleep, prepare for life.'
>
> The last twist of the knife.

It is the word *life*, there, which is the last twist of the knife for the suffering speaker. The progress from these staccato rhythms of extreme pain to the open, bold, affirming rhythms of

> From the wide window towards the granite shore
> The white sails still fly seaward, seaward flying
> Unbroken wings

is a huge moral progress. One should note also that in *Ash Wednesday* the early vision of the suffering women,

> My people humble people who expect
> Nothing.

becomes the lovely invocation both to the Hyacinth Girl and the Virgin :

> Lady of silences
> Calm and distressed
> Torn and most whole
> Rose of memory
> Rose of forgetfulness
> Exhausted and life-giving
> Worried reposeful
> The single Rose
> Is now the Garden
> Where all loves end
> Terminate torment
> Of love unsatisfied
> The greater torment
> Of love satisfied
> End of the endless

Journey to no end
Conclusion of all that
Is inconclusible
Speech without word and
Word of no speech
Grace to the Mother
For the Garden
Where all love ends.

I have been lecturing on Eliot's poetry for a whole term and part of another term to my students at Leicester, not preparing elaborate scripts, but reading the poems aloud and uttering my free thoughts on them, and one thing that has impressed me most is how the poems that come after illuminate the poems that went before, so that the best commentary on any poem of Eliot's is usually nothing that a critic has said, but some lines, phrases, or images in another poem that Eliot has written : so that, in fact, one comes to think of his poems as parts of a single long and continuous poem, on a single theme : using language which one would hesitate to use to an English audience, since an English audience tends to distrust metaphysical or theological formulations of purely critical insights, I would call the single theme the resacramentalization of that which has been profaned. The poignancy of loss, accepted religiously, suddenly glows as gain. And each important poem in Eliot's *œuvre* is not merely a record of stages in this spiritual progress, however sensitive, it is in itself a spiritual act, of a daring and unexampled sort. It is through the poems, by means of the poems, that the journey is made.

I would like to read to you the most beautiful of all his shorter poems, 'Marina'. Marina, you will remember, is the lost daughter in Shakespeare's strange play, the precursor of the other three late romances, *Pericles, Prince of Tyre*. Taken from a prose romance, perhaps worked up from some play of the 1590s or even the 1580s, *Pericles* has puzzled critics, even in Shakespeare's own time : Ben Jonson called it 'the mouldy tale of Pericles'. It has in it the theme of the lost daughter and the lost wife which is also the theme of Shakespeare's greatest romance play, *The Winter's Tale*. Pericles, wooing a king's daughter, having to answer a riddle successfully or die, finds that the terrible meaning of the riddle is that the princess has committed incest with her father. He flees back to his own kingdom, but is still threatened by the wrath of the wicked king. Wrecked on another shore, he wins a different princess in a joust with other knights. The vengeance of the wicked king still pursues him, and with his new wife, big with child, he puts to sea. There is a huge storm. The wife dies, or seems to die, in childbirth, she is set afloat. Pericles goes back to his own kingdom, to mourn for her. But his daughter Marina is saved, to be brought up by a magnate of Thorsus, later persuaded by his jealous wife to sell her to a brothel. Her virtue converts and abashes her would-be customers, including the governor of the city. The aged Pericles, on a last voyage, discovers not only the daughter but the wife safe and well. What was thought utterly lost has been found. And all sensitive readers of *Pericles* have felt that there is here some allegory of the spiritual life. I think that it helps one to appreciate this poem to remember that Eliot's first wife was lost to him: she was neurotic from the start, she took drugs, she went mad. And they had no daughters nor any other children.* Here is the poem:

What seas what shores what grey rocks and what islands
What water lapping the bow
And scent of pine and the woodthrush singing through the fog
What images return
O my daughter.

Those who sharpen the tooth of the dog, meaning
Death
Those who glitter with the glory of the hummingbird, meaning
Death
Those who sit in the sty of contentment, meaning
Death
Those who suffer the ecstasy of the animals, meaning
Death

Are become unsubstantial, reduced by a wind,
A breath of pine, and the woodsong fog
By this grace dissolved in place

What is this face, less clear and clearer
The pulse in the arm, less strong and stronger –
Given or lent? more distant than stars and nearer than the eye

Whispers and small laughter between leaves and hurrying feet
Under sleep, where all the waters meet.
Bowsprit cracked with ice and paint cracked with heat.
I made this, I have forgotten
And remember.
The rigging weak and the canvas rotten
Between one June and another September.
Made this unknowing, half conscious, unknown, my own.
The garboard strake leaks, the seams need caulking.
This form, this face, this life
Living to live in a world of time beyond me; let me
Resign my life for this life, my speech for that unspoken,
The awakened, lips parted, the hope, the new ships.

What seas what shores what granite islands towards my timbers
And woodthrush calling through the fog
My daughter.

I remember Leavis, lecturing to us on Eliot last term at Leicester, saying how perfect this poem is and how he wished, great as Dante is, that Eliot had leaned more on Shakespeare in his later poems and less on Dante. One notes here how he uses everything again and again. A line suggesting the laughter between the leaves of children who might have been born but never have been,

> *Whispers and small laughter between leaves and hurrying feet,*

looks forward to the children among the leaves in *Burnt Norton* :

> *Go, said the bird, for the leaves were full of children,*
> *Hidden excitedly, containing laughter.*

And if that looks forward, similarly, 'the woodsong fog' looks backward to the brown and yellow fog of the earlier poems,

> *The yellow fog that rubs its back upon the window panes ...*

> *The brown waves of fog toss up to me*
> *Twisted faces from the bottom of the street ...*

but it is, as I say, sacramentalized, no longer the poisonous chemical fog of the city, but a thick sea-mist, what in Scotland we call a *haar*, and bringing out the tangy invigorating smell of the pine trees :

> *... reduced by a wind,*
> *A breath of pine, and the woodsong fog ...*

Four Quartets are Eliot's greatest achievement in poetry, and a fitting culmination to his purely poetic efforts. Leavis, talking to us at Leicester, said they were very great religious poems indeed and he did not want them kidnapped by the Church of England, by our Protestant Anglican Establishment. Eliot was very unkind to Wordsworth, a greater poet than himself, great though Eliot is : there are four very obviously great English poets, poets of permanent world stature, Chaucer, Shakespeare, Milton, and Wordsworth; if I were to add a fifth, it would be Hardy.[1] Eliot, speaking of Wordsworth's later poetry, described it as the 'still, sad music of senility'. But the *Four Quartets* are, of course, in their attitude to time and eternity, to the transient and the permanent, basically Wordsworthian : they are about 'spots of time', as Wordsworth called them, the moments of intuition that occur perhaps three or four times in a human lifetime, and that are yet the master-lights

---

[1] Yeats is a greater poet than Hardy, but perhaps not a great *English* poet; and baffling, because of his Irish background and the home-made magic of his ideas, to most European readers.

of all our seeing. Where Eliot differs from Wordsworth is in the dramatiza-
tion, the sense of difficulty and conquest, the refusal to relapse into a benign
moralistic complacency: 'Old men should be explorers.' The *Four Quartets*
are also magnificent poems about poetry: about the paradox that when a
poet has learned to say something perfectly it is no longer what he wants to
say, for 'Last year's words belong to last year's language.' The sense of a
heroic struggle with language, of 'raids on the inarticulate', of every great
passage as an effort and a raid heroically brought off, this remains with us:
what Leavis called 'heroic sincerity'. And one has also the sense, perhaps
particularly in the third quartet, *The Dry Salvages*, of how nothing in Eliot's
intense and deep and yet in many ways perhaps frustrating and punishing
experience of life, is allowed to be lost: his American youth and childhood:

> *The rank ailanthus of the April dooryard . . .*

Whitman's open-hearted and open-ended democratism is at the opposite extreme from anything Eliot believed in, yet one recalls of course Whitman's
great poem about Lincoln's death:

> *When lilacs last in the dooryard bloomed . . .*

Again, in *The Dry Salvages*, we pick up the breath of pine and the woodsong
fog, the granite islands, of 'Marina':

> *The salt is on the briar rose,*
> *The fog is in the fir trees.*
> *. . . the whine in the rigging,*
> *The menace and caress of wave that breaks on water,*
> *The distant rote in the granite teeth,*

Reading Eliot's poems all through as a single work, one has this extraordinary
sense of 'what images return': the constant rehandling, reshaping, heighten-
ing, transformation, perhaps in the end sanctification of a very few crucial
experiences. In that sense, he is a deep but narrow poet: Leavis, in that
lecture to which I have already several times alluded, praised him for making
as a poet so much out of how very little, in the way of moments of joy and
transfiguration, life had given him. His history as a poet differs also from
that of almost any lyrical poet of genius I know in this respect. Most lyrical
poets start from joy and the senses, from a vivid response to external nature,
from positive celebration, and go on, as they grow older, to write poems
that are more concerned with human and social problems. For Eliot the full
flowering of his senses belongs to his winter:

> *. . . Now the hedgerow*
> *Is blanched for an hour with transitory blossom*
> *Of snow, a bloom more sudden*

Than that of summer, neither budding nor fading,
Not in the scheme of generation.
Where is the summer, the unimaginable
Zero summer?

The greatest passage in all Eliot's poetry is the passage in *Little Gidding* where, returning home as an Air Raid warden in the early morning after a night raid on London, he meets or evokes the ghost of a poet, which is in a sense a compound ghost, but is perhaps especially the ghost of Yeats. These two great poets had never been intimate friends. Richard Ellmann has an amusing anecdote about Yeats and Eliot being sat together, without Yeats realizing it, at a dinner at Wellesley College in the United States. Yeats turned to his neighbour on his left-hand side and through several courses discussed with him Eliot's poetry, both agreeing that he was overrated: then Yeats, who of course was both absent-minded and short-sighted, turned to his right-hand neighbour, asking him what *he* thought about Eliot. Eliot picked up his *placement* card, with his name on it, let Yeats peer at the name through his thick glasses, and politely begged to be excused from the discussion. In *After Strange Gods*, he had described Yeats as a sort of drug taker, keeping the feeble pulse of romantic poetry alive by injections of occultism: the devotee of a lower religion. It was in this same book, rather a scandal, but in its unusual rashness one of his most entertaining books, that he had also dismissed Hardy and Lawrence as heretics, and Hopkins as a minor and eccentric devotional poet, whose experiments in metrics were on the whole unfortunate. Eliot's attitude to great contemporaries, especially to Lawrence, scandalizes Dr Leavis, but if one has known the world of poets well – and I think I have known it more fully than Dr Leavis – one does not, of course, expect men of great creative talent and opposite gifts to be just to each other. Yeats for his part wrote about Eliot:

> Eliot has produced his great effect upon his generation because he has described men and women that get out of bed or into it from mere habit; in describing this life that has lost heart his own art seems grey, cold, dry. He is an Alexander Pope, working without apparent imagination, producing his effects by a rejection of all rhythms and metaphors used by the more popular romantics rather than by the discovery of his own, this rejection giving his work an unexaggerated plainness that has the effect of novelty. He has the rhythmical flatness of *The Essay on Man* – despite Miss Sitwell's advocacy I see Pope as Blake and Keats saw him – later, in *The Waste Land*, amid much that is moving in symbol and imagery there is much monotony of accent:
>
> *When lovely woman stoops to folly and*
> *Paces about her room again, alone,*
> *She smooths her hair with automatic hand*
> *And puts a record on the gramophone.*

I was first affected, as I am by these lines, when I saw for the first
time a painting by Manet. I longed for the vivid colour and light of
Rousseau and Courbet, I could not endure the grey middle-tint – and
even today Manet gives me an incomplete pleasure; he had left the
procession. Nor can I put the Eliot of these poems among those that
descend from Shakespeare and the translators of the Bible. I think of
him as a satirist rather than poet. Only once does that early work
speak in the great manner :

> The host with someone indistinct
> Converses at the door apart,
> The nightingales are singing near
> The Convent of the Sacred Heart,
> And sang within the bloody wood
> When Agamemnon cried aloud,
> And let their liquid siftings fall
> To stain the stiff dishonoured shroud.

Yeats goes on to say rather warmer things than this about *The Hollow Men*
and *Ash Wednesday*, but the tone remains one of admiring dislike. Eliot's
attitude to Yeats had been equally mixed; Pound introduced him to Yeats
some time in 1913 or 1914, and Yeats talked about nothing but ghosts and
George Moore, both of which subjects the young Eliot found very boring.
He thought of Yeats as a survivor merely from the 1890s till one of the Plays
for Dancers, performed in London, caught his admiration, and from then on
he thought of Yeats as a distinguished slightly older contemporary, and
made a point of offering him the freedom of his periodical, *The Criterion*.
But then there are the strange and malicious remarks in *After Strange Gods*.
Nevertheless, in 1940, a year after Yeats's death, he paid a noble tribute to his
fellow poet's greatness, and defended also that terrible epigram :

> You think it horrible that lust and rage
> Should dance attendance upon my old age;
> They were not such a plague when I was young;
> What else have I to spur me into song?

Yeats, Eliot said, was only being honest. One should remember that epigram
when listening to this great passage, that I am going to read you, from *Little
Gidding*, and one should also remember the great stanza from Yeats's
'Byzantium' about the purgatorial dance of the spirits newly released from
the fury and the mire of human veins :

> At midnight on the Emperor's pavement flit
> Flames that no faggot feeds, nor steel has lit,
> Nor storm disturbs, flames begotten of flame,
> Where blood-begotten spirits come

And all complexities of fury leave,
Dying into a dance,
An agony of trance.
An agony of flame that cannot singe a sleeve.

Here is the speech of the Yeatsian ghost in *Little Gidding*. Part of the model also (and the lines are in an English equivalent of Italian hendecasyllabics, of terza rima, with alternated feminine and masculine endings substituting for proper rhyme) is Dante's meeting in hell with his old teacher of rhetoric, Brunetto Latini:

And he: 'I am not eager to rehearse
* My thought and theory which you have forgotten.*
* These things have served their purpose: let them be.*
So with your own, and pray they be forgiven
* By others, as I pray you to forgive*
* Both bad and good. Last season's fruit is eaten*
And the fulfilled beast shall kick the empty pail.
* For last year's words belong to last year's language*
* And next year's words await another voice.*
But, as the passage now presents no hindrance
* To the spirit unappeased and peregrine*
* Between two worlds become much like each other,*
So I find words I never thought to speak
* In streets I never thought I should revisit*
* When I left my body on a distant shore.*
Since our concern was speech, and speech impelled us
* To purify the dialect of the tribe*
* And urge the mind to aftersight and foresight,*
Let me disclose the gifts reserved for age
* To set a crown upon your lifetime's effort.*
* First, the cold friction of expiring sense*
Without enchantment, offering no promise
* But bitter tastelessness of shadow fruit*
* As body and soul begin to fall asunder.*
Second, the conscious impotence of rage
* At human folly, and the laceration*
* Of laughter at what ceases to amuse.*
And last, the rending pain of re-enactment
* Of all that you have done, and been; the shame*
* Of motives late revealed, and the awareness*
Of things ill done and done to others' harm
* Which once you took for exercise of virtue.*
* Then fools' approval stings, and honour stains.*

From wrong to wrong the exasperated spirit
  Proceeds, unless restored by that refining fire
  Where you must move in measure, like a dancer.
The day was breaking. In the disfigured street
  He left me, with a kind of valediction,
  And faded on the blowing of the horn.'

I have spoken about Eliot as a poet, and indeed as much as possible by quotations allowed him to exhibit himself as a poet. He was a very competent playwright, but he deliberately diluted his poetry to make the verse of his plays easily speakable, and, indeed, in *The Cocktail Party*, when he wants for properly dramatic reasons an effect of high poetry he makes a character quote a long passage from Shelley. He is a very great poet, but as a dramatist he is not great if we compare him, say, with Ibsen, Tchehov, or Strindberg, and indeed, leaving aside Ibsen's verse plays, these dramatists even in prose seem to me more profoundly poetical than Eliot: their use of symbolism is deeper, they are nearer profound passions. Eliot's dramas are works of edification, intended to put across a Christian message inoffensively to a secular audience, and their very inoffensiveness robs them of the turbulence and power of his non-dramatic poetry. He has eliminated the man who suffers, except as a puppet or, as in the character of Becket, as an eloquent mask. His criticism is another matter. Leavis said to us at Leicester that if you think there are in every century quite a number of great critics, you will think Eliot one; if you think that in every century there are only two or three great critics, you will think Eliot most interesting and distinguished as a critic, but not great. He was certainly a most influential critic. Up to about 20 years ago, his influence worked in English universities for a perhaps undue stress on the virtues of the Metaphysical poets and the non-Shakespearean Jacobean dramatists, and for a very cavalier attitude towards Romantic and Victorian poetry. He wrote excellently on eighteenth-century poets, on Dryden and Johnson, but Leavis blames him for having praised Dryden rather than Pope. His great mastery of European literature makes his essay on Dante the best short introduction to that starry figure in English, and his essays on Pascal and Baudelaire are masterly. He attacked Milton in a way that Leavis approved of, but then cautiously recanted. He withdrew also a petulant early attack on Shelley and in a late short essay on Dante praises Shelley for being the greatest English master, in the unfinished 'Triumph of Life', of the Dantesque style. His attack on *Hamlet* is amusing, but more for what it tells us about Eliot, certain 'intractable' material that Eliot himself could not bring wholly to light in poetry, than as a criticism of Shakespeare. He had a great gift for cryptic formulations: 'objective correlative', 'a certain dissociation of sensibility'. Of his more general stances, his stand as a Royalist, a Classicist, an Anglo-Catholic, his hierarchical theory of culture, his reflections on the nature of a Christian society, one may say that they served the needs of a time as he honestly saw these needs, but the needs are no longer ours :

> ...'*I am not eager to rehearse*
> *My thought and theory which you have forgotten.*
> *These things have served their purpose: let them be.*'

In an interesting late essay, 'To Criticize the Critic', he said that he was still a member of the Church of England, would still like European monarchies to be preserved where they existed, but that the sharp distinction between romantic and classic attitudes of which he had made so much in his youth no longer seemed to him critically very useful. He repented, I think, of some of his more reactionary positions, the touches of anti-semitism, for instance, in his early poems, the notorious remark in *After Strange Gods* that a traditional society cannot absorb 'too many free-thinking Jews' :

> *... the shame*
> *Of motives late revealed, and the awareness*
> *Of things ill done and done to others' harm*
> *Which once you took for exercise of virtue.*

He lost his early whole-hearted admiration for Donne : he expressed a warm admiration for Tennyson's poetry, particularly *In Memoriam* : he made noble amends to Shelley. He even wrote an appreciative essay on Byron, a poet of whom one would expect him always morally and technically to disapprove. His most influential essays remain, probably, those on the Metaphysicals and the Jacobeans: though Leonard Unger, a great American Eliot scholar, thinks that Eliot on the whole misinterprets the Metaphysicals, reading them too much as if they were early ancestors of the French Symbolists, seeing the vividness of disconnected images, but not the logical pattern of the conceit or of the sophistical mock-argument of the Metaphysical poem taken as a whole. Yet his criticism, in its insights and its errors, has become part of our contemporary literary culture, just as much as the criticism of brilliant men, like Leavis, who oppose him :

> *We cannot revive old factions*
> *We cannot restore old policies*
> *Or follow an antique drum.*
> *These men, and those who opposed them*
> *And those whom they opposed*
> *Accept the constitution of silence*
> *And are folded into a single party.*
> *Whatever we inherit from the fortunate*
> *We have taken from the defeated*
> *What they had to leave us – a symbol:*
> *A symbol perfected in death.*

He was certainly a very great poet and a very great man of letters : fortunate in the poetry that he made out of so much defeat in his life. Perhaps all his poems taken together do constitute one grand symbol : a symbol, indeed, perfected in death.

9 · THE POETRY OF ROBERT GRAVES

Vision and Rhetoric, Faber and Faber, London, 1959; *The Changing World*, Harvill Press, London, 1947. (The late Manya Harari and Marjorie Villiers, joint editors and directors to the Harvill Press, showed a generosity to me in my early literary struggles in London which I would like here briefly to acknowledge.)[1]

If we wanted to introduce Robert Graves's poetry to some receptive and intelligent person who did not know much about it – and there are many such people, for Graves as a poet is merely a fine artist preoccupied with a rather strange personal theme, what he says has sometimes a good deal of philosophic interest, but he has neither a warning nor a consoling message for his age – where would we start? We would wish to illustrate the solid excellence of style in much of his poetry, its occasional intense lyricism, a certain defiant toughness of mood which it expresses; and we would also wish to hint at that strange personal theme. 'Ulysses' might be as good a poem to start with as another. It opens in a workmanlike way:

> To this much-tossed Ulysses, never done
>   With woman whether gowned as wife or whore,
> Penelope and Circe seemed as one:
> She like a whore made his lewd fancies run,
>   And wifely she a hero to him bore.

A cultivated reader would appreciate at once the rotundity and neatness of that, and the fashion in which the 'she' and 'she', standing for *illa* and *haec*, reproduce in a neat inverted antithesis (it is Penelope, though she is his wife, who makes his lewd fancies run, and Circe, though she is his whore, who bears a hero to him) the effect of an Ovidian elegiac couplet. It is of Ovid, in fact, that we think at once, rather than of later poets like Dante and Tennyson who have also seen what they could do with Ulysses. Once the reader, however, has settled down to expect a smooth Ovidian treatment, he will be

---

[1] This essay was first published in 1947, before *The White Goddess* had appeared or Graves had become fashionable. I let it stand as it was first written. I think *The White Goddess* is likely to distract one from what the poems actually do and say. And I still think the dualistic theme, or the theme of agonizing tension between mind and body, is central to Graves's poetry.

disturbed in the next stanza by two lines of bitingly vivid romantic imagery :
these women,

> Now they were storms frosting the sea with spray
> And now the lotus orchard's filthy ease.

The first of these images is too romantically beautiful for the Ovidian setting;
the second, with the violent epithet, 'filthy', too full of sharp self-disgust.*
The next stanza is a piece of angry moralizing :

> One, two, and many: flesh had made him blind,
>   Flesh had one pleasure only in the act,
> Flesh set one purpose only in the mind –
> Triumph of flesh, and afterwards to find
>   Still those same terrors wherewith flesh was racked.

And the last stanza clinches the thought : the brave hero, the great amorist,
was really to himself a *worthless* person, in all his successes he was fleeing
from something he was afraid of, yielding to a weakness that he despised.

> His wiles were witty and his fame far known,
> Every king's daughter sought him for her own,
>   Yet he was nothing to be won or lost.
> All lands to him were Ithaca: love tossed,
> He loathed the fraud yet would not bed alone.

Graves set out, like Ovid, to comment, from an unheroic point of view, on a
well-known heroic story; but his comments are more searching than Ovid's,
and though this poem can stand by itself, it also fits into the general body of
his work as a variation on his favourite theme, which is the relationship
particularly between love and sexuality, more generally between the spirit
and the body, more generally still between the mind and nature. That relationship Graves sees as sometimes a comic, sometimes a tragic, but always
essentially an *awkward* relationship; it is never happy and harmonious.

Graves is peculiar among poets in that (though unlike Leopardi, for instance, who had something of the same attitude, he is a man of robust
physical energy) he has a sense of awkward and unwilling attachment to his
own body; and that awkwardness and unwillingness are, again and again,
the main *theme* of his poems. He can treat the topic in a thoroughly amusing
fashion, as in the comic and rather indecent little poem which begins, 'Down,
wanton, down!' Addressing an intractable part of himself, he says, with a
sort of affectionate contempt :

> Poor bombard-captain, sworn to reach
> The ravelin and effect a breach –
> Indifferent what you storm or why
> So be that in the breach you die!

But his more common attitude to the body, to its lusts, to its energies, to its mortality, to the clogging foreign weight that it hangs about him, is a far more sombre one. In 'The Furious Voyage' it is a ship, on a great uncharted sea, containing no land:

> And it has width enough for you,
> This vessel, dead from truck to keel,
> With its unmanageable wheel,
> Its blank chart and its surly crew,
>
> Its ballast only due to fetch
> The turning point of wretchedness
> On an uncoasted, featureless
> And barren ocean of blue stretch.

In a perhaps less effective poem, 'The Castle', it is a sort of gothic bastille in which he is imprisoned:

> Planning to use – but by definition
> There's no way out, no way out –
> Rope-ladders, baulks of timber, pulleys,
> A rocket whizzing over the walls and moat –
> Machines easy to improvise –

Baudelaire (but Baudelaire was a sick man, aware that his body was breeding its own ruin has similar images in some rough notes of a dream: he explores a crumbling and gothic interior, full of labyrinths and tottering statues, a fabric which is at any moment going to fall and crush him, but from which there is 'by definition no way out'. But Graves is concerned not so much with the body's mortality as with what he regards as the bearable, just bearable, nastiness of ordinary physical life. Should we after all, he asks in one poem, be grateful

> That the rusty water
> In the unclean pitcher
> Our thirst quenches?
>
> That the rotten, detestable
> Food is yet eatable
> By us ravenous?
>
> That the prison censor
> Permits a weekly letter?
> (We may write: 'We are well.')
>
> That with patience and deference
> We do not experience
> The punishment cell?

> *That each new indignity*
> *Defeats only the body,*
> *Pampering the spirit*
> *With obscure, proud merit?*

Most of his emblems for the body, it should be noted, are *inorganic*: a ship, a castle, a prison cell. (In the little comic poem I have quoted, the male sexual organ, the 'poor bombard-captain' is a sort of obstreperous puppet-character like Mr Punch.) As a love poet, Graves is essentially a romantic, along the same lines as (though probably not consciously influenced by) the troubadours and the poets of the *dolce stil nuovo*: a critic like Denis de Rougemont would connect his hatred of the body with their alleged Catharism, and it is true that Graves, in his latest novel, shows a great interest in the Gnostics, for whom the real fall was the creation of the world. But I think Graves's philosophy, in so far as he has one, springs from a fact about his personal nature: the fact does not spring from a philosophy. This sense of awkward and unwilling attachment to his body is, as it were, a *given* factor for him. A critic, too, must take it as a given factor.

Much of Graves's poetry, then, will be concerned with the dissatisfaction of the lover with sex, of the spirit with the body, of the mind with nature; and yet with facing the fact that love is bound to sex, spirit to body, and mind to nature. It is revealing to read, in this connection, some of his abundant and on the whole unsatisfactory early verses. Graves's early work does not show much promise of his present strikingly individual and distinguished style. He became known first as a war poet. After the war he relapsed for a little into very weak writing in the Georgian bucolic style, and in the preface to 'Whipperginny' (1923) he describes some of these rustic pieces as 'bankrupt stock', and this whole manner as the result of a mood of 1918, 'the desire to escape from a painful war neurosis into an Arcadia of amatory fancy'. These escapist pieces have most of the qualities that we dislike today in the Georgians, the bucolic-hearty strain,

> *Contentions weary,*
> *It giddies all to think;*
> *Then kiss, girl, kiss,*
> *Or drink, fellow, drink.*

the manly beer-drinking note,

> *'What do you think*
> *The bravest drink*
> *Under the sky?'*
> *'Strong beer,' said I.*

and what Belloc, in 'Caliban's Guide to Letters', calls the prattling style,

> *No! No!*
> *My rhymes must go*
> *Turn 'ee, twist 'ee,*
> *Will-o'-the-wisp like, misty;*
> *Rhymes I will make*
> *Like Keats and Blake*
> *And Christina Rossetti,*
> *With run and ripple and shake,*
> *How pretty . . .'*

How pretty, indeed, we feel inclined to murmur. And today when we come upon this self-conscious rusticity, these awkward assumptions of innocence in verse, we remember the advice of Patrice de la Tour du Pin: 'Do not play, like children, with the parts of yourself that are no longer childish.' But if these escapist pieces are mostly rather mawkish, the war neurosis did not itself produce very memorable poetry. Consider this postscript to an otherwise rather sentimental 'Familiar Letter, to Siegfried Sassoon':

> *. . . to-day I found in Mametz wood*
> *A certain cure for lust of blood,*
> *Where propped against a shattered trunk*
> *   In a great mess of things unclean*
> *Sat a dead Boche: he scowled and stunk*
> *   With clothes and face a sodden green;*
> *Big-bellied, spectacled, crop-haired,*
> *Dribbling black blood from nose to beard.*

In a passage like that there are the roots of the horror which is a recurring theme in Graves's later poetry; just as in the bucolic pieces he seeks in nature something which, in later, better poems he will know he has not found. But though the passage is obviously extremely sincere, it is poetically unconvincing. Compare the amount of control in it with that shown in some verses on a similar theme by the most mature battle poet of the war that recently ended, Keith Douglas. Douglas is writing about another dead soldier, this time in the Western Desert:

> *Three weeks gone and the combatants gone,*
> *returning over the nightmare ground*
> *we found the place again and found*
> *the soldier sprawling in the sun.*
>
> *The frowning barrel of his gun*
> *overshadows him. As we came on*
> *that day, he hit my tank with one*
> *like the entry of a demon . . .*

Douglas's dead man has a picture of his girl in his pocket:

> *But she would weep to see to-day*
> *how on his skin the swart flies move,*
> *the dust upon the paper eye*
> *and the burst stomach like a cave.*

> *For here the lover and killer are mingled*
> *who had one body and one heart;*
> *and Death, who had the soldier singled,*
> *had done the lover mortal hurt.*

This is a very much better passage than Graves's, partly because Graves expresses more disgust (and mere disgust is itself disgusting); because the dead soldier in this passage is seen as a person, and the 'dead Boche' in the other a a mere object. There are also technical reasons why it is a better passage. Some of them have to do with the changing technique, not of poetry, but of war; mobile warfare, more than trench warfare, permits a certain control and detachment; Keith Douglas, not quite perpetually having his nose rubbed in the smell of death, is able to look on his dead man as an example of the fortunes of war and the large paradoxes of human life. The horrid foreground does not block all background. But also Douglas is beginning to write in a handier period, with neater tricks of rhetoric available to him. His lines move on the verb (the repetitions of 'gone' and 'found' in the first stanza), his visual images are conveyed by the antiseptically exact epithet and the isolated noun ('the *swart* flies', 'the *paper* eye', 'the *burst* stomach', 'the *frowning* barrel', and even, deliberately trite but appropriate, 'the *nightmare* ground'; and the two similes, 'like a *cave*', 'like the entry of a *demon*', at once natural and surprising). Moreover the deliberate formality of the language ('*nightmare* ground', '*swart* flies', '*weep*' instead of 'cry', particularly) and of the balanced syntax,

> *and Death, who had the* soldier *singled,*
> *had done the* lover *mortal hurt.*

give an effect of aesthetic distance. With Graves that effect is not created, he merely presents unpleasant raw material, too close to him to be art. And neither verbs nor nouns are used in Graves's passage so as to activate the line. He has one terribly feeble inversion ('things unclean'), and he makes his main descriptive effect,

> *Big-bellied, spectacled, crop-haired,*
> *Dribbling black blood . . .*

in the weakest way, by piling up adjectives. Yet we may well suppose that the ardours and horrors of the 1914–18 war, and his retreat into 'an Arcadia of amatory fancy' afterwards, provided Graves with his main poetic material; in his later work he has, we may say, been largely concerned with refining, controlling, and generalizing the practical attitudes that were forced upon him in these exacting years. He had a facile success as a war poet and a writer of bucolics; it is very much to his credit that he should have struggled through from that sort of success to one more lonely but very much more worth having.

Examples of his early style at its least satisfactory can be found in *Poems, 1914–1926*. Graves's second volume of collected poems, *Poems, 1926–1930*, has an epigraph from Laura Riding:

> *It is a conversation between angels now*
> *Or between who remain when all are gone.*

and his style in this volume has suffered the astonishing purgation that this epigraph suggests. The Arcadianism has gone. Nature and a self-conscious bucolic childishness are no longer considered as cures for a poetic, or a metaphysical unease that has become a far deeper and wider thing than any war-neurosis. In one of the rudest poems ever written about nature (a poem which, like much else in the volume, beautifully anticipates Auden's earliest manner), he says, with all the spite of a disillusioned lover (I quote the original version from that volume, not the revised version from 'No More Ghosts'):

> *Nature is also so, you find,*
> *That brutal-comic mind,*
> *As wind,*
> *Retching among the empty spaces,*
> *Ruffling the idiot grasses,*
> *The sheep's fleeces.*
>
> *Whose pleasures are excreting, poking,*
> *Havocking and sucking,*
> *Sleepy licking,*
>
> *Whose griefs are melancholy,*
> *Whose flowers are oafish,*
> *Whose waters, silly,*
> *Whose birds, raffish,*
> *Whose fish, fish.*

The total effect of such a passage is probably indescribable in prose. The poem, in fact, like most of Graves's later pieces, is very much itself and not what a critic can say about it. But if you read these lines out to yourself aloud, you will find they have a slow, sad movement, a melancholy perched on the edge of a yawn, a humour on the edge of a sigh, that lulls and depresses, that seems at once to confirm and contradict what the poem says: for this oafish, idiotic, and melancholy nature has its own perverse charm, too, conveyed much more intensely in these lines than in Graves's earlier straight poems about rustic life, in such volumes as *Country Sentiment*. There will also be, in very much of his later work, that knack of flat and final statement,

> *Whose birds, raffish,*
> *Whose fish, fish,*

as well as that ability to make a jocular manner go with a sad tone of voice, that ability to seem, whatever is being said, not entirely committed to it. Graves's reader had better be suspicious and alert; or else choose another poet.

Graves, in his volume of 1930, anticipates Auden's early manner so often and so startlingly – as in the beautiful poem that begins:

> *O Love, be fed with apples while you may,*
> *And feel the sun and go in royal array,*
> *A smiling innocent in the heavenly causeway –*

that we may wonder why he did not enjoy a revival of prestige in the 1930s, on the tail, as it were, of Auden's sumptuous early renown. The chief reason was probably that, unlike Auden (who has had a succession of messages), Graves has no obvious message for the age. He is probably most moving and most beautiful as a poet in these love poems which are concerned entirely with themes from his personal life. As far as politics are concerned, he has expressed, in a poem called 'The Tower of Siloam', his objection to becoming a prophet, an announcer of calamities:

> *It behoved us, indeed, as poets*
> *To be silent in Siloam, to foretell*
> *No visible calamity. Though kings*
> *Were crowned with gold coin minted still and horses*
> *Still munched at nose-bags in the public streets,*
> *All such sad emblems were to be condoned:*
> *An old wives' tale, not ours.*

About politics, as about war, as about life in general, his feeling seems to be that people are to do their duty and not to expect things to turn out well. His Belisarius hates the corrupt, cowardly Justinian, rather admires the straightforward virtues of the barbarians he is fighting against, but never thinks of ousting Justinian from his place, or going over to the other side; and Belisarius is a hero very much to Graves's taste. He has a poem about that period, 'The Cuirassiers of the Frontier': the soldiers who speak in it say

> *We, not the city, are the Empire's soul:*
> *A rotten tree lives only in its rind.*

Does Graves feel about the British Empire, or about western European civilization generally, more or less what he feels about Byzantium? He gives no hint about that. But whereas when he fought it was the horrors of war that came most closely home to him, in his later poetry he thinks more of the honour and nobility of a soldier's life, of the good fortune of an early death. As in the poem, 'Callow Captain', in which he may perhaps be thinking of the *persona* of himself, the young, gallant soldier, who stalks through *Goodbye to All That.*

> *A wind ruffles the book, and he whose name*
> *   Was mine vanishes: all is at an end.*
> *Fortunate soldier: to be spared shame*
> *   Of chapter-years unprofitable to spend,*
> *To ride off into history, nor throw*
> *   Before the story-sun a long shadow.*

Yet if he has managed, in retrospect, to purge war of its horror, horror of another kind has gathered in his later poetry around the love in which he sought an escape from war. His love poems are nearly all, though wonderfully touching, almost unbearably sad. That poem of which I have quoted three lines closes (I quote again the earlier version) sadly and sinisterly enough:

> *Be warm, enjoy the season, lift your head,*
> *Exquisite in the pulse of tainted blood,*
> *That shivering glory not to be despised.*
>
> *Take your delight in momentariness,*
> *Walk between dark and dark, a shining space,*
> *With the grave's narrowness, but not its peace.*

'The tainted blood', 'the shivering glory' (the uncontrollable shivering of the body in a fit of lust), 'not to be despised'. Even in a love poem Graves cannot repress his faint grimace of disgust at the body; and in the saddest of all his love poems, 'A Love Story', he describes how love had dispersed the winter whose horror besieged him, transformed it, how his loved one, 'warped in the weather, turned beldamish', how the horror came back again, and how he realized that it had been a mistake 'to serenade Queen Famine'. His advice, in fact, about love, as about other things, seems to be to make the most of the good in the evil, of the good moment which heralds the bad change. But his final note is always sad:

> *And now warm earth was Arctic sea,*
> *   Each breath came dagger-keen;*
> *Two bergs of glinting ice were we,*
> *   The broad moon sailed between;*

> *There swam the mermaids, tailed and finned,*
> *And love went by upon the wind*
>   *As though it had not been.*

Only the lucid wintry fantasy there, and the compelling canorous voice, only the romantic trappings of which Graves had never entirely divested himself, console us for the cruel thing said.

It would be wrong to think of Graves as an entirely pessimistic poet. He is pessimistic about the world that exists. He has no message for the age, in that he does not think that things will turn out well (as, in their different ways, Auden and Eliot do). Some writers, like Orwell, who expect things to turn out badly, are at least very much concerned about this : and that also gives them, in a sense, a message; it is their part 'to foretell visible calamity –'. Graves seems, on the whole, to think that it is in the nature of things to turn out badly, and only a fool would make a fuss about it. But there is some realm or other of subsisting value (in a recent poem, he calls it 'excellence') which the change, which is the badness, cannot touch : the ravaging worms

> *. . . were greedy-nosed*
> *To smell the taint and go scavenging,*
> *Yet over excellence held no domain.*
> *Excellence lives; they are already dead –*
> *The ages of a putrefying corpse.*

And in his last volume there is also a religious poem (largely translated from ancient Greek texts), 'Instructions to the Orphic Adept', in which it is suggested that complete self-recollection is a way of escape from change. The regenerate soul is admonished :

> *. . . Man, remember*
> *What you have suffered here in Samothrace,*
> *What you have suffered.*
> *Avoid this spring, which is Forgetfulness;*
> *Though all the common rout rush down to drink,*
> *Avoid this spring.*

In his poetry, Graves has obeyed these instructions; he has remembered what he has suffered, and, in remembering, has transformed pain into the excellence of art. He is a very fine poet, and a poet whose vision of some things, of love, of suffering, of pain, of honour, is much deeper, stronger, and calmer than the vision that most of us can claim. His temperament may estrange intimacy; his chief preoccupations may be irrelevant to our most urgent contemporary problems. And when he deals with the theme of the body in a prison he may be dealing with a theme rather excessively private (in the sense that readers, like myself, who have not a parallel feeling about their own bodies, have to make a rather conscious effort of sympathy). Nevertheless, in his later work in verse – as, indeed, in his better work in prose – he is a model for young writers of a strong and pure style. His journeys may lie rather aside from what we think of as our main roads; but his is a very pure and individual talent, which, if we do care at all for good and honest writing, we ought not to ignore or decry.

1O · AUDEN
IN MIDSTREAM

Vision and Rhetoric, Faber and Faber, London, 1959. *Poetry London*, XI (September–October, 1947).

'With his unattractive stock-in-trade, and his clap-trap,' says Kathleen Raine, 'Auden, nevertheless, as none of the rest do, touches the human heart.' The unattractive stock-in-trade is, I suspect, for Miss Raine the facile use of generalizations – the taking of a leading idea from Freud, from Marx, and now from Kierkegaard, and seeing how it works out in a different context. It is the adoption, by a powerful but not a very scrupulous intellect, of any convenient 'working scheme'. (The first section of *The Orators*, with its startling application of Dante's ideas about love, as the only human motive, to the problems of public-school life, is an admirable example of Auden's pragmatism at its most fruitful and illuminating level.) God, like the libido, or like the dialectic, is for Auden chiefly a useful generalization; assuming the existence of God, he finds it possible to solve certain problems. The clap-trap is the unction, the over-persuasiveness, the mixture of blarney and bullying that goes with this sort of pragmatism. Hugh Sykes Davies, an excellent critic, who writes too little, has hinted at the morally repellent side of Auden's attitudes ... the element that has something in common even with Buchmanism. 'It is not possible,' Sykes Davies says,

> to adopt a new theory or a new loyalty overnight for valid reasons, and the reasons for such overnight changes are always invalid. The crisis in the patient's ideas and feelings does not arise from observation and speculation, but from internal psychological problems, of course unperceived; and the solution is determined not by observation and speculation, but by the needs of the psychological condition ... Every convert is psychologically ill ... Morally, he disgusts because the act of conversion solidifies personal neuroses into social form. *In time, converts band together in such numbers that they, the diseased, can interfere with the healthy unconverted – and they are always anxious to do this.*

It must be admitted that it is almost too easy to apply this generalization to Auden. He has, since he began, been threatening his readers with a variety of calamities – disease, madness, death in war or revolution, and now eternal damnation. He has, as he admits himself,

> ... *adopted what I should disown*
> *The preacher's loose, immodest tone.*

Yet, when all this is said, Auden does remain the most considerable poet of his generation. He does, as Miss Raine says, touch the human heart. He cannot be dismissed just by saying that one doesn't believe what he says, and doubts (because he is too emphatic about it) whether he really believes it himself. Auden's attitudes, reduced to average prose, would result in a writer as unpleasant as, say, Middleton Murry. But they are not reduced to average prose. They are *used* for rather extraordinary poetry.

Let us take an example of the clap-trap – the gift for sinisterly effective Kiplingesque slogans: 'We must love one another or die.' Has anybody thought of a more nasty and horrid motive for our loving one another?* (Just what would a love vamped up on such prudential considerations be really worth?) But it has its effectiveness as a slogan, as *telling* clap-trap, just because it leaves to the reader the choice of the level at which he wishes to interpret it. There is the level of mere platitude: 'Isolated people wither away.' There is a level of frightful cynicism: 'Though all my impulses are selfish, I need other people as a source of new energy.' 'I am so lonely, that I must love you, though there is nothing in you to love.' There is the level of fear: 'I had better love you, for otherwise you may kill me.' There is even an honest level, as in Christ's answer to the rich young man who asked what should he do to inherit eternal life. 'I admit that to try to love anybody, in a quite undiscriminating way, is a terrible strain and a sacrifice. But you are not forced to. You can always die ... the more usual, and perhaps the more dignified choice.' But the total effect of such slogans is *mainly* frightening, revealing a ghastly hollowness, but putting up a sort of façade in front of it, or suggesting a cheap way out ...

What touches the human heart is certainly not Auden's solutions (which are other people's solutions, ready-made solutions, taken over) but the situation in which Auden, and most of us, more often than we care to admit, find ourselves: that of complete isolation. Isolation is the disease, and Love, however much he cheapens the word, can still remain the word that suggests a remedy:

> *Released by Love from isolating wrong*
> *Let us for Love unite our various song,*
> *Each with his gift according to his kind*
> *Bringing this child his body and his mind.*

That is from *For the Time Being* and, according to the Christian framework of this oratorio, Love in the first line would mean charity, in the wide sense, and Love in the second God, or more precisely the Christ-child; but the effectiveness of the passage is partly due to the fact that, owing to the vague echo of the Counter-Reformation – the note of Dryden and Purcell – in the style, we *also* think of sexual love in the first line and of Cupid in the second. Thus to 'bring this child my body', while it *ostensibly* means to bring the Christ-child a body dedicated to chastity, *also* suggests bringing Cupid a body dedicated to pleasure; this faint and trembling ambiguity creates more effective poetry than a merely Christian, or a merely pagan statement possibly could. We are aware of the death from which Auden's Love ('Winter and Love,' says one very subtle poet, 'are desperate medicines') is an escape; we forgive him a great deal because we, too, are aware of the 'isolating wrong'. Admittedly, Auden's escape has never been into personal love in the ordinary sense; rather into something larger and vaguer and more full of energy than the ordinary human situation – the dialectic (loss of oneself in history), the libido (loss of oneself in sexual ecstasy), and now God (surrender of one's will to another much more powerful one). He has been seeking situations less painful and complicated, with less of a prosaic drag about them, than this. His success as a poet, perhaps, is his failure to remain satisfied with his escapes. The pathos, what touches the human heart, is that after all these efforts the great waves move away, and the poet is as much alone as ever, lying awake in bed and regarding the other body

> ... *mortal, guilty, but to me*
> *The entirely beautiful.*

Something like this perhaps is true – whether wholly intended by Auden or not – about Auden's Prospero, a Gerald Heard type, in 'The Sea and the Mirror'. That he quite fails (as Antonio maliciously suggests) to break his wand. There is an obvious comparison. Shakespeare was not intensely or especially a religious writer, yet in that conventional little epilogue to *The Tempest* with, as Walter de la Mare says, 'its curiously apt overtones',

> ... *now I want*
> *Spirits to enforce, art to enchant,*
> *And my ending is despair*
> *Unless I be relieved by prayer,*
> *Which pierces so, that it assaults*
> *Mercy itself, and frees all faults ...*

in that, we feel a consciousness of the 'last things', so habitual that it does not need, so to say, to write itself up.

Auden's Prospero, on the other hand, in what might be an expansion of this passage, writes himself up to some tune.

> *When the servants settle me into a chair*
> *In some well arranged corner of the garden*
> *And arrange my mufflers and rugs, shall I ever be able;*
> *To stop myself from telling them what I am doing –*

Sailing alone, out over seventy thousand fathoms?
Yet if I speak, I shall sink without a sound
Into unmeaning abysses. Can I learn to suffer
Without saying something ironic or funny
About suffering?

I would say, no; the old gentleman will be talking ... (In passing, these three lines I have emphasized show one weakness in the style of this volume – an excessive bookishness. They are like bad Aldous Huxley. They irritate because Auden's Prospero has given no evidence, sententious, loquacious, and sometimes eloquent as he is, that he is at all capable of thinking of anything very effectively ironic or funny to say; and people may be irritated, too, at the notion of suffering as a rather expensive and special luxury for the truly high-minded.)

But one sees the differences. Shakespeare is a dramatist but his people are not, in quite this sense, incessantly dramatizing themselves. For Auden the dramatic gesture (not the dramatic incident) is all important. Everything he would do would be this special sort of thing, with its sharp rhetorical edge to it – 'Leave for Cape Wrath tonight!' or, 'Seeing our last of Captain Ferguson'. Yet ordinary common little people pray and repent, and feel the emptiness of their small successes, just as they work for a political party, or go to bed with their wives; it was not, after all, Auden who invented religion or sex or politics. Like Miranda, Auden finds novelty everywhere and everywhere assimilates it; as with her brave new world, ''tis new to *him*'. This is part of what Laura Riding and Robert Graves meant by calling him a synthetic, not a traditional, writer. Everything has to be questioned, everything explained. This partly explains the queer and rather unfeeling detachment Spender has noted: for Auden's Prospero,

A stranger's quiet collapse in a noisy street
Is the beginning of much lively speculation,

not the beginning of doing anything practical for the stranger.

That everything is seen from the outside, and as new, and as having to be explained (that is, as having to be set against a wider background, which is assumed, so that there may be explanations) is one reason, perhaps, for certain faults of taste and feeling which are rather noticeable in *For the Time Being*. He ignores the fact that lives of ordinary routine, which look dull and simple from the outside, from the inside, broken down into their day-to-day detail, may seem interesting and complicated enough. And this causes him occasionally to indulge in a peculiarly unpleasant mixture of spiritual and social snobbery:

The solitude familiar to the poor
Is feeling that the family next door
The way it talks, eats, dresses, loves, and hates
Is indistinguishable from one's own.

Both the facts, and the values implied here, seem to me wrong. It is the upper classes in all ages, who have tended to conventionalize their behaviour; Goldsmith somewhere has an acute remark about the manners of the gentry being the same all over eighteenth-century Europe – one must look both for national characteristics, and individual eccentricities, among the peasantry. I am sure, I am much more *like* any other middle-class intellectual of my age, than a plumber in Bradford is like a plumber in London. Secondly, I do not see what is wrong with the family next door being like my family. Real conversation, real intimacy, is, in fact, only possible when two people share a general background of behaviour, and indeed of reading, and of taste, which is so much taken for granted that it need not be talked about. The individualism which Auden *seems* to be advocating here is rather like that which, along so many English streets, jostles together the fake-Tudor or neo-lavatorial pub, the commercial Renaissance bank, and the jazz-modernistic cinema. I prefer the amenity of the Georgian crescent. An even more snobbish (and very badly written) passage is this:

> *Redeem for the dull the*
> *Average Way*
> *That common ungifted*
> *Natures may*
> *Believe that their normal*
> *Vision can*
> *Walk to perfection.*

It is not really such a colossal and crushing tragedy not to be Auden; and the best of us are very common and ungifted, in very many directions, and the most limited of us is capable of sacrifice and love.

This stuffiness is all the more depressing when one remembers Auden's former gift, in a poem like 'August for people and their favourite islands', of summing up, quite easily and lazily, the whole atmosphere of a place and the people there; and he seems to have lost that, and to have lost the unaffected pleasure he once felt in the sight of people being easily and lazily themselves; America could have offered him Coney Island, instead of these depressing and unconvincing generalizations, but the American scene, the American atmosphere, the speech habits of America, appear not to exist for him. I think there is a reason, a sociological one. The façade of English life is a very composed one, the flaws in the surface are difficult to detect, and one of the things that made Auden before the war a poet of such extreme social significance was his ability to put a finger on points of extreme, but hidden, stress. But America does not present a composed façade; it makes a cult, almost, of the incongruous; it is almost blind to the incongruous; and American writers tend, like Henry Adams, or the Southern Regionalists, either to invent a manner adapted to a composed society which does not exist, but ought to, or like Sinclair Lewis, in his earlier and less regrettable days, to shout at the top of their voices to draw attention to incongruities which, even for the least sensitive English observer, would be glaring enough. A writer like Auden for instance, or like Rex Warner, might do a fruitful parody of a leader in *The Times*, *The Economist*, or the *Spectator*; but a leader in the *Saturday Evening Post* parodies itself. There is a degree of rusticity which exhausts the resources of language. In America, I suppose, there are only three alternatives: one surrenders, one becomes hysterical and hoarse like Mark Twain or Sinclair Lewis, or one withdraws. Auden seems to have withdrawn, and America, for all it exists for him, might be a desert island. There is only one outbreak of the old beautiful malice and mischief, a poem which I first read in a scribbled copy over a bar in Cairo:

> *In the Retreat from Reason he deserted on his rocking horse*
> *And lived on a fairy's kindness till he tired of kicking her,*
> *He smashed her spectacles and stole her cheque-book and mackintosh*
> *Then cruised his way back to the Army.*
> George, you old numero,
> How did you get in the Army?

That is nicely done. But, on the whole, and at least for the time being, Auden seems to have lost that promise he had once of being our best poet in a conversational style (that is, our best poet with an adult social sense) since the Byron of 'Don Juan' or perhaps even since Pope.

On the other hand, Auden is steadily increasing his mastery over the actual craft of verse. There is almost no form, no metre at which he is not capable of having a pretty competent try. His most interesting metrical innovation in 'The Sea and the Mirror' is the borrowing of syllabic metre from Marianne Moore. He uses this in what is perhaps his most perfect single poem to date, 'Alonso to Ferdinand'. Each line has nine or seven syllables, the stanzas have an elaborate and difficult rhyme scheme, but since stressed can rhyme with unstressed syllables the number of possible full rhymes in English is greatly extended; the general effect of the metre, in Auden's use of it, is to give an effect of careful but successful concentration, like a military slow march with the soldiers counting their steps, or like counting your steps when you are dancing a slow waltz. His use of the metre is quite unlike Miss Moore's, who always has the air of balancing, say, a pile of plates which are always about to topple over but never quite do; the air of doing something surprising, difficult, acrobatic, sometimes almost (elegantly) clownish ... indulging, as she does, in lines of varying length and slyly concealed rhyme patterns. Auden's use of the metre is more straightforward, his effect, smooth, grave, and majestic. I think syllabic metre is a very important and useful innovation in English verse ... much more so, for instance, than Hopkins's type of metre, which tends to distort the natural syntax and cadence of the English language, and can only be used effectively, indeed, in Hopkins's own peculiar type of rhetoric. It would be a mistake, of course, to attempt to read 'Alonso to Ferdinand' without any stresses at all; what the reader will find himself stressing is what the French call the 'mobile accent' ... or those words on which, from the sense pattern (of the individual line, not of the sentence or paragraph) there is a natural rhetorical stress. That stress, however, will be a modulated one, so as not to rack the slow and grave syllabic pattern.

With this advance in metrical accomplishment there goes, however, that tendency towards an impressive vagueness, even towards a triteness or woolliness, of metaphor and simile first noticed by Julian Symons. The contrast with the tightness of Auden's earliest poems is striking and from some points of view depressing. 'My dear one is mine as mirrors are lonely.' That, as reviewer after reviewer has pointed out, is a very lovely line. But just how does my dear one being mine resemble mirrors being lonely? (To anybody with some knowledge of how poems are composed, it must seem possible that Auden may have written first, 'My dear one is mine *though* mirrors are lonely,' and then, by the alteration of a syllable, created at once a more metaphorius and a more mysterious line.) It might be a mere comparison of degree: mirrors are so lonely that they reflect everything which is in front of them, and my dear one just as completely reflects me (or I may be, indeed, comparing myself to the mirror; I am as lonely for my dear one as a mirror is for everything, and for me there is nothing else, my dear one is everything). That is enough to satisfy the syntax, but the sadness and the beauty of the line come partly, I think, from the fact that mirrors are so obvious a symbol both of understanding and separation; I am reflected completely outside the mirror; or, in love with you, I reflect you completely, but you are free, as a person, to move away, while I still possess – for a little time – your image. And if *both* you and I are like mirrors, we only know each other as reflected in each other, and being in love is important as a way of possessing oneself. But this possession is illusory, for the surface never melts away, never quite dissolves even in love, and we can never, like Alice, enter the looking-glass kingdom, and wander together there, hand in hand. All these ideas are more or less relevant, and there are probably others I have missed. The point is that one can't, of course, stop to work them all out while actually reading the poem. One has the impression, merely, of something moving, intricate, and perhaps true, and passes on. This intricate vagueness has its own fascination and I cannot agree with Symons in regarding it as mere laziness on Auden's part. He knows very well, I should think, its peculiar effectiveness.

I have been delaying coming to grips with Auden's thought. William Empson has a striking little poem, 'Reflections from Rochester', in which he says that the mind

> ... now *less easily decides*
> *On a good root confusion to amass*
> *Much safety from irrelevant despair.*
> *Mere change in numbers made the process crass.*

Auden is not a thinker in the sense that Empson is; but what he has really been doing all along is seeking, in politics, or psychology, or religion, for a good root-confusion which would make the despair (which is, I think, his centrally important experience) irrelevant. Partly for that reason his politics, his psychology, and now his religion are always off-centre. And they are, in fact, confusing. They are ways both of explaining and of attempting to get rid of – but also to infect others with a personal sense of guilt. He does seek in that sense, in Sykes Davies's phrase, to solidify personal neuroses. The particular type of religious thinking to be found in *For the Time Being* is not new in his work. It is to be found in the famous poem that begins,

> *Sir, no man's enemy, forgiving all*
> *But will, his negative inversion, be prodigal ...*

and that ends with the rather undergraduate line,

> *New styles of architecture, a change of heart.*

It is a religion of emotional conversion, and, among historical forms of Christianity, it resembles Lutheranism more than either Roman Catholicism or High Calvinism. It makes much more of God's will and less of His reason, much more of the individual's direct response to God and less of the idea of fellowship in a Church, than Roman Catholicism, but it does allow some scope for man's emotions (if not for his reasonable will) to co-operate with God, and it does not go all the way with that type of extreme Protestantism which makes man's salvation or damnation *entirely* dependent upon God's particular election. The general effect of such a religion would be to make men feel that, whether or not necessarily wicked, they are certainly weak, and perhaps it is better to sin strongly and to repent strongly than to be puffed up with a sense of one's strength and virtue. (Herod, the good administrator, in Auden's oratorio, is the man who tries to rely on his own will and reasoned moral standards; he is rather venomously treated. Caesar, in another poem, stands for all man's attempts to stand on his own feet – in science, in culture, in philosophy, as well as in politics – and it is made clear that from Auden's standpoint all these are equally wicked and disastrous.) The dangers of this particular type of religion, with its emphasis on some sort of emotional surrender, are seen more clearly in 'The Sea and the Mirror'. Antonio's great crime is that he has not surrendered to Prospero,

> *Your all is partial, Prospero;*
>   *My will is all my own;*
> *Your need to love shall never know*
> *Me; I am I, Antonio:*
>   *My choice myself alone.*

But if Prospero can be a symbol for God, he might also be a symbol for Hitler. No man has the right to compel another man's love, unless he can prove himself worthy of it; no God either, for that matter, unless he can prove that, as well as being powerful, he is good. 'God is not without sin. He created the World', says an old proverb from the East, and it is not very noble to worship a God just because he is powerful and can harm us. Auden, indeed, does show that he is aware of this dilemma:

> Alone, alone, about a dreadful wood
> Of conscious evil runs a lost mankind,
> Dreading to find its Father lest it find
> The Goodness it has dreaded is not good ...

but his solution is Kierkegaard's, that of the emotional leap in the dark, not Milton's, that of justifying the ways of God to man. We have seen some of the results of the emotional leap in the dark in politics (and German politics have suffered greatly from the tradition of passive obedience that goes with Lutheran pietism) and German politics, when Hitler played Prospero, suffered greatly from the lack of a few Antonios. Auden has perhaps found a temporary solution for a number of his own personal difficulties, but I do not think that he has lighted on a very useful root-confusion for the rest of us. He seems to me, on the whole, to be *less* illuminating than in the days of his psychological and political probings.*

He is not, I think, fundamentally a religious poet, any more than, for example, Milton was.[1] A person with the genuine piety, the sense of mystery and awe, of, say, Dr Johnson could never have made out of the truths of the Christian religion the purely mythological pattern – the argumentative deity and the cannonading angels of *Paradise Lost*. The artist and the dialectician were strong enough in Milton to make use of this dangerous material and the artist and the dialectician are strong enough in Auden. But I find no evidence anywhere in this book of Auden's, any more than anywhere in Milton, of any profound *personal* spiritual experience; such as one finds, for instance, in David Gascoyne's *Noctambules* or in some short poems of Kathleen Raine's. He is not a religious poet in that sense, and though *For the Time Being* has some affinities with *The Rock*, I do not see Auden going on to write something like *Four Quartets*. His gifts are of another sort, and his strength is of another sort. Antonio's mockery is true,

---

[1] I hope this does not sound too paradoxical. The distinction is between grasping a theology as a coherent parable, or a coherent system of ideas, which is what Milton and Auden do, and having a certain kind of personal experience, a sharp and immediate sense of goodness or of evil. Or perhaps it might be described as the difference between generalized and personal experience, between accepting a set of ideas because on the whole they seem to fit, and being absolutely gripped and held by a certain sort of experience. Neither Auden nor Milton seem to be gripped and held. They choose, rather, to grip and hold. They could let go.

Because they could let go, poets like Auden and Milton are more anxious to persuade than poets, like Herbert, or Vaughan, or Crashaw, of actual religious experience. One has had it, and can merely attempt to record it.

Antonio, sweet brother, has to laugh.
How easy you have made it to refuse
Peace to your greatness! Break your wand in half,
The fragments will join; burn your books or lose
Them in the sea, they will soon reappear
Not even damaged: as long as I choose
To wear my fashion, whatever you wear
Is a magic robe . . .

We can allow no peace to Auden's greatness. He will not be satisfied until he has written something which is utterly moving, persuading, convincing, to *everybody*, and, of course, he will never do this. There will always be the schoolboy who doesn't attend, the scout who skips the parade, the man who chooses dying instead of loving, the heckler with the awkward question, the fellow conjuror chiefly interested in how he does the trick – there will always be Antonio. Prospero, again and again, will have to postpone the breaking of his wand. But, after all, is it to be regretted? There are so many professional mystagogues; so many dull preachers; so many cheapjacks with their bottled spiritual cure-alls; but of all poets writing today, there is only Auden with just that range and scope. His strength is not in what he accepts, but in what he discards. It lies just as much in a certain fundamental ruthlessness as in the love about which he talks so vaguely and so much. He is a much greater man than his ideas; as a poet, a major voice, as a thinker, about on the level of Middleton Murry. Because he has a major voice, what he says will always be relevant, without having to be, in a sense, true. (In one sense, it always will be true; it will always be a possible synthesis of an unusually wide reading and experience – it will always be pragmatically true, a possible 'working scheme'.) 'All I have is a voice . . .'

11 · AUDEN'S LATER MANNER

Vision and Rhetoric, Faber and Faber, London, 1959 (contains some material adapted from short reviews in the *New Statesman*).

Of all the poets whom I have dealt with in this volume [*Vision and Rhetoric*], I feel that I have treated Auden least fairly. Irritation not so much with his ideas as with his manner of entertaining ideas has, through the years, when I have had occasion to deal with him, betrayed me into a carping, petulant, suspicious tone; and I am now beginning to see that to argue whether his ideas were right or wrong had as little to do with the strict function of a critic of poetry as treating, for instance, Dryden's *Religio Laici* or Tennyson's *In Memoriam* as pamphlets about natural religion, to be supported or refuted by logical arguments. I tended, in all my earlier writing about Auden, to take elements in a composition for statements in a pulpit, or a witness-box. I nagged at a social attitude which irritated me, where I should have taken the social attitude as 'given', and reverted to it only when I thought some inadequacy in it helped to explain some inadequacy in what was poetically made of it. Let me try, now, to make some belated slight amends.

He does remain, of course, the most considerable Anglo-American poet of his generation. As Richard Hoggart says, in an admirable recent British Council Pamphlet about him, one still hesitates to accord him major status – to put him 'up there', as it were, with Yeats, with his own early master, Hardy, with Eliot – but he does remain, at 50 or so, the most exciting and promising 'younger poet' of our generation. Nobody else of around the same age – except in his narrower but perhaps sometimes deeper mode, William Empson – rivals him in speculative agility or technical adroitness. And Empson has written only three or four new poems since 1940. Nobody at all, of all poets who are active now, rivals Auden in fertility of invention. And yet, I suppose, over the last ten years or so few of us have been wholly happy about the way his poetry has been going. I shall say nothing about *The Age of Anxiety*. A learned Italian critic, Signor Melchiori, in his book *The Tight-rope Walkers*, thinks of it as a triumph in a new baroque manner, square and solid in construction, but with lavish extravagant ornamentation; it uses a very primitive metrics, that of Anglo-Saxon poetry, for a very sophisticated theme: and I remember a fine scholar saying to me, when it first came out, 'If one is seeking to be "mannerist", to play on one's sense of the jarring inappropriateness of subject to handling, of content to form, why not instead try out the metre of *Hiawatha*?' But two volumes of shorter poems, largely of 'light' poems, *Nones* and *The Shield of Achilles*, deserve both a warmer welcome and a more respectful consideration.

Let me take the second of these volumes first, *The Shield of Achilles*. And let me relate it to the two aspects of Auden's work which have most worried recent critics. One of these is a growing lack of personal immediacy; the other is an over-piling of verbal ornament. That lack of immediacy is very noticeable, for instance, in the first seven poems in *The Shield of Achilles*, the set called 'Bucolics'. These are like the notes of a very intelligent lecturer in human ecology done into verse. Thus, when we turn to the poem (among the poems on plains, mountains, and so forth) on islands, we do not get a vivid image like Pound's

> *Tawn foreshores*
> *Washed in the cobalt of oblivions.*

We get instead reflections, pungent, intelligent, but faintly chilling, on penal colonies and dying Pacific races :

> *Once, where detected worldlings now*
> *Do penitential jobs,*
> *Exterminated species played*
> *Who had not read their Hobbes.*

Nothing could be neater but (as in the fine 'Ode to Gaea' in another section) it is our world seen from an aeroplane. The poet, on the whole, brackets his personal life off from his poetry. We find ourselves longing for some concentration of direct experience, out of which the generalizations could grow.

Auden, of course, has always been a generalizer. He has never been interested either in his own experience, or the experience of other people, for its own sake; he has been interested in it as an instance of a general case, of the sort of thing that happens. He has a classifying mind; he is at the very, very extreme opposite pole from a poet like Hopkins with his passionate concentration on *haecceitas*, thisness, 'sakes', 'selving', and 'unselving', 'inscape'. The worry that critics may have had about his attitude to language in his recent books is not about this 'given' element in him; it is about a painstaking frivolity, a preoccupation with ornament. He does manfully defend the baroque mode :

> *Be subtle, various, ornamental, clever,*
> *And do not listen to those critics ever*
> *Whose crude provincial gullets crave in books*
> *Plain cooking made still plainer by plain cooks ...*

Walter Bagehot was one of 'those critics' and I agree with Bagehot that the way to make a basket of fish poetical is *not* by calling it, as Tennyson did in *Enoch Arden*,

> ... *Enoch's ocean-spoil*
> *In ocean-smelling osier* ...

Or that way of handling it *does*, of course, make it 'poetical' : but in a soppily vulnerable way, a way for the tough and wry who hate poetry to kick at.

Let us consider, with this suspicion of 'the poetical' in mind, such a passage as this of Auden's from his recent work :

> *The horn gate and the ivory gate*
> *Swing to, swing shut, instantaneously*
> *Quell the nocturnal rummage*
> *Of its rebellious fronde, ill-favoured,*
> *Ill-natured and second-rate,*
> *Disenfranchised, widowed and orphaned*
> *By an historical mistake* ...

But for the Fall, the basic sense of that passage is, our dreams would not be Freudian dreams – would not be so shabby, guilty, and incoherent as they are (the shabbiness expressed by 'noctural rummage', 'rebellious fronde', and so on : the Fall, ironically, by 'an historical mistake'). The rhetoric, the mechanism of persuasion, in such a passage is one of expansion; the plain, underlying prose sense is 'like gold to ayery thinness beat'; the lines *look* as if they were making more portentous and complex statement than they are making.

The title poem of *The Shield of Achilles*, a grim meditation on power politics, perhaps on the *Iliad* itself as what Simone Weil called 'the Poem of Force', had a bleak impressiveness : three victims being (not exactly) crucified :

> *The mass and majesty of this world, all*
> *   That carries weight and always weighs the same*
> *Lay in the hands of others; they were small*
> *   And could not hope for help and no help came:*
> *   What their foes liked to do was done, their shame*
> *Was all the worst could wish; they lost their pride*
> *And died as men before their bodies died.*

That impresses me poetically, impresses me morally, and yet there is something about the attitude implied in it that very frighteningly raises the whole question, in the context of which in the 1930s one always, perhaps obtusely, would discuss Auden's poetry, of the power of poetic perception to influence events. An hour or so before I copied out these lines I read, in the *Manchester Guardian*, a translation of passages from M. Alleg's book, *La Question*. M.

Alleg is the editor of a Communist newspaper, who was tortured by para-
chutists in Algeria. His torturers told him that they were modelling themselves on the Gestapo, that they hoped to torture Frenchmen, including
liberal or radical political leaders, in France, too, and be done with the Republic. I reflected that if there is any country in Europe which men of other
countries have turned to as a centre of civilization, have loved second to
their own countries, it is France. I reflected also that as at least a sympathizer
with Communism M. Alleg must have in his time turned a Nelson eye to the
possibility that men were being tortured behind the Iron Curtain; and yet,
standing up to torture himself, he seemed to speak not as a partisan but for
all men. In a sense, Auden speaks also in these lines for all men – but hope-
lessly? In the 1930s, he seemed often ahead of events, warning of what we
might still do to dodge our fates. In a poem like *The Shield of Achilles*, he is
like the chorus in a Greek tragedy, which makes all the appropriate moral
comments, but knows it cannot prevent the awful thing happening. By
classical standards, this should make him a more universal poet; and by revealing starkly what is worst in us, he may in fact, in such a poem, be
nerving us to pursue what is better. And yet, in a cruder way, did he not
move us more when he took sides more, when he seemed to speak with even
crude power, like an orator? Was 'the preacher's loose, immodest tone',
which he once often protested against, not part of his early power over one?

In fact, the vein which I often find most attractive in Auden's later poems
is not this harsh, bleak vein but one of playfulness. There was much of this
in the volume which preceded *The Shield of Achilles*, the volume called
Nones, the most variously pleasurable for me of all Auden's more recent
volumes. Nones is the daily office of the Church originally said at the ninth
hour, or three o'clock in the afternoon; it was between the sixth and the
ninth hour, while Christ hung on the Cross, that there was a darkness over
the earth, the sun was darkened, and the veil of the Tempest was rent. So far,
certainly, the title does not suggest a mood of cheerfulness. But there is another meaning of the word more directly relevant to the mood of at least
the lighter pieces in the book. 'Nones' is the old spelling of 'nonce'. Many of
the poems in *Nones* are nonce-poems (poems inspired by recurring gradua-
tion ceremonies): many of these are also full of nonce-words:

> On the mountain, the battering torrent
> Sunk to a soodling thread,[1]

for instance; the once battering but now faltering torrent sunk, I suppose, to
a soothing and dawdling thread. One is half tempted on reading such lines to
wonder whether Auden's inspiration has itself begun to soodle, but, if there
was little or nothing in *Nones* in Auden's old, urgent, hortatory vein, that

---

[1] John Fuller (*A Reader's Guide to W. H. Auden*, 1970, 215) points out that the
word 'soodling' had been used previously by John Clare. Other examples of
rustic – particularly north Midlands – words are in fact to be found in Auden.

was because of a feeling that all 'sane affirmative speech' has been so 'pawed-at' and 'profaned' by newspapers and politicians that the only civilized tone of voice for a poet today is

> ... *the wry, the sotto voce,*
> *Ironic and monochrome.*

And in fact Auden has rarely written with more confident ease than in the lighter pieces in *Nones*. He hits just the note he wants to, even when he is seeking to hold the restless attention of an audience of undergraduates:

> *Between the chances, choose the odd;*
> *Rear* The New Yorker, *trust in God;*
> *And take short views.*

Whether under the ease of the surface of such poems there is a slackness of will is another question; also, how far irony and humour at this level can unconsciously betray an undue complacency of spirit. There is a *New Yorker* side to Auden, and the recipe for the *New Yorker* type of humour is to step far enough back from the routines we are all immersed in to feel sophisticated about them; but not far enough back to cease to be one of the boys. But Auden can be one of the boys at several levels and there is a quite different snob highbrow pleasure, for instance, in recognizing the tessellations of Horatian syntax in these lines addressed to Brian Howard:

> ... *what bees*
>
> *From the blossoming chestnut*
> *Or short but shapely dark-haired men*
> *From the aragonian grape distil, your amber wine,*
> *Your coffee-coloured honey ...*

To read a volume like *Nones* is, in fact, to recognize once again that Auden is more adroit – almost unscrupulously adroit, perhaps – than anyone else now writing verse; he can be back-slapping, ominous, port-winy, or abstruse, as the occasion demands. Yet even where he does not aim at major statements, there are major themes, above all the Christian theme, in the background; the frivolity is in a sense permissible because the last things, death, judgment, hell, heaven, are always in Auden's mind, and the worldly hopes men set their hearts upon have been rejected. In the interim, there is nothing against a little harmless enjoyment. Auden's type of Christianity strikes me, as I have said in an earlier essay, as being a sophisticated Lutheranism. He does not exactly say to us, *Pecca fortiter*, but to avoid despair he has put most of his money on Grace since he knows he is going to fall down on Works. One trouble about such a type of Christianity is that to the outsider it might not seem to make much practical difference:

But that Miss Number in the corner
Playing hard to get ...
I am sorry I'm not sorry ...
Make me chaste, Lord, but not yet.

Humility consists of recognizing one's impurity, but also provides an excuse for going on being impure:

The Love that rules the sun and stars
Permits what he forbids.

I saw the poem from which these lines come first in typescript. Auden had sent it to a Roman Catholic lady, a friend of mine, who was editing a literary magazine and she was embarrassed, much admiring Auden's work generally, but feeling that the allusions to St Augustine and Dante in that jazzy context were in desperately bad taste; I agreed with her then, but now feel that I was silly and squeamish. It is one of the strengths of Auden's handling of the theme of Grace and Original Sin that he does not worry about shocking *les bien pensants*. And when he expresses, as he sometimes does, his more intimate and personal convictions, he can be very moving, as in these lines from one of the most beautiful of all his recent poems, the loveliest poem in *Nones*, 'In Praise of Limestone':

Dear, I know nothing of
Either, but when I try to imagine a faultless love
Or the life to come, what I hear is the murmur
Of underground streams, what I see is a limestone landscape.

Nones was a disconcerting book, but I would say it more often embodied positive values (it is certainly a value that somebody can go unashamedly enjoying himself today, as Auden seems to) than *The Age of Anxiety*, where the theme of our awkward *malaise* was all too faithfully mirrored – Yvor Winter's 'fallacy of imitative form' – in the elaborately maladroit handling. From all sorts of official and respectable points of view, *Nones* was a quietly outrageous little book, and one liked it all the more for that. Deliberately slackening down a little when everybody else is keyed up, taking a humorous view of guilt and anxiety as part of the set-up – 'throwing it away', as the actors say of a strong line – is, after all, a defensible human attitude when everybody else is getting shrill, frightened, and nasty. But one's admiration for Auden, from first to last, remains mingled with doubts. From his beginnings he could be spotted as a potentially major talent: will the moment come, or has it come already, or is it too late for it to come now, when we shall look back on all that he has done and salute a major achievement? Or will he always remain for critics the problem prodigy, the boy who 'might have gone anywhere', but who always, when the obvious goals were pointed out to him, chose to go somewhere else?

12 · EVASIVE HONESTY: THE POETRY OF LOUIS MACNEICE

Vision and Rhetoric, Faber and Faber, London, 1959. (Written fresh for that volume but adapts some material from short reviews in the *New Statesman and Nation* and *The Times Literary Supplement*.)

It is probably an error, at least of tact, to bring into an appraisal of a living poet one's impression of his personality as a man. But there is a real sense, as Roy Campbell once remarked about Dylan Thomas and about William Empson, in which good poets are, when you meet them, like their works; they talk and behave in a way you expect them to. And it follows, conversely, that one's impression of the personality of a notable poet may throw some light on his work.

In any case, this personal impression will be a superficial one; I have talked or listened to MacNeice, at BBC pubs, at his friend William Empson's, at the Institute of Contemporary Arts when I have taken the chair for him, I suppose half a dozen times in the last ten years; and I have seen him often in pubs or at parties without talking to him. He gives a paradoxical impression of at once extreme and genial sociability, and remoteness. His talk flows easily and wittily, and his remarks on people, on ideas, on works of literature come out with an unpremeditated spontaneity. At the same time, one has often the impression that he is thinking at the back of his mind about something else; that the alertness and the sparkle are very much on the surface of his mind, that his *ripostes*, however apt, are almost absentminded, that a whole elaborate apparatus of thinking and feeling is behind a fire curtain.

Something like this I feel also about his poetry. Nothing could be more vivid, more frank, more candid, even in a sense more indiscreet than some of his best poetry. All the cards seem to be, even casually, on the table. At the same time, reading his poems one has the feeling sometimes that one has been subjected to an intelligence test; or that his hands, as he deals the cards on the table, move with disquieting speed. To use another metaphor, he is both in life and in poetry a man whose manner, at once sardonic and gay, suggests that he is going, perhaps, to let one in on a disquieting secret about something; one finds that he hasn't. The quality that one is left remembering, the poetic as well as the personal quality, is a kind of evasive honesty. Both the strength and the weakness of his best poems, like the strength and the weakness of the personal impression he makes, rest on the sense that a good deal is held in reserve. What it is, I have only a faint idea; but I have a feeling that he would be a more important poet, if it were less fully held in reserve, yet that the strength even of his slighter poems depends on one's intuition that there is so much of it.

He is a poet, I think, whom it is sensible to discuss in terms of his conscious attitude to life, his moral tastes and preferences, what he feels about the problematic world we are living in, since that mainly, and only occasionally deep personal feelings, seems to be what his poems are about. When his *Collected Poems* came out in 1948, he was the poet of the 1930s in whose work the years of the Second World War did not seem to have brought about a sharp break. C. Day Lewis, for instance, in the 1930s was often writing, to my mind rather unsuccessfully, either in a manner diluted from Hopkins or in a manner taken over from Auden's coarser scoutmaster vein. He was writing about the 'state of the world', rebelling against it. At some period in the 1940s, one noticed that he was writing, much more successfully, in a manner that owed something to Hardy, something to Browning and Clough, and that he was writing about the personal life. As for Auden himself, he has run through styles almost as Picasso has, he has reminded one of Laura Riding, Byron, Rilke, Yeats, he has perversely forced interesting matter into what seems a strangely inappropriate mould, like the Anglo-Saxon alliterative metre of *The Age of Anxiety*; the very beautiful purely personal manner with its long lines and its florid vocabulary which he has forged for himself in recent poems like 'In Praise of Limestone' is composite, not simple; through the kaleidoscope of successive styles, we now see that he has had a more consistent attitude all along than we thought. MacNeice's attitude has always been a firmly fixed one, and his style has changed only from a young man's concentration on images to an older man's care for structure. His short poems have been much more often successful than his poems of a certain length (the only two of his longer poems that I admire quite whole-heartedly are two from the middle of the 1930s, *Eclogue for Christmas* and *Death and Two Shepherds*). In this again, he is not exceptional; the number of poems of more than three or four pages which are completely successful in their way is, I suppose, a very small fraction indeed of the number of poems of three or four stanzas which are completely successful in theirs. There is a case, in fact, for thinking of MacNeice as a poet who has sacrificed an unusual gift for concentration to a misguided ambition to deploy himself at length. But, failures or successes, MacNeice's poems express from his beginnings to now an attitude to life which is admirably coherent: that of the man who is out at once to enjoy life and to shoulder the responsibilities. The typical attitude is one of a sane and humorous, and sturdily self-confident, social concern.

What may put some readers off is that this is so much (polished, learned, alarmingly witty though MacNeice is) the decent plain man's attitude.

Decency, measure, courage, a lack of patience, a making of the best of good things while they last, and a facing up to bad things when they have to be faced, these are the good insider's virtues. MacNeice's standpoint is the standpoint of common sense. He is subtle enough, however, to realize that the standpoint of common sense can be defended only through dialectic and paradox; he does not try to fight the plain man's battles with the plain man's weapons. It is on an acceptance of paradox that his own consistency is based (he was very interested in his youth in the paradoxes of the modern Italian idealists, not only Croce, but Gentile):

> Let all these so ephemeral things
> Be somehow permanent like the swallow's tangent wings.

Thus one of MacNeice's favourite figures (as he has noted in a lively and perceptive essay on his own work) is oxymoron: the noun and epithet that appear to contradict each other. He might himself be described in that figure as an intolerant liberal or a large-hearted nagger. He wants a world in which all sorts and conditions of men can have their say; but when their say, as so often, proves slack, or insecure, the say of

> The self-deceiving realist, the self-seeking
> Altruist, the self-indulgent penitent,

he loses his patience. It takes all sorts to make a world, certainly, but making is an activity, and the sorts he approves of must really put their shoulders to the wheel, must really creatively work to *make* it. More broadly, to underline yet again this paradoxical consistency, one might say that it is MacNeice's taste for variety, contrast, obstinate individuality – combined with his feeling that all these things, all 'the drunkenness of things being various', must somehow join in the 'general dance' – that unifies his vision of the world. (The problem of the One and the Many, like the problem of Essence and Existence, crops up again and again in MacNeice's poetry. The swallows are ephemeral existents but the pattern their tangent wings make seems to claim to be an eternal essence. Perhaps the submerged nine-tenths, both of his poetry and his personality, is a speculative metaphysics, of an unfashionably ambitious sort.)

The danger of MacNeice's liberal, humanistic attitude, so admirable in so many ways in itself, is that it is too often, especially in his longer poems, liable to slacken down into mere moralizing. Take such a passage as this:

> ... it is our privilege –
> Our paradox – to recognize the insoluble
> And going up with an outstretched hand salute it.

One agrees, of course, at some though not all levels, with what is being said (one does not agree, but this is certainly not an application MacNeice will have had in mind, that one should greet the apparently insoluble political divisions of our time, as Browning greeted the Unseen, with a cheer). One is unhappy about the way of saying. Is not the tone of voice, too flat in one sense, and too stretched in another, the orator's tone rather than the poet's? When, in a long, ambitious poem, full of such moralistic passages, I come for instance on this,

> The paradox of the sentimentalist
> Insisting on clinging to what he insists is gone,

I do feel, I confess, a sense of relief. The tone is right, there, these two lines are tight, witty, hit straight home. The moral *fact* is presented, the moral judgment is left (as I think it should be) to the reader.

Readers of that collected volume of 1948 often found themselves, I imagine, like myself, lingering a little wistfully over the dash, vividness, and gaiety of the earlier poems. But the later poems also deserved careful reading. MacNeice was tired, as he explained in a prose piece written about that time, of 'journalism', and tired of 'tourism', tired of the poem as a mere footnote to experience; he aimed now at making all the parts of a poem fit coherently together, even if that involved the sacrifice of the brilliant inorganic image and the witty irrelevant sally. 'Thus the lines,' he wrote, 'that I am especially proud of in my last book are such lines as these (of the aftermath of war in England):

> The joker that could have been at any moment death
> Has been withdrawn, the cards are what they say
> And none is wild ...

or (of a tart):

> Mascara scrawls a gloss on a torn leaf

(a line which it took me a long time to find).' Both passages are essentially exploitations of the poetic pun. A card in a gambling game that can become any other card is called 'wild'; the joker, which is not really a proper member of the pack, is often used in this way as a 'wild' card. But the wider connotations of death as a cruel practical joker, or as a wild beast in the jungle waiting to spring on one, emotionally reinforce what might have been a mere piece of knowingness. The second pun, I think, is even subtler. Mascara scrawls either a sheen on a torn piece of foliage (the tart's sad eyelid shaped like a leaf) or a commentary on a torn page (from a diary say, a record of illicit self-indulgence to be destroyed). And the tart herself is like a leaf torn from the living tree of life, and the false gloss of the mascara on her eyelid is a commentary on her fate. Such Empsonian economies certainly demanded harder work from MacNeice's readers than his old pieces of 'tourism',

... impending thunder
With an indigo sky and the garden hushed except for
The treetops moving,

or his old pieces of 'journalism', his shrewd remarks in passing,

... that a monologue
Is the death of language and that a single lion
Is less himself, or alive, than a dog and another dog.

The danger, however, that MacNeice at the end of the 1940s seemed to be facing was that of sometimes relapsing – as a relaxation from the strain of much close writing and as a sop to his sense of moral urgency – into the very 'monologue' which in these lines he deplores. How far, in the last ten years, has he surmounted that danger?

Perhaps he did not wholly surmount it. In 1952, he brought out *Ten Burnt Offerings*, a set of fairly longish poems which had been originally conceived for radio (they took about 15 minutes each to broadcast). In that book, one had a sense of an inner flagging battling with an obstinate ambition. The relevance of the themes of these ten poems, both to common problems of our day and to what one took to be MacNeice's personal predicaments, seemed real but oddly oblique. The themes of the poems were themes that might have suited a prose essay: the paradox of Elizabethan culture, the dung and the flower: the harsh roots of modern ethics in Greek and Hebrew guilt and sacrifice: Ulysses and Jacob as twin competing symbols of searching and driven man: Byron as the romantic for whom the conscious pursuit of liberty becomes the subconscious pursuit of death. Such a range of topics was impressive; but it had a touch about it, also, of the Third Programme producer with his fatigued fertility in 'new approaches'. The language showed, sometimes, that fatigue. When MacNeice wrote about the Elizabethans,

Courtier with the knife behind the smile, ecclesiastic
With faggots in his eyes,

it was impossible to forget how much more freshly they said the same sort of things about themselves:

Say to the Court it glows
  And shines like rotten wood;
Say to the Church it shows
  What's good and doth no good.

A wider reach can imply a shallower local penetration. As if aware of the dangers of a stretched thinness, MacNeice was fecund in metaphor:

> *... because your laugh*
> *Is Catherine wheels and dolphins because Rejoice*
> *Is etched upon your eyes, because the chaff*
> *Of dead wit flies before you, and the froth*
> *Of false convention with it ...*

Nothing could be gayer than the 'Catherine wheels and dolphins'. But were the more painful connotations of 'etched' (a needle on the iris?) intended or relevant. Are 'chaff' and 'froth', themselves examples of conventional dead metaphor, appropriate because 'dead wit' and 'false convention' are what they refer to – but even if so, is there not still an unpleasant though faint clash between the 'froth of false convention' and the real and beautiful sea-froth churned up three lines back, by 'dolphins'? The ornamentation, in fact, in this book had often the air not of emerging spontaneously from the theme, but of being trailed over it, like roses over a trellis. A trellis, to be sure, would be nothing without roses, but the gaunter outlines of MacNeice's thought, often half-hidden here, were interesting in themselves. His language was best where it was barest: as in the section on Byron in Lowland Scots,

> *I maun gang my lane to wed my hurt,*
>   *I maun gang my lane to Hades,*

or the aside about history,

> *... the port so loved*
> *By Themistocles, great patriot and statesman,*
> *Great traitor five years on,*

or the statement of the poet's own predicament:

> *This middle stretch*
> *Of life is bad for poets; a sombre view*
> *Where neither works nor days look innocent*
> *And both seem now too many, now too few.*

Even in these fine lines, there was something to question about the texture. 'A sombre view of the situation' is a worn politician's phrase; was it being accepted with a sort of fatigue, or alluded to with a sort of irony? Bareness, at least, seemed in the early 1950s to be MacNeice's growing-point: his danger, that facility of the practised writer which is so very different from spontaneity – the temptation to write because one can, not because one must.

In *Autumn Sequel*, which came out in 1954, it seems to me that he yielded almost fully to that temptation. Certainly in calling these twenty-six Cantos of that very intractable metre in English, *terza rima*, 'a rhetorical poem', MacNeice rather cunningly anticipated one's own verdict, that the poem was a triumph not only of skill but of determination. Of course, for MacNeice 'rhetoric' is not, as for Sir Herbert Read, the natural enemy of poetry, but, in the traditional sense of the word, the art of eloquent and persuasive writing, or, as for Hopkins, 'the common teachable element in poetry'. *Autumn Sequel* was partly an exercise, a deliberate display of skill. And it was an exercise written with a particular medium in view (though it had not, in fact, been commissioned in advance by that medium). The bulk of the poem was, in fact, broadcast on the Third Programme before it was published, and a passage from the fourth Canto, about the dangers and rewards of radio for the creative writer, is both an example of the tone of the poem at its most effective and partly a definition of that tone:

> *... as Harrap said*
> *Suggesting I might make an air-borne bard*
> *(Who spoke in parentheses and now is dead),*
> *'On the one hand – as a matter of fact I should*
> *Say on the first hand – there is daily bread,*
> *At least I assume there is, to be made good*
> *If good is the right expression; on the other*
> *Or one of the other hands there is much dead wood*
> *On the air in a manner of speaking which tends to smother*
> *What spark you start with; nevertheless, although*
> *Frustration is epidemic (take my brother,*
> *He simply thinks me mad to bother so*
> *With people by the million) nevertheless*
> *Our work is aimed at one at a time, you know ...'*

Throughout the poem MacNeice was at his best in the recording, as there, of conversation. Harrap's mannerisms of hesitation and deviousness, partly *mere* mannerisms, partly a technique for checking 'stock responses' in himself, are caught more fully than either a novelist or a realistic prose dramatist could afford to catch them. MacNeice makes us listen for the sake of listening, listen for the essential quality of something, instead of listening to see what comes next.

Harrap's remarks also suggest why *Autumn Sequel* makes a paradoxical, and in the end rather disturbing and unsatisfying, combined impression of impersonality and intimacy. A poem written for the ear – and though the poem was not commissioned in advance, it cannot have come as a very great surprise to MacNeice that the Third Programme should decide to broadcast it – must take every trick as it comes and some tricks, the less obvious ones, two or three times over. It must be painted in poster-colours. Its visual images should have the punch and the concentrated exaggeration of good descriptive journalism. Its shifts from one topic to another must be as smooth as a change of gears. Its moral reflections must be made explicit, must be hammered in, even at the cost of stridency. Its human characters must establish themselves at once in clear outline even at the cost of oversimplification and flattening out. All the goods must be in the shop-window; for the listener, with no text in front of him to go back over and puzzle about has not, even ideally, access to the rest of the shop. Technically, *Autumn Sequel* is exactly what a long poem conceived primarily in terms of radio ought to be. Criticisms of it, therefore, must fundamentally be criticisms of the limitations of radio as a primary medium for poetry. The paradoxical 'limiting judgment' about *Autumn Sequel* is that the more MacNeice apparently succeeds in taking us into his confidence, the more we admire his public skill in 'putting himself over'. The poet throughout, even and perhaps especially at his moments of most extreme genial informality, has been on parade. *Autumn Sequel* was not only, as MacNeice himself rightly commented, less 'occasional' than its predecessor of the late 1930s, *Autumn Journal*; it was also much less the poetic equivalent of a journal, like Amiel's, written primarily for the writer's own eyes.

The poem's nearest traditional equivalents, perhaps, were those poems of the late eighteenth and early nineteenth centuries which mingled moral reflections, natural descriptions, and sketches of human character in a blank verse subdued to the tone of polite conversation, like *The Task* or *The Excursion*. *Autumn Sequel* is, in a slightly brittle way, much *brighter* reading than such poems. The easy amble of pedestrian blank verse does not keep many modern readers alert; and the very difficulty of *terza rima*, and its apparent unsuitability for a sustained conversational use, enable MacNeice to keep us waiting restlessly for the next rhyme, the next glide at a tangent to a new topic. Yet perhaps readers will not return to *Autumn Sequel* as they find themselves returning even to the flatter patches of Cowper or Wordsworth. Everything, here, is on the surface. No nail is not hit on the head; and what we miss – in spite of what I have said earlier about my feeling that there is a great bulk of MacNeice that is permanently submerged, that never surfaces in poetry – is the sense of an area of unused resource outside the poem. (Of unused *conscious* resource: that may explain my apparent contradiction of myself, for it is the unconscious sources, probably, that MacNeice is always scary of tapping.) This, for all its abundant and sometimes too facile archetypal imagery, the sinister Parrot gabbling the cult of flux, the Garden, the Quest, the mountain which must be climbed 'because it is there', is above all a poetry of consciousness, as also of an admirable social conscientiousness. It lacks the beauty of necessity.

A few short quotations may illustrate, in a more particularized fashion, some of the poem's flaws and felicities. MacNeice is at his best a witty writer, but his wit can lapse into a pointless allusive facetiousness:

> ...Oxford in October
> Seems all dead stone (which here hath many a Fellow...

'Stone dead hath no fellow': our memories are jogged flatteringly, but then we reflect that 'stone dead' does not mean 'dead stone' and that the impeachment of the Earl of Strafford has nothing really, at all, to do with what Mac-

Neice is talking about. A similar fault is a recurrent facile smartness. Visiting Bath, MacNeice tells us at length that he does not like the eighteenth century :

> *Accomplishments were in, enthusiasm out,*
> *Although to our mind perhaps it seems a pity,*
> *That prose and reason ran to fat and gout ...*

A deeper and today a more usual observation would be that in its greatest writers, in Swift, in Pope, in Gray, in Cowper, in Johnson, the prose and reason ran to spleen, melancholia, or actual madness; MacNeice is attacking an Austin Dobson view of the eighteenth century which nobody now holds.

Here and there also in the descriptive passages of *Autumn Sequel* one feels that MacNeice is very much the Third Programme feature-writer, mugging up the background in advance, and determined to discover something quaint. But more usually MacNeice is at his best in the descriptive passages, as here, on Oxford stone :

> *... I roll on*
> *Past walls of broken biscuit, golden gloss,*
> *Porridge or crumbling shortbread or burnt scone,*
> *Puma, mouldy elephant, Persian lamb ...*

I have noted already his excellence in the recording of conversation Some passages expressing personal feeling, notably those on the character, death, and funeral of the poet Gwylim (an archetypal joyous maker, modelled, with the warts rather carefully left out, on Dylan Thomas) are genuinely moving, though, because MacNeice is shy about the direct expression of feeling, when he does express it directly he often seems just on the verge of becoming sentimental. One respects also the passages of moral exhortation, on the importance of being and making, of struggling and giving and loving, of not yielding to drift. The whole poem is extremely readable, but it is in these personal and moral passages that one gets farthest away from the sense of something extremely skilful, but also too consciously and too wilfully 'contrived'.

Both *Ten Burnt Offerings* and *Autumn Sequel* gave me, then, the sense that a fine talent was forcing itself. I read with far more genuine pleasure MacNeice's most recent volume, *Visitations*, in which he seemed to have got back for the first time in ten years or so the bite that he had in the 1930s; and in which he got away also from the snare of the blown-up, big poem, of a length suitable for broadcasting. In these new short poems or sequences of short poems he had freed himself from the twin temptations of moralizing at the drop of a hat, and of ad-libbing. His mood, from the beginning of the book, was agreeably cantankerous (it is very difficult to discuss him, except in oxymorons!) :

Why hold that poets are so sensitive?
A thickskinned grasping lot who filch and eavesdrop ...

He attacked snooty reviewers (or the snooty reviewer in himself):

Yet the cold voice chops and sniggers,
Prosing on, maintains the thread
Is broken and the phoenix fled,
Youth and poetry departed.

Acid and ignorant voice, desist.
Against your lies the skies bear witness ...

It is time, perhaps, that I did stop prosing on about him, that my own acid and perhaps ignorant voice did desist. I have said already, I think, all the general things I want to say. I should say finally that one would not have registered so sharply the degree of one's dissatisfaction with some of Mac-Neice's recent poetry unless one had a very high respect for, and therefore made very exacting demands on, the range and flexibility of his art and the integrity and scope of his mind. He has tried, with a strain of conscious effort, to make himself into the wrong sort of major poet. I think that if he had only waited a little more patiently for the pressure to gather, for the poem to force itself upon him, he might have been a major poet of the right sort. He has brought intelligence and poetry together; but the intelligence has too often seemed something superadded to the poem, rather than something used up in its proper shaping.

13 · 'NOT WRONGLY MOVED . . .' (WILLIAM EMPSON)

Vision and Rhetoric, Faber and Faber, London, 1959; *The Times Literary Supplement* middle page article, no. 2797, 7 October 1955.

Towards the end of William Empson's long expected, and long delayed, *Collected Poems* there is a short and moving poem called 'Let it Go'. It is one of the only three poems he wrote during the Second World War, when he was very busy at the Far Eastern Section of the BBC.

> *It is this deep blankness is the real thing strange.*
> *The more things happen to you the more you can't*
> *Tell or remember even what they were.*
> *The contradictions cover such a range*
> *The talk would talk and go so far aslant.*
> *You don't want madhouse and the whole thing there.*

From these six lines, a critic, new to Empson's work, and starting this collection of poems – like dishonest readers of detective stories – at the end instead of the beginning, might deduce a great deal about the poet's art and temperament and moral attitudes.

In Empson's tone and diction, such a critic might first notice an apparent casualness. The six lines at first sound like a few touching but slightly disjointed remarks flung out by a very tired man in conversation. Yet, having had that impression, he may then notice that they are a formal whole; the metre is regular, the rhyme-scheme strict, the rhymes themselves exact. And he will notice also that Empson, though here imitating the effect of conversation, is by no means slavishly bound by a conversational word-order. He inverts that here twice, and in both cases for rhetorical emphasis:

> *It is this deep blankness is the real thing strange.*

> *Tell or remember even what they were.*

The prose order would be 'the real strange thing' and 'even remember'; though, in fact, the first of these two lines is, like many of Empson's lines, covertly elliptical – it opens out as 'It is this deep blankness (that) is the real thing (that is) strange.'

The next thing our critic with a fresh eye might notice is that the throw-away mannerism, the artifice of the off-hand statement, of the lucky stray shot, conceals – or rather holds down, and reveals with polite indirectness – an enormous pressure of inner disturbance. The phrase 'deep blankness' points to the state which psychologists call protective emotional fatigue; but points to it, unexpectedly, with gratitude. And the phrase 'madhouse and the whole thing there' is similarly an eloquently reticent paraphrase for what psychologists call 'total recall'. The poem is about deciding not to go mad, or about being grateful to Nature for her odd, her sometimes rather flat and depressing way of stopping us from going mad. The use of the word 'madhouse' instead of 'madness', which would have been the more obvious choice, contributes to the peculiar tone of pragmatic irony. Poets can talk about their 'madness' rather smugly, remembering Plato's theory of inspiration or Dryden's:

> Great Wits are sure to Madness near alli'd
> And thin Partitions do their Bounds divide ...

Even if these associations are not present, the word 'madness' has a ring of awe and pity. But 'madhouse' is a brutal word (it has not even the remoteness of 'asylum' or the gentility of 'mental hospital'). Empson's use of 'madhouse' reminds us that it is weak and inept to go mad if you do not have to; you get shut up and your friends, however kind they are, tend to feel superior. 'The whole thing there,' if we compare it with 'total recall', has the same flavour of tart common sense. A 'total recall' suggests an experience which might be terrific but would also be awe-inspiring: 'the whole thing there' sharply reminds us that emotional problems, like all problems, should be tackled piecemeal. Though it deals with a mood of apathy, the poem does not express such a mood. It expresses a firmness of moral decision. And in an odd way the poet's fatigue bears witness to his energy, and his deliberate façade of blankness to the range of his experience and the power of his passions. There are clues, here, that will help us with much more complex poems. When Empson writes in 'Ignorance of Death',

> Otherwise I feel very blank upon this topic,
> And think that though important, and proper for anyone to bring up,
> It is one that most people should be prepared to be blank upon,

only a fool would take this as an expression of complacency, obtuseness, or indifference. And when, discussing the poetic schools of the 1930s, he writes jauntily in 'Autumn on Nan-Yueh':

> Verse has been lectured to a treat
>   Against Escape and being blah.
> It struck me trying not to fly
>   Let them escape a bit too far,

he might be having a dig at some of his young poetic disciples of our own decade.

Many young poets have in the past five years or so, in this country, been profoundly influenced, and rightly so, by an admiration for what could, most broadly, be called Empson's 'tone of voice': its assurance, its moderation, its sanity. But some of the verse produced by this discipleship has been, to say the least, prosy. Empson is a master of the line that makes its point by not making it, by a sort of terse reticence, the line like,

The contradictions cover such a range ...

It seemed the best thing to be up and go ...

There is not much else that we dare to praise ...

but, when he wants to, of something that Matthew Arnold himself would recognize as 'the grand style';

Matter includes what must matter enclose,
Its consequent space, the glass firmament's air-holes.
Heaven's but an attribute of her seven rainbows.
It is Styx coerces and not Hell controls.

His flat manner has been easier to learn than his grand manner; and in a conversation with some young poets about Matthew Arnold's 'touchstones', Empson, indeed, once himself suggested that 'the grand style' was a thing most good poets could lay on for a line or two when it was wanted, and by itself no sure test of a poet's rank. Yet his own flatness,

Blame it upon the beer
I have mislaid the torment and the fear,

gains its authority from the possibility of the grand style always in the background. His love of sanity springs not from phlegm but from a passion, obstinately sustained in 'a mad world'. His advice to us to be sensible and pragmatic springs from a deep awareness of the attraction of various kinds of emotional excess. When his young disciples have endured as sturdily as he has the ravages of time and the contradictory tugs of temperament they may begin at last to speak to us, in his tones, with something of his authority.

Empson is proverbially a 'difficult' poet. He has written elaborate notes to many of his own poems; and his best poems do deserve to be considered individually, and in detail. In a short, general survey of his poetic achievement, like this, however, the detailed examination of individual poems would be out of place. What may be more humbly useful, and what is perhaps new, is to sketch the kind of moral framework within which, in the broadest meaning of the phrase, Empson's poems 'make sense'; to consider them as the expression of a coherent attitude to life. Empson is a poet who has a religious temperament, a scientific world view, the attitude to politics of a traditional English liberal of the best kind, a constitutional melancholy and a robust good-humour, a sardonic wit, a gift for expressing the diffidence and passion of romantic personal attachments, a belief in pleasure, a scepticism about abstract systems, and a sharply practical impatience with anything he considers cant. The total complex of his attitudes has more in common with that of the attitudes of an essayist like, say, Montaigne than with that of most other poets. Many subjects have 'poetic' interest for him that to other writers would appear matters for prose disquisitions. He resembles the metaphysical poets (the greatest single ancestral influence on his work has been the poetry of Donne) in his power to fuse the activities of 'thinking' and 'feeling', in his power of finding or making connections between apparently disparate objects and themes, and also in not being (in the broader sense of the word, as it is used by philosophers rather than literary historians) in the least 'metaphysical'. It has often been pointed out, recently, that a poet like Spenser, who is not metaphysical in the literary historian's sense, has something like a coherent metaphysics (or a coherent traditional philosophy), whereas a poet like Donne has not. Empson's attitude towards philosophy in the strict sense of the word is one of scepticism, sometimes good-humoured and sometimes impatient:

> Two mirrors with Infinity to dine
> Drink him below the table when they please.
> Adam and Eve still breed their dotted line,
> Repeated incest, a plain series,
> Their trick is all philosophers' disease.

Empson's note to this is: 'Two mirrors have any number of reflections (the self-conscious mind): a dotted line is used for "and so on". The mind makes a system by inbreeding from a few fixed ideas.' Like one of his intellectual masters, I. A. Richards, Empson has a profound distrust both of 'systems' and of 'fixed ideas'.

The philosophical attitude has its place, in the scale of human interests, somewhere between the religious attitude and the practical attitude; and both men of religious genius and men of practical genius have often shown an impatience, something like Empson's, with philosophy. What is profoundest in Empson's religious attitude is expressed, more compactly than anywhere in his poems, in the quotation at the beginning of them from the Buddhistic 'Fire Sermon':

> When he is weary of these things, he becomes empty of desire.
> When he is empty of desire, he becomes free. When he is free he
> knows that he is free, that rebirth is at an end, that virtue is ac-
> complished, that duty is done, and that there is no more returning
> to the world; thus he knows.

Empson's practical attitude, on the other hand, is perhaps expressed more compactly than elsewhere in the masque 'The Birth of Steel' (with additions by other hands) which he wrote for performance before the Queen when she visited Sheffield University. The final choruses, with their gaily plebeian rhymes, glorify that industrial revolution which is the hard gritty core round which British greatness, art, culture, manners, and all the rest of it must now be built :

Men :
Puddling iron, casting iron,
Is the work of this environ;
And it suits the British lion
Puddling iron.

Women :
Blending steel, rolling steel,
That's the way to get a meal,
And we're right ahead of the field,
Blending steel . . .

The reader who finds it hard to reconcile the moods which these two quotations evoke should note perhaps in the extract from 'The Fire Sermon' the remarks about duty – 'that virtue is accomplished, that duty is done'. He might remember also Santayana's phrase about 'the long way round to Nirvana'. There certainly does seem to be a sense in which, for Empson as for the Buddhists, all existence not only involves suffering but *is* suffering. But, like the Buddhists, also, he refuses to believe that there is any short cut away from suffering. We must see that 'duty is done'. And, apart from its constitutional melancholy, there is perhaps in Empson's temperament something 'mere English', unaffected by Eastern profundities; a Yorkshire doggedness, a plain man's common sense, a cheerfulness that keeps breaking in.

The aristocratic tradition and the Christian tradition have both, at times, attracted him :

We could once carry anarchy, when we ran
Christ and the magnificent milord
As rival pets; the thing is, if we still can
Lacking either.

There are times also when he seems to feel that any religious attitude is at best a piece of gallant make-believe in a universe neither hostile nor friendly but neutral, in which man is an isolated creature. In a fine early poem, 'The Last Pain', he solemnly and eloquently recommends such make-belief, the postulating and sustaining, as objective, of values that one knows in one's heart not to be objective :

Feign then what's by a decent tact believed
And act that state is only so conceived,
 And build an edifice of form
 For house where phantoms may keep warm.

Imagine, then, by miracle, with me,
(Ambiguous gifts, as what gods give must be)
What could not possibly be there,
And learn a style from a despair.

Empson's later statement of this position in 'Your Teeth are Ivory Castles'
is more complex. There is a hint that something, after all, might 'possibly be
there'; and a far greater liberality about the range of attitudes which, if con-
sistently adhered to, might make possible some sort of 'good life' :

... though you
Look through the very corners of your eyes
Still you will find no star behind the blue;

This gives no scope for trickwork. He who tries
Talk must always plot and then sustain,
Talk to himself until the star replies,

Or in despair that it could speak again
Assume what answers any wits have found
In evening dress on rafts upon the main,

Not therefore uneventful, or soon drowned.

Among a number of younger critics there is a doctrine current that
Empson's best poems are half a dozen of his early ones, those in which he
makes a magnificent Donne-like use of metaphors and images from mathe-
matical physics and from natural history; it seems to me that he is a con-
sistently good poet, though, of course, not always at the top of his form;
and that what his later poems lost through a greater relaxation or expansive-
ness (some of them, like 'Autumn on Nan-Yueh', are positively chatty), they
gain through a wider range of reference, a deeper warmth, a more direct
and contemporary human appeal. It is unfashionable to deal with a contemporary poet, as Empson has been dealt with here, in terms of his 'ideas', even
in terms of his 'message'; yet it seemed justifiable in the case of a poet whose
mind is so original and distinguished, whose preoccupations are, basically,
those of so many thoughtful and sensitive men of our time. The passages already quoted have illustrated the assurance but perhaps not the range of his
verbal art. He can write like Pope, and as well as Pope :

Still stand uncalled-on her soul's appanage;
Much social detail whose successor fades,
Wit used to run a house and to play Bridge,
And tragic fervour to dismiss her maids.

He can write with an intense lyrical pathos,

> *... But oh*
> *The lovely balcony is lost*
> > *Just as the mountains take the snow.*

His talent is, as he himself once said in a broadcast, perhaps a 'narrow' one; it is also deep.

14 · A POETRY OF SEARCH (STEPHEN SPENDER)

Vision and Rhetoric, Faber and Faber, London, 1959; Middle page article–review on Stephen Spender's *Collected Poems, 1928–1953* in *The Times Literary Supplement*, 28 January 1955.

'A poet may be divinely gifted with a lucid and intense and purposive intellect; he may be clumsy and slow; that does not matter, what matters is integrity of purpose and the ability to maintain the purpose without losing oneself. Myself, I am scarcely capable of immediate concentration in poetry. My mind is not clear, my will is weak, I suffer from an excess of ideas and a weak sense of form. For every poem that I begin to write, I think of at least ten which I do not write down at all ...'

A poet, if he can strike the right balance between modesty and candour, between due humility and proper pride, is sometimes his own profoundest critic. Stephen Spender's *Collected Poems* should be read not only along with the poet's concise and charming introduction, but along with his more elaborate essay, from which the above quotation is taken. 'The Making of a Poem', published in *Partisan Review* in 1946. Spender there describes the patient compositional tactics of an intuitive poet of the slow introvert type. He describes how he is always given something to start with (is given more than he can use, endless sketches and ideas in notebooks) and how, having chosen among many possible beginnings, he works forward from the given element in a poem, not so much by a logical process as by a series of patient gropings, exploring and retreating from blind alleys, towards the completed poem, 'the final idea'. This groping forward, for Spender, is partly a matter of reviving, around two or three given lines, or disconnected sets of lines which he feels to be potentially parts of the same poem, or perhaps sometimes round a single phrase, past experiences with all their emotional associations. Thus, for Spender, the Muses are the daughters of Memory. Imagination is a function of Memory, and he would not agree with Landor that 'Memory is not a Muse'.

'It is perhaps true [he writes] to say that memory is the faculty of poetry, because the imagination is itself an exercise of memory. And our ability to imagine is our ability to remember what we have already once experienced and to apply it to some different situation ... Here I can detect my own greatest weakness. My memory is defective and self-centred.'

Poets, Spender goes on to say, are men not saintly (they have not renounced ambition) but men 'ambitious to be accepted for what they ultimately are as revealed ... in their poetry ...' Since there can be no cheating, the poet, like the saint, stands in all his works before the bar of a perpetual day of judgment. But the poet is like the saint at least in that he has renounced 'the life of "action" which ... is in fact a selective, even a negative kind of life'.

It is easy to see in the light of such statements why, when Spender's poems first appeared, they were hailed with such enthusiasm by critics like Sir Herbert Read who look on the Romantic movement as the last great unifying force in European literature. Like the great romantics, Spender sees the poet as a man dedicated, set apart. We are reminded, not indeed of Coleridge's transcendentalism, but of Keats on 'negative capability', and of Wordsworth on 'emotion recollected in tranquillity', on the life-enhancing quality of certain remembered 'spots of time' and on the association of ideas. When Spender says, 'There is nothing we imagine which we do not already know,' we could, indeed, give the remark a Colerigian or Platonic turn, but we may be pretty sure he himself does not intend to give it such a turn. He is not what he himself calls a 'visionary' poet, like Blake or Coleridge, or like Rimbaud, or Rilke, or Yeats. His feet are on the ground. No myth, or hunger for myth, obsess him. He is a sensitive agnostic, whose soul indeed might be described as naturally religious or even *naturaliter Christiana* – few living poets have such a spontaneous and patient sympathy even with uncomely weakness and even with deserved suffering – but who feels it would be intellectually dishonest to accept the consolations of faith. Even on a secular level Spender is not a man to be contained by rigidities. If his poems of the Spanish Civil War annoyed Roy Campbell, they also annoyed Communists, because of their tenderness towards cowards and deserters, their refusal to strike heroic attitudes, or to regard war, even for a cause assumed to be just, as anything but the most horrible necessity. Spender's deep sympathy in these poems is with the individual who wishes, however self-centredly, to escape.

It is, in fact, this 'self-centredness' which Spender rightly regards as in some ways a weakness of his that also gives him his peculiar uncomfortable honesty; and it is his deepest link with those masters of lyrical or symbolic autobiography, the great romantic poets. Auden, in one of the introductions to the admirable anthology, *Poets of the English Language*, which he edited along with Professor Normal Holmes Pearson, has the following acute remarks on the ethos of the romantic poet: 'The divine element in man is now held to be neither power nor free-will nor reason, but self-consciousness. Like God and unlike the rest of nature, man can say "I" : his ego stands over against his self, which to the ego is a part of nature. In this self he can see possibilities; he can imagine it and all things being other than they are; he runs ahead of himself; he foresees his death.'

This passage might almost be a commentary on one of the most penetrating
of Spender's early poems:

> *An 'I' can never be a great man.*
> *This known great one has weakness*
> *To friends is most remarkable for weakness:*
> *His ill-temper at meals, of being contradicted,*
> *His only real pleasure fishing in ponds,*
> *His only real wish – forgetting.*
>
> *To advance from friends to the composite self,*
> *Central 'I' is surrounded by 'I eating',*
> *'I loving', 'I angry', 'I excreting',*
> *And the great 'I' planted in him*
> *Has nothing to do with all these,*
>
> *Can never claim its true place*
> *Resting in the forehead, and calm in his gaze.*
> *The great 'I' is an unfortunate intruder*
> *Quarrelling with 'I tiring' and 'I sleeping',*
> *And all those other 'I's' who long for 'We dying'.*

No poet is totally unaffected by the climate of his age, and the tone of this
poem, its irony and the flatness of its pessimism, would have puzzled the
great romantics. There is a deep inherited wish in Spender to yield to the
romantic afflatus; there is also a strong contemporary impulse to question it
and check it. He knows that, for the taste of the age, his emotions can be
triggered off too easily. 'The Pylons' and 'The Funeral', two poems which
he reprints with reluctance in this collection, 'for the record', are instances
of how dangerously in Spender's work the platform speaker, shy and hesitant
and at a certain level very 'sincere', but fatally responsive to the mood of
his audience, can take over from the poet. Aware of this danger, Spender
lets his finger hover very delicately indeed round the trigger. The typical
quality of his style, arising from this paradoxical combination of a desire to
'let himself go' and a fear of 'letting himself go' is a stumbling eloquence of a
sweeping gesture suddenly arrested; or sometimes, starting off in a mood of
careful constriction, he works rather flatly or awkwardly towards a sudden
concentration – a concentration the more striking because of the painful
effort with which it has been arrived at. It might be said that, unlike the great
romantics, Spender is 'self-conscious', in the colloquial sense, *about* his self-
consciousness. It remains true that his poetry, like theirs, is an exploration of
the possibilities of the self and a search for the 'unfortunate intruder', the
great 'I' that transcends these.

It is this centring of the poetic process on the quest for the transcendental
ego – or for the inner perspective, a vanishing one, from which everything
can be understood and forgiven – that explains aspects of Spender's work

that have exasperated more robust or perhaps more simple-minded critics. He often shows sympathy towards characters, actions, or feelings not in themselves admirable; towards, in the Spanish Civil War poems, the shirker rather than the fighter; towards, in the poems grouped in this volume under the theme of 'love and separation', the traditionally ridiculous figure of the cuckold rather than towards simply happy lovers; towards that kind of liberalism commonly described as muddled or as wanting to have its cake and eat it too rather than towards coherent and consistent attitudes like those of the Communist, the Conservative, or the Pacifist; towards moods of hysteria rather than towards states of balance; towards people who become symbolically significant after they are dead rather than towards people who fulfil themselves while living; towards self-pity rather than stoicism, weakness rather than strength, failure rather than success. Yet critics, like Roy Campbell or Peter Russell, who have been infuriated by what they consider the unvirility of such attitudes, ought to ask themselves whether they are not in fact traditionally Christian attitudes – of humility about one's own weakness and charity for the weaknesses of others; and whether 'tougher', more 'manly' attitudes, of Nietzschean sort, may not have in them something of vulgar kowtowing to strength, crude male self-gratulation, worship of success, 'the bitch goddess'.

Let us admit, however, that the greatest poetry is heroic, and that there was sense in what Yeats said about passive suffering not being a theme for poetry. The answer, on Spender's behalf, would be that suffering is an inescapable feature of our time and that in a persistent active sympathy with suffering, a refusal to withdraw from imaginative participation in it, there *is* something heroic. It would be easy, of course, in Spender's case as in Byron's, to jeer at 'the pageant of his bleeding heart'; but it is a gentle heart, and the age has given it something to bleed for. It may at times, to be sure, bleed a little too easily, and we may wonder whether the bleeding really hurts. Spender's feelings are near the surface, and he is often a little ashamed that they are so near the surface. He might, perhaps, have integrated his feelings more fully if he had not been born in the land of the straight bat, the jolly good show, and the stiff upper-lip; or if he had belonged to some country like Spain or Germany where the direct expression of emotion is not thought shameful, and where it is not obligatory for poets to have 'a sense of humour'. Yet, as has been hinted above, the real answer to those who object to the emphasis in Spender's poems on weakness – on 'I eating', 'I tiring', 'I sleeping' – is that these, our vulnerabilities, belong for him to the self of possibilities, they are not ultimately real, they are transcended by the 'central "I"'. And the search for that, the playing of the cards through weakness up to strength, is his own special and distinctive courage as a poet. On a more technical level, of course, a similar remark might be made about Spender's verse craftsmanship. It is his consciousness of his 'weak sense of form' – and uncertain taste for language – that makes him work so hard on his poems, that makes him doubt whether even anthology pieces are quite 'finished'.

Louis MacNeice once described Spender as a poet patiently pressing *clichés* into poetic shape with steady and powerful hands. His syntax does, indeed, often seem either flat or awkward, his diction threadbare; and side by side with this drabness or clumsiness there goes a basic element of *cliché* of another sort, an eloquence that is real, but too like the eloquence of an orator. Yet, out of fumblings, out of over-emphatic gestures, the great white bird of poetry suddenly takes wing:

> *Not palaces, an era's crown,*
> *Where the mind dwells, intrigues, rests;*
> *Architectural gold-leaved flower*
> *From people ordered like a single mind,*
> *I sing. This only what I tell:*
> *It is too late for rare accumulations,*
> *For family pride, for beauty's filtered dusts;*
> *I say, stamping the words with emphasis,*
> *Drink from here energy and only energy,*
> *As from the electric charge of a battery,*
> *To will this Time's change.*
> Eye, gazelle, delicate wanderer,
> Drinker of horizon's fluid line . . .

With the two lines not italicized, an extraordinary change of quality or dimension seems to come over the early poem of which this is the onset. The first 11 lines are, indeed, skilful, vigorous, and persuasive rhetoric; the line,

> *Drink from here energy and only energy,*

is a particularly memorable one. Yet there is in the choice of words, in the order of words, in these first 11 lines something not exactly vulgar, but a little strident, a little stale: 'an era's crown', 'dwells', 'rare accumulations', 'family pride', 'beauty's filtered dusts' – there is something in such phrases which suggests either a leading article or a conventional old-fashioned 'literariness'. 'This only what I tell' may irritate, for it is an ellipsis that may not (at a first try) fill out to make good sense. 'This is only what I tell' is not the required meaning, but 'This only is what I tell'. It would be a captious criticism, perhaps, to say that 'the electric charge of a battery' strikes us to-day as too much of a period image, like pylons, or arterial roads. It is sounder to say that throughout these first 11 lines we have a certain uncomfortable feeling of being 'got at'. But then, by its lyrical concentration,

> *Eye, gazelle, delicate wanderer . . .*

utterly transforms these partly hostile impressions. The first 11 lines become 'right' again, for what they lead up to, for what they set off.

In quite a number of the earlier poems of this volume there are such moments of magical transformation. Many of the later poems, however, more lucidly organized round more coherent sets of feelings, have no need of such moments. In Spender's earlier work we can spot the moment when the poem, which has been roaring along the runway, suddenly soars. In beautiful late poems like 'Seascape' or 'Missing my Daughter' what holds us, frail and almost vanishing in its detail, yet delicately strong in its total composition, like a David Jones water-colour drawing of flowers in a glass bowl against a window, is the shining transparency of the single vision:

> *The shore, heaped up with roses, horses, spires,*
> *Wanders on water, walking above ribbed sand ...*

Or the reflection of a child in a mirror already reflecting roses and the child's imagined image, the sense of her absence:

> *The door, in a green mirage,*
> *Opened. In my daughter came.*
> *Her eyes were wide as those she has,*
> *The round gaze of her childhood was*
> *White as the distance in the glass*
> *Or on a white page, a white poem.*
> *The roses raced around her name.*

In such late poems we feel that the essential purity of Spender's vision has become purged at last of a youthful turbidness, of an awkward and contorting shyness, and of an encumbering, too facile, rhetoric.

15 · LAWRENCE DURRELL

Notes on Literature, no. 126 (January 1972), issued by the British Council.

(1) POETRY AS STYLE

A malicious critic once remarked that in his most widely successful prose work, *The Alexandria Quartet*, Lawrence Durrell had genius without taste, but that in his poems he had taste without genius. I am using for this commentary the poems of Durrell's included in *Penguin Modern Poets 1*, in which the other two poets, R. S. Thomas and Elizabeth Jennings, are temperamentally and in their general beliefs about life, I would think, very unlike Durrell, but like him in their chastity of diction in verse and their delicate modulation of rhythm to suit sense. There is a very beautiful stanza, for instance, at the end of Elizabeth Jennings's 'Song at the Beginning of Autumn':

> *But I am carried back against*
> *My will into a childhood where*
> *Autumn is bonfires, marbles, smoke;*
> *I lean against my window fenced*
> *From evocations in the air.*
> *When I said autumn, autumn broke.*

It will be noticed that in this stanza an extreme regularity of rhyme and metre (a reader who judges rhyme by the eye may not at first notice that 'against' is an exact rhyme with 'fenced') works along with a perfectly natural speaking tone of voice. The stanza moves on the noun and the verb (there are no adjectives). There is only one noun of an abstract and conceptual sort – 'evocations'. The verb 'broke', strong at the end of the last line, could mean *either* that when the poet said the word 'autumn' or evoked the concept of autumn, the whole concept broke in her hands (her window was fencing her against it) *or* that it broke into a sudden, dramatic, firework blaze or flowering. The two poets, so far as I know, have never met or corresponded with each other: but this is a Durrellesque stanza.

Generally, R. S. Thomas uses more adjectives than Durrell, but a stanza of Thomas's from this Penguin volume also strikes me (I do not, in either case, suggest any direct influence) as oddly Durrellesque. The title is rather like Elizabeth Jennings's title, 'Song at the Year's Turning'; the stanza is the second of a three-stanza poem :

> *Love deceived him; what is there to say*
> *The mind brought you by a better way*
> *To this despair? Lost in the world's wood*
> *You cannot stanch the bright menstrual blood.*
> *The earth sickens, under naked boughs*
> *The frost comes to barb your broken vows.*

Again there are few adjectives ('better', 'bright', 'naked', 'broken', are felt as functionally informative: and 'menstrual' sends a noise up like a howl). I think I hear a bit of Welsh sing-song in Mr Thomas that I do not hear in Miss Jennings. But whoever edited this first volume of *Penguin Modern Poets* had a remarkable intuition of stylistic affinity, affinity in taste, in diction and feeling for the play between natural speech rhythm and metrical regularity, in three British poets who had never met each other and might even dislike each other intensely (though I think they would have a respect for each other's craft and art in verse) if they did.

Let us look now at Durrell in this reduced stylistic context, and context of worry about style, that I have set up. He thinks a great deal about style in his poems and writes about it : a poem called 'Style' :

> *Something like the sea,*
> *Unlaboured momentum of water*
> *But going somewhere,*
> *Building and subsiding,*
> *The busy one, the loveless.*
>
> *Or the wind that slits*
> *Forests from end to end,*
> *Inspiriting vast audiences,*
> *Ovations of leafy hands,*
> *Accepting, accepting.*
>
> *But neither is yet*
> *Fine enough for the line I hunt.*
> *The dry bony blade of the*
> *Sword-grass might suit me*
> *Better: an assassin of polish.*
>
> *Such a bite of perfect temper*
> *As unwary fingers provoke,*
> *Not to be felt till later,*
> *Turning away, to notice the thread*
> *Of blood from its unfelt stroke.*

Various things might be noticed about this poem. Though the images are all from nature, it is a poem about art, which takes its models from art. The first stanza about the sea suggests the lyrical mode in poetry, with its surging, rhythmical expression of pure emotion. The second stanza suggests the dramatic, particularly the tragic mode, the 'ovations of leafy hands' suggesting the clapping of the audience, the whole metaphor suggesting that drama turns the individual trees of the audience into one great forest and then splits the forest with the heartrending tragic mind. The two last stanzas, about the dry sword-grass that cuts the careless hand, which only long after touching the sword-grass notes that it is bleeding, suggests the kind of poetry that Durrell wants to write himself. A more controlled, sharper, more epigrammatic poetry than the simple direct lyric or the great tragedy, something a little perhaps like the poetry of Landor or the poetry of the great Alexandrian poet, Kavafy, whom Durrell much admires. One will admire first of all the 'polish' of such poetry but it is an 'assassin'; springing from a sense of intimate pain, it will arouse, though not immediately, one's own sense of intimate pain. Durrell, in fact, is often gay in his poems, nor is he always elegant like Landor and Kavafy: his character sketches have sometimes a Browningesque roughness, other poems like 'The Ballad of the Good Lord Nelson' are full of boisterous humour. But his more typical poems are ones in which an elegant and concise evocation of the beauty of landscape, the pleasures of life, leaves a sense of a touch of bitterness lurking under the flowers. It might not be wholly inaccurate to describe them as the poems of a sad hedonist, of a man to whom riches and harmony always suggest loss. Yet this is perhaps a limiting account. In Durrell, this latent sadness or bitterness is balanced also by a kind of religiousness, often expressed in pagan Greek terms.

(2) LANDSCAPES AND MYTHOLOGIES

This religiousness comes out in a fine poem in the *Penguin Modern Poets* selection, 'Delos', addressed to the dancer Diana Gould. It is about the island of Delos, a great religious centre in ancient Greece. The poem begins with a wonderful evocation of the small Greek islands, seen, as with a god's eye view, on a chart, from the sky:

> On charts they fall like lace,
> Islands consuming in a sea
> Born dense with its own blue;
> And like repairing mirrors holding up
> Small towns and trees and rivers
> To the still air, the lovely air ...

The poem goes on to speak in its second section of the statues of the dead which, through art, somehow, if they do not conquer death, give a kind of religious grace and piety to our idea of death:

> *The statues of the dead here*
> *Embark on sunlight, sealed*
> *Each in her model with the sightless eyes:*
> *The modest stones of Greeks,*
> *Who gravely interrupted death by pleasure.*

The last line in that passage shows the great condensation and weightiness of which Durrell is capable. These modest statues of the dead seem to sail out into sunlight but with sightless eyes, in the gravity of their beauty (and I think there is a subdued pun on the idea that they are graven images, on the idea of their engraved beauty) break into the idea of inescapable death which would otherwise obsess because they transform that idea into the serious pleasure of art. The sentence I have just written is complicated and clumsy. But I think the reader who now reads Durrell's simple and elegant line again,

> *Who gravely interrupted death by pleasure.*

will find that everything I have laboriously spelt out is *implicit* in that line. Yet, though Durrell's lines often have this weight, they could be described as 'modest lines', just as he describes his Greek statues of the dead as 'modest stones'. Though he is often a rather showy and even flashy writer in prose, he is never brassily rhetorical, he never shows off in poetry.

This particular poem does not end, however, with this grave, religious confrontation of death. It ends with a splendid invocation of life, in three images: sails voyaging out to sea, women voyaging out to confront all the risks of life, and a guiding star, more than a mere physical star, which gives such voyages their aim; and we voyage, after all, from a sacred island:

> *And in harbours softly fallen*
> *The liver-coloured sails –*
> *Sharp-featured brigantines with eyes –*
> *Ride in reception so like women:*
> *The pathetic faculty of girls*
> *To register and utter a desire*
> *In the arms of men upon the new-mown waters,*
> *Follow the wind, with their long shining keels*
> *Aimed across Delos at a star.*

One or two felicities should be noticed there. The ships, 'sharp-featured', 'with eyes' are not merely symbols of the human quest but seem themselves humanized, personified. Even their slightly grotesque 'liver-coloured sails' relate these artefacts to the organic world and Durrell, with his great love for Elizabethan literature, may be remembering that the liver of Shakespeare and his contemporaries was the seat of the deep emotions, both love and wrath. The 'pathetic faculty of girls' does not mean that we should pity the girls but that they have a faculty for pathos, for feeling, which may be sorrow indeed but may also be joy. Durrell is a fine Greek scholar and the adjective of Greek derivation that contrasts with 'pathetic' is 'drastic' (related to the idea of drama), suggesting a faculty not for feeling but for decisive and perhaps dangerous action. Durrell is never a poet of the drastic, but of what Wordsworth calls a 'wise passiveness', of the acceptance both of joy and sorrow.

Yet this is perhaps too simple an account of Durrell's attitude. He is not, after all, a contemporary of Wordsworth, but of Sartre; a man much influenced in his youth by Freud, and by Freud's disciple Groddeck, very much influenced as a poet both by the style of his slightly older contemporary W. H. Auden and by Auden's 'clinical' attitude to the human condition. (T. S. Eliot was very kind to Durrell in his youth, but I find little direct influence from Eliot in Durrell's poetry, though Durrell's early novel, published in Paris, *The Black Book*, bears a strong resemblance to *The Waste Land* – particularly, one might add, to the first drafts of *The Waste Land*, longer and grimmer than the 'official' version, edited and published by Eliot's widow, Mrs Valerie Eliot, in 1971. There is the same obsession in *The Black Book* and in the first drafts of *The Waste Land* with the pathos and fascination of the sordid, the same combination of a horror of, and an obsession with, sexual appetite divorced from love.) But let us look now at Durrell, the poet, as a 'modernist'.

(3) DURRELL THE 'MODERNIST'

As a poet, Durrell is not 'modernist' in technique. He eschews free verse, shock tactics of any sort, abrupt transitions, like those of Pound and Eliot, between one area of subject-matter and another quite contrasting one; nor does he, like William Empson, indulge in deliberately elliptical syntax and sophistical-paradoxical argument (he loves Shakespeare's sonnets, which are difficult though not in a metaphysical way, and, in a fairly long acquaintance with him, I have never heard him express any interest in John Donne or Donne's school). He is not even modernist in diction, though he is not deliberately archaic; like most well-educated Englishmen who have lived most of their lives abroad, he speaks very correct but slightly old-fashioned English. If he uses slang or colloquial phrases in conversation, or sometimes in his novels, the slang is that of the early 1930s or even the 1920s. But the diction of his poetry, even of his occasional comic poems, one would describe as more or less 'timeless'. Durrell's 'modernism' in poetry is a matter, then, not of presentation but of sensibility and ideas.

In the *Penguin Modern Poets* selection two poems especially seem to me to express this modernism of sensibility and ideas, one 'On Seeming to Presume' (which gave the title to one of Durrell's volumes) and the other 'Je Est Un Autre' of which the title – literally in English translation, 'I *is* an Other' (not 'I *am* an Other') – is from one of the prose poems of Rimbaud, the most revolutionary figure in the French poetry of the later nineteenth century. What Rimbaud's ungrammatical sentence perhaps implies is that one's ego (the self that perceives) either transcends or is alienated from one's *moi* (the self, or multiplicity of selves, that is perceived). The I who is another in Durrell's poem is the sinister figure in a black hat who, in their European cities, has watched the poet watching him, and has also been watching the poet. He can never be caught and accosted but he leaves clues behind, black cigars burning on the pavement, he knows all about the poet's love affairs, he can be heard laughing sinisterly in the next room, and now that the poet is writing a poem about him, he seems to watch its composition, the madness of the French pre-Symbolist poet Gérard de Nerval in his eyes. In a sense this sinister alienated other is more the true poet than the poet himself. And the visual images suggest something else modern, the dark Gothic romanticism of pre-Second World War German films like *The Cabinet of Dr Caligari*. The figure in the tall black hat, with the black cigars, with his coat tails disappearing round corners, haunts us even if we cannot give a rational explanation of him. He is a projection of the spy in us who spies upon ourselves.

'On Seeming to Presume' is a less grotesque and sinister but in some ways a much sadder poem. It sees man thrust from the womb where he felt at home slowly and painfully developing first a libido, then a rational selfishness, then a superego or self-punishing moral sense – symbolized by Durrell as 'I will', 'I must', 'I ought' – but with this moral sense seeming to exclude himself further and further 'from the true/Participating love'. He defies his moral sense, gives rein to lust and hate, insists on the will to live for its own sake, is caught in Hamlet's predicament of 'To be or not to be' :

> He wrings his hands and cries
> 'I want to live,' but dies.

And the last two stanzas reflect sadly that it was lovers who first composed in mind, before begetting in body, 'this poor unstable/Derivative of clay .../ That bears the human label'. The average 'caliban of gloom' cannot be helped by 'king or saint', his fate is to be 'swaddled in despair' (swaddled like the newly born babe at the beginning of the poem) in a factory or a furnished room, crying throughout his 60 years of life for his apparent presumption in being born into a world that has no place for him. This is one of the saddest of all Durrell's poems; it is 'modernist' in fitting in both with Freud's late, and not generally accepted, theory of the death-wish, and also with Sartre's bitter description of man as a 'useless passion'. I would not take either of these poems, fine and powerful as they are, as an ultimate statement of Durrell's poetic vision. He has, in spite of his awareness of the sadness in things, a natural zest for life. He is a little like Dr Johnson's friend, Mr Edwards, who wanted to be a philosopher but cheerfulness would always keep breaking in. But I have emphasized in these notes a certain deeper, sadder, and more thoughtful side in his poetry, since its musicality, its charm, its evocation of the Mediterranean landscape are more likely to strike on a first reading. As a poet Durrell has not been ignored but has been a little underestimated. It is worth, by contrast to the usual estimate, emphasizing the depth of his feelings and the searching seriousness of his thoughts.

Vision and Rhetoric, Faber and Faber, London, 1959; *British Book News Supplements*, Longmans for the British Council, 1957.

(1)

When Dylan Thomas died in New York in his 39th year at the end of 1953, he had been a poet of considerable reputation for 20 years and, with the recent publication of his *Collected Poems*, was at the height of his fame. The collected volume was known to have sold, even before his death, more than 10,000 copies, an enormous figure by contemporary English or American standards. He was one of the two or three poets of his time whose name, like that of Eliot or Auden, was familiar to the man in the street. Shortly after his death, the success over the air and on stage of his dramatic prose fantasy for radio, *Under Milk Wood*, introduced his work to an even wider audience than that which appreciated his poetry. It was not only, however, as a writer that Thomas was known to a wide public. He had a remarkable gift as an entertainer, and was a first-rate broadcaster, particularly of his own short stories based on his childhood in Wales. He was an extremely gregarious man, and had a very warm and lovable personality. His death produced a spate of tributes in prose and verse from scores of friends and acquaintances. And even for those who did not know him personally, Thomas had become, as few poets of our age have become, a kind of legend. He corresponded, as most poets do not, to some popular ideal, vision, or fiction of what a poet, in real life, should be. He was the pattern of the poet as a bohemian, and this was in many ways a misfortune for him. Had he been a more aloof, a less gregarious, a more prudent man; had he been less ready to expend himself in casual sociability; had he had less of a knack, in his later years, for earning money quickly and spending it even more quickly; in any of these cases, he might have lived longer and produced more; but he would not have been, in any of these cases, the writer that he is.

Thomas achieved, and has retained, a popular fame as a poet in spite of the fact that many of his poems are, at least on an intellectual level, extremely hard to comprehend. The design of at least many of his earlier poems is notably obscure; many of his later poems are much clearer in outline than his earlier work, but they are still full of puzzling details. Yet he is one of the few modern poets who can be read aloud to a large, mixed audience, with a confidence in his 'going down'. There is a massive emotional directness in his poems that at once comes across. And the more critical reader, who may be suspicious of what seems a direct attack on his feelings below the level of the intellect, soon becomes aware that Thomas's obscurity is not that of a loose and vague but of an extremely packed writer. In one of the best short studies that has been written of Thomas since his death, David Daiches quotes what is certainly at a first glance, an almost totally opaque passage.

> Altarwise by owl-light in the halfway house
> The gentleman lay graveward with his furies;
> Abaddon in the hangnail cracked from Adam,
> And, from his fork, a dog among the fairies,
> Bit out the mandrake with tomorrow's scream ...

Daiches comments :

> The careful explicator will be able to produce informative glosses on each of these phrases, but the fact remains that the poem is congested with its metaphors, and the reader is left with a feeling of oppression ... But it must be emphasized that this is not the fault of a bad romantic poetry, too loose and exclamatory, but comes from what can perhaps be called the classical vice of attempting to press too much into too little space.

In spite of this excessive congestion of much of his poetry, Thomas obviously did succeed in communicating in verse, to a very large public by modern standards, something which that public felt to be important. What was that something, and how did Thomas get it across? It was certainly something very different from the public personality, the personality of an entertainer, which Thomas conveyed in a prose book, *Portrait of the Artist as a Young Dog*. Thomas was not, like Byron or Yeats, for instance, the poet as actor; he did not dramatize his personal life in his poetry, or build himself up as a 'character'. He did these things in conversation, and in the sketches and short stories, brilliant improvisations, which were fundamentally an extension of his genius for conversation. His poems are exceedingly individual, but they are also impersonal; when he writes about his childhood he is not so much recalling particular experiences as transforming them into a vision of innocence before the Fall. Yet at the same time, he is a concrete rather than a generalizing poet; he does not, like Auden, take a more or less abstract theme and proceed to relate it, in a detached way, to particularized observations about man and society. Both the appeal and the difficulty of his poetry come from the fact that it is a poetry of unitary response. Many of the best modern writers have been concerned with a kind of split in the consciousness of our time between what men think and what they feel or would like to feel, between what men suppose to be true and what they would like to believe, between what men feel is a proper course of action and what they feel is an attractive one. These urgent contemporary themes of stress, doubt, division in the self, tragic irony, and tragic choice, do not enter into Dylan Thomas's poetic world. It is a world quite at one with itself. At the heart of his poetic response to experience there is a baffling simplicity.

(2)

It is Thomas's poetry that makes him important and, because of this baffling simplicity at the heart of it, his personal history, outside the history of his poems, can perhaps throw very little direct light on his achievement as a poet. His prose works, with the exception of *Under Milk Wood*, also throw little light on his poetry. They are second-level achievements, representing Thomas as the brilliant entertainer rather than the dedicated poet; they stand also, as so much of Thomas's personal life did, for that search for distraction which the concentrated nature of his dedication to poetry made necessary. Thomas's poetry is the main theme of this essay, but I shall precede my consideration of it by a few brief remarks on Thomas's life, his personality, and his achievements in prose.

Thomas was the son of a Swansea schoolmaster, a teacher of English in a grammar school, who had himself poetic ambitions; Thomas's father must have had remarkable gifts as a teacher, for many of the leading figures today in Welsh literary life were, at one time or another, his pupils. The Welsh, like the Scots, have a very strong family sense, and in his later years memories of holidays with farmer uncles meant a great deal to Thomas. He was not a particularly brilliant schoolboy, but he did very well at English, took an enthusiastic part in amateur dramatics, and wrote neat and very conventional poems for his school magazine. His father would have liked him to work hard to gain a scholarship to a university, but he did not do so. On leaving school he became for a short time a reporter on a Swansea newspaper, a job which must have combined for him the appeal of bohemianism with that of the outer verges of literature.

Thomas's Welshness is an important part of his make-up. He never spoke or understood the Welsh language, and he very early taught himself to speak English not with the slight Welsh sing-song but with what he himself described mockingly as a 'cut-glass accent'. He disliked Welsh nationalism, and, indeed, all types of nationalism, but Wales remained to him home. His knowledge of the Bible, and his fundamentally religious – emotionally rather than intellectually religious – attitude to life were typically Welsh; his bohemianism was partly a reaction against the severe puritanism of much of middle-class Welsh life. His sense of verbal music, his feeling for the intricate interplay of vowel and consonant, and also, in prose and conversation, his love of the extravagant phrase and the witty exaggeration were Welsh. He was un-English also in his universal gregariousness, his unwillingness to make social discriminations, his complete lack of class-consciousness.

He first became known as a poet through contributing poems to, and winning prizes from, the poetry page of *The Sunday Referee*, edited by Victor Neuberg. *The Sunday Referee* finally financed the publication of his first volume, *Eighteen Poems*. Thomas was thus flung on the London literary world, particularly its bohemian side, as a boy of 20, and in his early years in London he depended a great deal on the generosity and hospitality of friends. In his later years, however, his wide range of secondary gifts, as a broadcaster, a writer of sketches and short stories and film scripts, even as a comic journalist, were bringing him in a considerable yearly income; this tended, however, to be spent as soon as it was earned, and his payment of income tax was perpetually overdue. He lost, in later years, his taste for London life, and spent as much time as he could with his wife and children at Laugharne. It was monetary need that drove him to undertake the American poetry reading tours, which both he and those who organized them found a considerable strain as well as a stimulus, and on the last of which he died. John Malcolm Brinnin's book about these tours is obviously almost agonizingly accurate in its descriptions of many embarrassing episodes, but it is a portrait of a sick man under the strain of financial and moral worry, and of being perpetually on public show, and it should not be taken as giving a fair idea of the character or personality of Dylan Thomas as his English friends knew him. In particular it conveys a vivid impression of the element of stress, but no impression at all of the element of fulfilment, in Thomas's married life; Brinnin's remarks about this should be corrected by Roy Campbell's that Thomas and his wife were 'always in love, even years after marriage to the day of his death. They would quarrel like newly-weds on the slightest pretext with never a dull moment and make it up in two minutes.'

In America, Thomas tended to drink whisky rather than beer, though he knew spirits were bad for him. In England and Wales, he stuck on the whole to beer, not for its own sake, but as what his friend Vernon Watkins calls 'a necessary adjunct to conversation'. The tempo of his English life was slower, more genial, and less harassed than that of his tours in America. The charm of his rambling, vivid, extravagantly anecdotal conversation comes out in *Portrait of the Artist as a Young Dog* and in many of his broadcast sketches. The warmth of his personality, his zest in every kind of human oddity, his love for his fellow men, come out in his last completed work, *Under Milk Wood*. Here, more than in any other prose work of his, he managed to combine his prose gift for humorous fantasy based on realistic observation with his poetic gift for a piled-up richness of evocative language. *Under Milk Wood* is also, purely formally, notable as an invention. It derives not from any literary model, but from the radio form of the 'feature', in narrative and dialogue, evoking the spirit of a place; it turns that form into literature. It also makes more broadly and obviously apprehensible than, perhaps, any of Thomas's poems do that 'love of Man ... and praise of God' which, in the introduction to the *Collected Poems*, Thomas wrote of as underlying all his work. *Under Milk Wood* is not, in the ordinary sense, dramatic. The characters are not confronted with choices; they behave according to their natures, mean, thriftless, or generous, and are to be accepted, like natural objects, for being what they are; and the movement is not dramatic, but cyclical, from early morning through day to night.

There are perhaps two moral centres in *Under Milk Wood*: the Reverend Eli Jenkins, with his touching 'good–bad' poems and his gentle appeals to a gentle God to look kindly on human failings; and the old blind sea-captain, the fire of whose lust and love – it is typical of Thomas's unitary response to refuse to distinguish between these – is not quenched even by the waters of death and of utter forgetfulness. Thomas was as a man, like the Reverend Eli Jenkins, utterly without malice. Reading *Under Milk Wood* it is possible to understand what a famous newspaper, in a remarkable obituary notice of Thomas, meant by asserting that he had the courage to lead the Christian life in public. 'The harlots and the publicans shall go into heaven before you.'

(3)

In an early statement about his poems, published in Geoffrey Grigson's poetry periodical of the 1930s, *New Verse*, Thomas spoke of the process of writing a poem as one of stripping away darkness, of struggling up to light; and also of that struggle as taking place through a dialectic of images. In his preface to his *Collected Poems*, on the other hand, he spoke, as we have seen, of his poems being written 'for the love of Man and in praise of God'. These two statements help us to measure a certain progress, or development, in a poetic achievement which is too often thought of as having been one of more or less stationary self-repetition. In many of his early poems, Thomas does, in fact, seem immersed, in a way that is bewildering to the reader and may have been bewildering to himself, in an attempt to grasp the whole of life, human and natural, as an apparently confused but ultimately single process. In his later poems, he more often seems to be, quite consciously and much less bewilderingly, *celebrating* that process – celebrating it, as Daiches says, religiously, and with sacramental imagery.

Perhaps also it is wrong to speak of him as celebrating some particular process; an American critic has suggested that what Thomas can be thought of as celebrating is the fact, or notion, of process in general, Eliot's 'three things', 'birth, and copulation, and death', seeing them as cyclical, seeing every birth as involving death, every death as involving birth, seeing also human life and natural process as exactly equated.

Such a set of clues certainly helps us a good deal with Thomas's earlier poems:

> *The force that through the green fuse drives the flower*
> *Drives my green age; that blasts the roots of trees*
> *Is my destroyer.*
> *And I am dumb to tell the crooked rose*
> *My youth is bent by the same wintry fever ...*

Thomas, there, is massively identifying the body of man with the body of the world. The forces, he is saying, that control the growth and decay, the beauty and terror of human life are not merely similar to, but are the very same forces as, we see at work in outer nature. But how is Thomas able to hold and move us by saying this? In a way, it is a platitude: it is a statement, at least, which most of us would accept without too much excitement or perturbation up to a point, or with qualifications. Man, as an animal, is part of nature; is that a new or startling idea? My own answer, when many years ago I first considered the puzzle of the extremely powerful impact of this passage, was this. The man–nature equation here gains strength from an inter-transference of qualities between – or, more strictly, of our emotional attitudes towards – man and nature. We feel a human pity for Thomas's 'crooked rose', and, on the other hand, the 'wintry fever' of an adolescent's unsatisfied sexual desires acquires something of the impersonal dignity of a natural process.

It is still, I think, the best clue that we have at least to Thomas's earliest volume, *Eighteen Poems*, to think of him as engaged in this way in bestowing on something humanly undignified, adolescent frustration, natural dignity:

> *I see you boys of summer in your ruin.*
> *Man in his maggot's barren.*
> *And boys are full and foreign in the pouch.*
> *I am the man your father was.*
> *We are the sons of flint and pitch.*
> *O see the poles are kissing as they cross.*

The American critic, Elder Olson, interprets the whole poem from which this stanza comes – the first poem in Dylan Thomas's first book – as a dialogue between perverse youth and crabbed age, with the poet occasionally intervening as an impersonal commentator. Olson's ingenuity leaves out, however, the most obvious thing. The poem is not only *about* the boys of summer in their ruin, but *by* one of them. It seeks to give oratorical emphasis and nobility of gesture to a subject which literature can usually touch on only furtively or with condescending pity – the subject of the sexual frustrations suffered by, and also the agonizingly intense erotic imaginings that obsess, in an advanced and therefore in many ways repressive civilization like our own, the middle-class adolescent male. Thomas began to write his poems in his late 'teens. It is in his late 'teens that the sexual desires of the male are at their most urgent, and that his sexual potency is at its greatest, it is in his late 'teens also, in our society, that he has least chance of satisfying or exercising one or the other in a normal fashion. What Thomas is doing in many of his earliest poems is finding poetic symbols adequate to this experience, which is centrally important in most masculine life-histories, but which it is difficult to treat not only with literary, but even with ordinary, decency. He also expresses the wider sense of traumatic shock, a shock at once of awe and horror, which is likely to accompany, for any young male in our civilization, the full imaginative realization of 'the facts of life'. He went on to do things more broadly significant than this; but this, in itself, was a significant achievement.

(4)

Thomas's second volume, *Twenty-five Poems*, brought him on the whole more praise and more fame than his first. Edith Sitwell, in particular, saluted it with enthusiasm in a memorable short review in *The Observer*. Yet like many second volumes of verse – and like all second novels! – *Twenty-five Poems* is in many ways unsatisfactory. It shows Thomas experimenting with new themes, new images, new styles. Two poems in the book have, indeed, been much praised, but to me it seems undeservedly. One is 'And Death Shall Have No Dominion', which strikes me as a set of large but rather empty rhetorical gestures, a poem in which the poet faced by the harsh fact of death is not properly confronting it but 'cheering himself up'. The other is Thomas's one political poem, 'The Hand That Signed the Paper'. That ends with this stanza:

> *The five kings count the dead but do not soften*
> *The crusted wound nor stroke the brow;*
> *A hand rules pity as a hand rules heaven;*
> *Hands have no tears to flow.*

That stanza has been praised as an example of a poet splendidly and successfully mixing metaphors; may not some, with all respect, find it rather an example of bathos?

There are other poems in *Twenty-five Poems* like 'Should Lanterns Shine', which show us that Thomas had been reading both Rilke, probably in translation, and Yeats:

> *And from her lips the faded pigments fall,*
> *The mummy cloths expose an ancient breast* ...

> *I have heard many years of telling,*
> *And many years should see some change.*

> *The ball I threw while playing in the park*
> *Has not yet reached the ground.*

Such lines show a minor good taste in a composite manner which is essentially *not* Thomas's. He had become, in his second volume, much more uncertain about the way he was going than in his first, and there is one poem which expresses his doubts admirably. Was, perhaps, his poetic method a method of self-deception?

I have longed to move away
From the hissing of the spent lie
And the old terrors' continual cry
Growing more terrible as the day
Goes over the hill into the deep sea;
I have longed to move away
From the repetition of salutes,
For there are ghosts in the air
And ghostly echoes on paper,
And the thunder of calls and notes.

I have longed to move away but am afraid;
Some life, yet unspent, might explode
Out of the old lie burning on the ground,
And, crackling into the air, leave me half-blind.
Neither by night's ancient fear,
The parting of hat from hair,
Pursed lips at the receiver,
Shall I fall to death's feather.
By these I would not care to die,
Half convention and half lie.

Thomas very rarely used in his poetry the wit and humour of his personal conversation and his narrative prose. But here he manages to evade deep fears by mocking at shallow fears: '... night's ancient fear,/The parting of hat from hair' is simply a grotesque image of man's being so frightened that his hair stands on end and pushes his hat off: as in a comic drawing by such a cartoonist as H. M. Bateman. The 'receiver' is simply a telephone receiver, and the poet's lips are 'pursed', as in a melodrama, because he is receiving a horrifying message. 'Death's feather' has no deep, obscure symbolic meaning but is simply an allusion to the humorous Cockney phrase: 'You could 'ave knocked me down with a feather!' (That, I think, is its use here; but it is quite a favourite phrase of Thomas's, and what he has often in mind is the custom of holding a feather to a dead man's lips to make sure he is no longer breathing.) These thrillerish fears, or self-induced, half-pleasant shudders, are 'half convention and half lie'. Neither the poetic imagination, nor sane, practical common sense, can afford to pay much attention to them. But the spent lie from which some life, yet unspent, might explode as it lay burning on the ground, is another matter; so are the ghosts, the ghostly echoes on paper, the repetition of salutes.

This, in fact, is the one poem of Thomas's whose subject-matter is poetical self-criticism. The poet is pondering whether he ought to make a bonfire – accompanied by small fireworks, perhaps dangerous ones – of childish fears, obsessions, and superstitions; a bonfire, also, in his writing of poetry of 'given' phrases, lines, and images – 'ghostly echoes on paper' – about whose source and meaning he is not clear. He is wondering whether he ought to become, like so many of his contemporaries of the 1930s, an 'adult' and 'socially conscious' poet. He decides that he cannot afford to make this bonfire for the reason that the poetic lie, the undue fearsomeness and rhetoric – the 'ghosts' and the 'repetition of salutes' – are somehow bound up with the possibility of the full, life-giving poetic vision. The old lie, exploding, might leave him half-blind; the terrors from which he wants to move away are somehow inextricably linked with an image full of peace, dignity, and beauty:

> ... as the day
> Goes over the hill into the deep sea.

I have been trying here to follow Riding's and Graves's ideal technique of making a poem's drift clear by expounding it, at greater length, mainly in its own words. If the reader agrees with me about the poem's drift, he will admire the insight into his own poetic scope which Thomas shows in this poem. He was right to take the risk of regressiveness, rather than cut the tangle of links that bound him with his childhood; the obsession with childhood, even with its fictions and fantasies, was to lead him in the end to a rediscovery of innocence.

The most important and most obscure poems in *Twenty-five Poems* are, however, the ten sonnets beginning 'Altarwise by owl-light'. Elder Olson has argued very persuasively that these sonnets evoke in succession pagan despair, the new hope consequent upon the birth of Christ, the Christian despair consequent upon the Resurrection; very ingeniously, but perhaps a little less persuasively, he has suggested that these ideas are expressed through an almost pendantically exact symbolism drawn from the movements of the constellation Hercules, standing both for man, and for the manhood of Christ. For other readers, the sonnets had always seemed the most baffling of Dylan Thomas's works, though to a sympathetic reader the Christian overtones and the occasional presence of the 'grand style' were obvious from the start. There are fragments in these sonnets – which as wholes remain, in Daiches's phrases, oppressive and congested even after one has grasped and accepted the main lines of Olson's exposition – more nobly eloquent than anything else Dylan Thomas ever wrote:

> This was the crucifixion on the mountain,
> Time's nerve in vinegar, the gallow grave
> As tarred with blood as the bright thorns I wept ...

> Green as beginning, let the garden diving
> Soar, with its two black towers, to that Day
> When the worm builds with the gold straws of venom
> My nest of mercies in the rude, red tree.

The sonnets, a failure as a whole, splendid in such parts as these, are important because they announce the current of orthodox Christian feeling – feeling rather than thought – which was henceforth increasingly to dominate Thomas's work in poetry.

(5)

Thomas's third volume, *The Map of Love*, which contained prose pieces as well as poems, appeared in 1939, on the verge of the Second World War. It had a great and in many ways unfortunate influence on some of the younger English writers of that time, in particular on the movement called at first the New Apocalypse, and later, when it became a wider and even more shapeless stream of tendency, the New Romanticism. The prose pieces in *The Map of Love* were not at all like the straightforwardly descriptive and narrative, funny and pathetic pieces of *Portrait of the Artist as a Young Dog*, which came out in the following year, 1940. They were much influenced by the belated English interest in the French Surrealist and Dadaist movements. David Gascoyne's excellent short book on Surrealism had appeared two or three years before *The Map of Love*, and more recently there had been Herbert Read's anthology of Surrealist texts and paintings published by Faber. The prose pieces in *The Map of Love* are not strictly Surrealist – they are too carefully worked over, as to their prose rhythms, and so on – but they have a semi-Surrealist flavour in their superficial incoherence, their reliance on shock tactics, and the cruelty or obscenity, or both, of much of their imagery. They are failures on the whole, artistically, but they have a real interest in relation to the total pattern of Thomas's work. They are his *pièces noires*, the pieces in which he accepts evil : they are one side of a medal of which the other side is Thomas's later celebration of innocence, and the benignity of the Reverend Eli Jenkins. In writing these pieces, Thomas was grappling with, and apparently succeeded in absorbing and overcoming, what Jungians call the Shadow.

Perhaps because of the comparative failure of these prose pieces, *The Map of Love* was the least popular of Thomas's volumes. It cannot have been printed in large numbers, or have gone into many impressions, for it is almost impossible – where with the other volumes it is fairly easy – to procure a second-hand copy of it. Yet it contains some of Thomas's most memorable poems, chief among them the elegy 'After the Funeral' for his elderly cousin, Ann Jones. This is a piece of baroque eloquence : in the poet's own words,

> ... *this for her is a monstrous image blindly*
> *Magnified out of praise* ...

There are, however, three or four lines towards the end which transcend the baroque manner and which rank with the passages already quoted from the sonnets as among Thomas's finest isolated fragments.

Their appeal is simple, human, and direct :

> *I know her scrubbed and sour humble hands*
> *Lie with religion in their cramp, her threadbare*
> *Whisper in a damp word, her wits drilled hollow;*
> *Her fist of a face died clenched on a round pain;*
> *And sculptured Ann is seventy years of stone.*

Other, slighter poems in *The Map of Love* have interest as explorations of new aptitudes. A slight but charming poem, 'Once it was the colour of saying' gives a foretaste of one of Thomas's main later themes, the reminiscent celebration, through the evoking of a landscape that the perspective of time has made legendary, of childish innocence :

> *Once it was the colour of saying*
> *Soaked my table the uglier side of a hill*
> *With a capsized field where a school sat still*
> *And a black and white patch of girls grew playing ...*
> *The gentle seasides of saying I must undo*
> *That all the charmingly drowned arise to cockcrow and kill.*
> *When I whistled with mitching boys through a reservoir park*
> *Where at night we stoned the cold and cuckoo*
> *Lovers in the dirt of their leafy beds,*
> *The shade of their trees was a word of many shades*
> *And a lamp of lightning for the poor in the dark;*
> *Now my saying shall be my undoing,*
> *And every stone I wind off like a reel.*

The 'capsized field' there – looking as if it had been upset or overturned on the hillside, and also, from the distance, just the size of a schoolboy's cap – is a delightful example of the subdued punning which a careful reader of Thomas soon learns to look for everywhere. Yet even as late as 1939, Thomas's voice was still not always quite his own. Or rather, he had his own voice, but he would still from time to time try on other people's to see how they fitted. Asked, for instance, who was the author of the following stanza from *The Map of Love*, an intelligent reader might well name C. Day Lewis or W. H. Auden. The turn and the mood of the last two lines, in particular, suggests that preoccupation of most of the poets of the 1930s with harsh historical necessity, which Dylan Thomas on the whole did not share :

> *Bound by a sovereign strip, we lie,*
> *Watch yellow, wish for wind to blow away*
> *The strata of the shore and drown red rock;*
> *But wishes breed not, neither*
> *Can we fend off rock arrival ...*

It was biological necessity, rather, that preoccupied Thomas. That comes out in the last poem in this volume, flatly melancholy in its tone, but displaying a gift, new and unexpected in Thomas, for the forceful gnomic statement :

Twenty-four years remind the tears of my eyes.
(Bury the dead for fear that they walk to the grave in labour.)
In the groin of the natural doorway I crouched like a tailor
Sewing a shroud for a journey
By the light of the meat-eating sun.
Dressed to die, the sensual strut begun,
With my red veins full of money,
In the final direction of the elementary town
I advance for as long as forever is.

(6)

Among many critics of Thomas, there has been a tendency to attempt to enclose him within a formula; that of the man–nature equation used here to throw light on *Eighteen Poems*; that of adolescent sexual excitement used here for the same purpose; that of the disorderly breeder of images, struggling from sleep to wakefulness, and so on. There has been no general agreement about which formula is right, but there has been a general agreement that some formula would be, and also that there is a remarkable similarity about all Thomas's poems. I have been trying, in this sketch, to deal with each volume of Thomas's in turn, almost as if I had been reviewing it when it first came out. I hope I have conveyed my impression – an impression which, when it first came solidly home, very much surprised me – that in tone, in style, in subject-matter Thomas is a much more various, a much less narrowly consistent poet, and that in attitude to life he is much more a developing poet, than people make him out to be. In *Eighteen Poems*, for instance, there is, in the ordinary sense of these words, no human or religious interest; the sonnets, at least, in *Twenty-five Poems* have a remarkable religious interest; and 'After the Funeral' and some other poems in *The Map of Love* have a human interest that is new.

Thomas was found unfit for military service and spent most of the years of the Second World War in Wales, coming up to London from time to time to see friends, do broadcasting work, or meet publishers. He never tackled the war directly as a subject, but at least two of his poems, the obscure but powerful title poem of *Deaths and Entrances* and the famous 'A Refusal to Mourn' have, for background, the bombing raids on London. I have been told that some work he did on a documentary film on the bombing raids, which in the end was found too grim for public release, had a profound effect on his imagination; an effect that may partly explain the retreat, in many of his later poems, to the themes of childhood innocence and country peace. Certainly, in these years, Thomas did more and more tend to turn, for the central themes of his poetry, to his Welsh childhood. The same episodes which, in *Portrait of the Artist as a Young Dog*, had provided material for comedy, now, more deeply explored, brought forth a transformation of memory into vision; a vision of a lost paradise regained.

Thomas's last English volume of new poems, *Deaths and Entrances*, came out in 1946. It increases the impression of variety, and of steady development, which the earlier volumes, read in the order of their appearance, give. It contains a remarkable number of successful poems of notably different kinds. One kind, in particular, at once caught the fancy of a wide public. It is a kind which, very roughly, throwing out words at a venture, one might call the recaptured-childish-landscape, semi-fairy-tale, semi-ode kind: more concisely, the long poem of formal celebration. Such, for instance, are seven late poems by Thomas: 'Poem in October', 'A Winter's Tale', 'Fern Hill', 'In Country Sleep', 'Over Sir John's Hill', 'Poem on His Birthday', 'In the White Giant's Thigh'.[1] All these poems have a larger and looser, a more immediately apprehensible rhythmical movement than most of Thomas's earlier work. They do not aim at dark, packed and concentrated, but at bright, expansive effects. Their landscapes are always partly magical landscapes. Their common flavour can, however, perhaps be better conveyed by a series of quotations than by such remarks:

> ... *Bird, he was brought low,*
> *Burning in the bride bed of love, in the whirl*
> *Pool at the wanting centre, in the folds*
> *Of paradise, in the spun bud of the world.*
> *And she rose with him flowering in her melting snow ...*
>
> (A Winter's Tale)

> *It was my thirtieth year to heaven*
> *Woke to my hearing from harbour and neighbour wood*
> *And the mussel pooled and heron*
> *Priested shore*
> *The morning beckon*
> *With water praying and call of seagull and rook*
> *And the knock of sailing boats on the net webbed wall*
> *Myself to set foot*
> *That second*
> *In the still sleeping town and set forth ...*
>
> (Poem in October)

> *I hear the bouncing hills*
> *Grow larked and greener at berry brown*
> *Fall and the dew larks sing*
> *Taller this thunderclap spring, and how*
> *More spanned with angels rise*
> *The mansouled fiery islands! Oh,*
> *Holier than their eyes,*
> *And my shining men no more alone*
> *As I sail out to die ...*
>
> (Poem on His Birthday)

[1] The last three of these are not in *Deaths and Entrances* but in *Collected Poems*.

Now as I was young and easy under the apple boughs
About the lilting house and happy as the grass was green,
  The night above the dingle starry
    Time let me hail and climb
  Golden in the heydays of his eyes,
And honoured among wagons I was prince of the apple towns
And once below a time I lordly had the trees and leaves
      Trail with daisies and barley
  Down the rivers of the windfall light.

(Fern Hill)

The dust of their kettles and clocks swings to and fro
Where the hay rides now or the bracken kitchens rust
As the arc of the billhooks that flashed the hedges low
And cut the birds' boughs that the minstrel sap ran red.
They from the houses where the harvest kneels, hold me hard,
Who heard from the tall bell sail down the Sundays of the dead
And the rain wring out its tongues on the faded years,
Teach me the love that is evergreen after the fall leaved
Grave, after the Beloved on the grass gulfed cross is scrubbed
Off by the sun and Daughters no longer grieved
Save by their long desires in the fox cubbed
Streets or hungering in the crumbled wood: to these
Hale dead and deathless do the women of the hill
Love for ever meridian through the courters' trees

And the daughters of darkness flame like Fawkes fires still.

(In the White Giant's Thigh)

Neither the style nor the mood of these passages would have been easily predictable even by an exceptionally acute critic of Dylan Thomas's earlier verse. The mood is close to some of the verse of Vaughan and some of the prose of Traherne, or to take a closer and more contemporary comparison from another art, there is something in this glowing transformation of everyday things – a boy in an apple tree, a young man going out for an early walk in a seaside town on his birthday – that recalls some drawings by David Jones or some paintings by Stanley Spencer. One would not, with the same confidence, mention Wordsworth or Blake; there is a kind of massiveness and sobriety in Wordsworth's explorations of childish memory, there is a naked directness in Blake's *Songs of Innocence*, that we do not find here. Thomas, like Vaughan, Traherne, Spencer, or Jones, could be described affectionately as 'quaint', his vision of paradise as a 'touching' one; such epithets would be out of place if one were discussing Blake or Wordsworth.

The style, also, has changed. Its main mark is no longer an obscure concision, a dense packing of images, but a rapid and muscular fluency that puts one in mind sometimes of a more relaxed Hopkins, sometimes of a more concentrated Swinburne. The tone of voice is a deliberately exalted one. The seven poems I have mentioned, and some of which I have quoted, are likely to remain Thomas's most popular pieces. But for the special effect he is aiming at in them he has eliminated that quality of cloudy pregnancy which, rightly or wrongly, was for many readers one of the main fascinations of his earlier poems. It is not that these eloquent, sincere, and moving long poems are in any sense shallow; they make us gloriously free of a visionary world; yet there does remain a sense, if the Irishism is permissible, in which the depths are all on the surface. The poems give what they have to give, grandly, at once. One does not go back to them to probe and question. A passion for probing and questioning can, of course, vitiate taste. Yet there will always remain critics (by his own confession, William Empson is one) to whom these lucid late successes are less 'interesting' than other late poems, more dense and obscure, much less certainly successful but carrying the suggestion that, if they *were* successful, their success might be something higher still.

The quality that Thomas jettisoned in these late, long poems, rightly for his purposes, was a quality of dramatic compression. The little poem of *Deaths and Entrances* is, for instance, almost certainly on the whole a failure: if only for the reason that Thomas does not provide us with clues enough to find out what exactly is happening in the poem, and yet does provide us with clues enough to make us bother about what is happening. The setting is certainly the bombing raids on London:

> On almost the incendiary eve
> Of several near deaths,
> When one at the great least of your best loved
> And always known must leave
> Lions and fires of his flying breath,
> Of your immortal friends
> Who'd raise the organs of the counted dust
> To shoot and sing your praise,
> One who called deepest down shall hold his peace
> That cannot sink or cease
> Endlessly to his wound
> In many married London's estranging grief.

To read that stanza is like seeing a man making a set of noble gestures on a tragic stage and not quite catching, because of some failure of acoustics, what he is saying. Yet the gestures *are* noble, and I would claim that the last line in particular,

> In many married London's estranging grief,

is a fragmentary achievement of a kind of poetry higher in itself than the dingles and the apple boughs and the vale mist riding through the haygold stalls and even than the very lovely heron-priested shore; a kind of poetry which grasps and drastically unifies an unimaginably complex set of inter-related pains. Such a line suggests the immanence in Thomas, in his last years, of a poetry of mature human awareness.

There are some shorter poems in *Deaths and Entrances* that seem similarly to reach out for, and sometimes to grasp, a mature human awareness. Among them are the beautifully constructed 'The Conversation of Prayer', 'A Refusal to Mourn the Death, by Fire, of a Child in London' (of which William Empson has given a masterly exposition); the two very short, which are also among Thomas's few very personal, poems, 'To others than You' and 'In My Craft and Sullen Art'; the plangent *villanelle*, with its Yeatsian overtones, addressed by Thomas to his dying father, 'Do Not Go Gentle into That Good Night', of which the intended sequel, recently reassembled by Vernon Watkins from Thomas's working notes, would have been an even more striking poem: and with less certainty 'There Was a Saviour'.

One of these poems, 'The Conversation of Prayer', is worth looking at on the page as an example of Thomas's extraordinary virtuosity as a creator of textures. I have emphasized the hidden rhymes:

> *The conversation of* prayers *about to be* said
> *By the child going to* bed *and the man on the* stairs
> *Who climbs to his dying* love *in her high* room,
> *The one not caring to* whom *in his sleep he will* move,
> *And the other full of* tears *that she will be* dead.
>
> *Turns in the dark on the* sound *they know will* arise
> *Into the answering* skies *from the green* ground,
> *From the man on the* stairs *and the child by his* bed.
> *The sound about to be* said *in the two* prayers
> *For sleep in a safe* land *and the love who* dies
>
> *Will be the same grief* flying. *Whom shall they* calm?
> *Shall the child sleep* unharmed *or the man be* crying?
> *The conversation of* prayers *about to be* said
> *Turns on the quick and the* dead, *and the man on the* stairs
> *Tonight shall find no* dying *but alive and* warm
>
> *In the fire of his* care *his love in the high* room.
> *And the child not caring to* whom *he climbs his* prayer
> *Shall drown in a grief as* deep *as his true* grave,
> *And mark the dark eyed* wave, *through the eyes of* sleep,
> *Dragging him up the* stairs *to one who lies* dead.

Apart from the extraordinary complexity of this rhyme scheme, the reader should notice that the vast majority of the words in the poem, most of the exceptions being participles, are monosyllables. The only word that is more than a disyllable is 'conversation' and it is also the most abstract word in the poem and the word that, as it were, states the poet's theme. No doubt any skilful craftsman might invent and carry through a form like this as a metrical exercise. But Thomas's poem does not read at all like an exercise; most readers, in fact, do not notice the rhyme-scheme till it is pointed out to them. Again, most poets would find it hard to construct a series of stanzas mainly in monosyllables without giving an effect of monotony. Thomas's line is so subtly varied as to defy an attempt at rule-of-thumb scansion. It is a four-stress line, with feet very freely substituted, and in one case the four feet are four anapaests but with a dragging effect, because of their setting, that anapaests do not usually have:

For the man/*on the* stairs/*and the* child/*by his* bed.

Usually, however, the effect is far more subtle:

Who climbs/*to his* dy/*ing* love/*in her*/hígh roòm.

There we have an iambus, an anapaest, an iambus and an unstressed two-syllable foot followed, according to English custom, by a two-stress foot. And that, to be sure, seems to make *five* stresses; but because 'high' chimes loudly with the first syllable of 'dying', earlier in the line, the word 'room' has actually only a secondary stress. Such minutiae are dry reading except for the teacher of metrics, but since Thomas has been accused by some critics, such as Geoffrey Grigson, of careless and slapdash writing, it is worth providing an almost mechanical demonstration of his mastery of his craft.

Yet the craft exists only for the sake of the art. 'The Conversation of Prayer', perhaps one of the most perfect of Thomas's short poems, may have been neglected because the idea around which it moves is, at least in Protestant countries, becoming marginal to our culture. It is the idea of the reversibility of grace; the idea that all prayers and all good acts co-operate for the benefit of all men, and that God, in His inscrutable mercy, can give the innocent the privilege of suffering some of the tribulations which have been incurred by redeemable sinners. The man in this poem might be the father of the boy, or he might have no connection with him; or the man and the boy might be the same person at different stages of their life histories. Both pray, and there is a sense in which prayer is eternally heard. The boy prays for 'sleep unharmed', for a night undisturbed by bad dreams, and the man whose wife or lover is dying prays that she may be better. The prayers, as it were, cross in the air, the man is granted his wish, for one night at least the sick woman is happy and well again, but the sleeping boy has to endure all the man's nightmare of climbing up the stairs to discover the loved one dead. Only this idea makes sense of the poem. How, it may be asked, could Thomas, bred a Bible Protestant, and never interested in abstruse notions, have come across it, or worked it out for himself? Perhaps it is an idea that all men who really struggle with prayer do, at least implicitly, work out for themselves. For, though Thomas's attitude to life was, as he grew older, an increasingly religious, and in a broad sense an increasingly Christian one, he was certainly not a poet, like Eliot for instance, to whom dry theological and metaphysical speculations were, in themselves, poetically exciting. His world was not a conceptual world and his coherency is not a conceptual coherency. Across the page in the *Collected Poems* from 'The Conversation of Prayer' there is the famous 'A Refusal to Mourn', whose drift Empson has summed up as 'a pantheistic pessimism'. Thomas's longest personal religious poem, 'Vision and Prayer', offers us a naked confrontation of the desire for utter extinction with the hope of personal salvation. The last line of 'A Refusal to Mourn',

After the first death, there is no other,

has a resonance and authority both for unbelievers and believers. At one level, the meaning may be, as Empson suggests, that life is a cruel thing and that the utter finality of physical death is welcome; but the logically contradictory Christian overtones – 'Do not let us fear death, since, once the body is dead, the soul lives for ever' – cannot possibly be excluded. We must respect the baffling simplicity of Thomas's unitary response and not impose abstract categories on him.

One poem in *Deaths and Entrances*, 'The Hunchback in the Park', a more descriptive and 'realistic' poem than Thomas was in the habit of writing, may help us, perhaps, to grasp this simplicity by watching it operate at a less profound level. This begins with a long but not obscure two-stanza sentence :

> *The hunchback in the park*
> *A solitary mister*
> *Propped between trees and water*
> *From the opening of the garden lock*
> *That lets the trees and water enter*
> *Until the Sunday sombre bell at dark*
>
> *Eating bread from a newspaper*
> *Drinking water from the chained cup*
> *That the children filled with gravel*
> *In the fountain basin where I sailed my ship*
> *Slept at night in a dog kennel*
> *But nobody chained him up ...*

The boys in the park, of whom Thomas is one, mock and torment the solitary hunchback who, ignoring them, seeks happiness in a dream in which the park stands for all the richness of life from which he is locked out; and the boys are locked out from the poetic understanding of that richness which the hunchback has attained to through deprivation and pain. They are part of the richness, and how should they understand it (that may be part of the implication of the phrase, 'the wild boys innocent as strawberries', which several critics have found sentimental)? Hunter and hunted; mocked and mocker; boys and hunchback; growth and decay, life and death, dream and reality : all sets of polar opposites are, for Thomas, at some level equally holy and necessary, holy is the hawk, holy is the dove ... This theme, the coincidence of opposites, runs through all Thomas's work and the end of this poem states it clearly : how the hunchback, the 'old dog sleeper'

> Made all day until bell time
> A woman figure without fault
> Straight as a young elm
> Straight and tall from his crooked bones
> That she might stand in the night
> After the lock and chains

> All night in the unmade park
> After the railings and shrubberies
> The birds the grass the trees the lake
> And the wild boys innocent as strawberries
> Had followed the hunchback
> To his kennel in the dark.

Other poems in *Deaths and Entrances* show Thomas experimenting along still other lines. 'Ballad of the Long-Legged Bait' is his only poem, with the partial exception of 'A Winter's Tale', of which the movement is primarily a narrative one. It is a phantasmagoric narrative like Rimbaud's *Bateau Ivre*. Its immediate impact is extremely confusing. Elder Olson has worked out a logical structure for it. The poet goes fishing in a magic boat, using a naked woman for a bait, and all the sea creatures eat her up, and then as in the Book of Revelation, 'there is no more sea'. She is a woman, and she is also his heart, and he has been sacrificing the desires of his heart to restore a lost Eden. In the end, Eden is restored, and so is the woman, and the heart in its lost innocence; the poet steps out of the boat, now on dry land and

> ... stands alone at the door of his home
> With his long-legged heart in his hand.

The poem, thus, for Olson is a kind of small allegory about the struggle inside Thomas, a typically Welsh struggle, between natural sensuality and puritan mysticism. Thomas himself, more modestly, over a bar in New York, said that the poem is about how a young man goes out fishing for fun and games, for all the excitements of the wild free life, and finds in the end that he has caught a wife, some children, and a little house. The poem, even with the help of these clues, remains unsatisfactory – it leaves one feeling a little sea-sick – but it is yet another example of Thomas's eagerness, throughout his poetic career, to go on extending his range. And as a whole *Deaths and Entrances* does remain one of the two or three most impressive single volumes of poetry published in English over the last ten years.

(7)

Let us now try to sum up. In the few years since his death, Dylan Thomas's reputation as a poet has undoubtedly suffered at least a mild slump. He was always far too directly and massively an emotional poet, and in the detail of his language often too confusing and sometimes apparently confused a poet, to be acceptable to the analytical critics of the *Scrutiny* school who to-day exercise a far wider influence on general English taste than they did four or five years ago.* Quite apart from that, there is quite generally in literary history a time lag, sometimes of as long as 20 or 30 years, between a notable writer's death and the attempt to reach a balanced judgment on him. The difficulty, also, at least at the level of attempting to explain in prose what the poet is doing, of Dylan Thomas's work has meant that the three short books so far published about him, by Henry Treece in his life-time (a revised edition has been published since Thomas's death), and since his death by Elder Olson and Derek Stanford, have been much more concerned with exposition of his sense than with attempts to 'place' him or even to illustrate in detail his strictly poetic art. Stanford thinks he may rank in English liter-ary history rather as Gray ranks; this may be too high an estimate, for where is Thomas's long poem of mature moral interest, where is his 'Elegy Written in a Country Churchyard'? But he might well rank as Collins ranks; he has written some perfect poems, his poetic personality is a completely individual one, he brings in a new note. One might call Gray a minor major poet; one might call Collins a major minor poet. That, possibly, is also Thomas's rank, but at the same time we should be profoundly suspicious of this class-room, or examination-school, attitude to poets. There is a very real and profound sense in which poets do not compete with each other. No true poet offers us something for which anything else, by any other true poet, is really a substitute. It is enough, for the purposes here, to insist that Thomas was a good poet and worth our attention; and to attempt to define, and make vivid, his specific quality.

The reaction against Thomas, since his death, has, in fact, really been con-cerned to deny that Thomas was a good poet; or to assert that he might have been a good poet, but cheated poetically, in a way that disqualifies him. Thus, John Wain has remarked that a meaning, or a set of meanings, can nearly always be got out of Thomas's poems but that the critic's worry is whether Thomas ever cared much what the meanings were so long as the thing sounded all right. Even more sharply, in his witty and provocative Clark Lectures, *The Crowning Privilege*, Robert Graves condemns Thomas as a poet who takes care of the sound and lets the sense take care of itself:

Graves compares Thomas to a soldier firing off a rifle at random while a confederate in the butts – the confederate being the gullible reviewer of contemporary poetry – keeps on signalling bulls and inners, whether or not the
bullet has come anywhere near the target.

How much justice is there in such strictures? There are certainly poems
by Dylan Thomas of which many readers must find even the main drift, as
sense, hard to grasp; there is hardly any poem of Thomas's of which some details, at least, are not likely to puzzle most readers. But I hope I have shown
two things: that in Thomas's best poems there is a coherent meaning, and
that it is not always mechanically the same meaning. It is simply not true
that he went on writing, with variations of form and imagery, the same
archetypal poem over and over again; he grew and changed, at his death was
still developing, in the direction of a wider and more genial human scope. The
importance of *Under Milk Wood* is that it shows him, at the very end of his
life, transforming into a kind of poetry that humorous apprehension of life
which, in *Portrait of the Artist as a Young Dog*, is still something quite
separate from poetry. Had he lived, he might have worked into his poetry
the shrewdness and the gaiety that make him a first-rate entertainer. His
feeling for life, at the end, was growing, not shrinking; and the separated
elements of it, the outer and the inner being, the legendary sweet funny
man and the fine solemn poet, were growing together.

Let me end this sketch by quoting a short, a very personal poem of
Thomas's, which warns us wholesomely against the kind of undue famili-
arity to which his public legend, the memory of his personality, the critic's
dangerous passion for summary judgments, might all invite us:

TO OTHERS THAN YOU

Friend by enemy I call you out.

You with a bad coin in your pocket,
You my friend there with a winning air
Who palmed the lie on me when you looked
Brassily at my shyest secret,
Enticed with twinkling bits of the eye
Till the sweet tooth of my love bit dry,
Rasped at last, and I stumbled and sucked,
Whom I now conjure to stand as a thief
In the memory worked by mirrors,
With unforgettably smiling act,
Quickness of hand in the velvet glove
And my whole heart under your hammer,
Were once such a creature, so gay and frank
A desireless familiar
I never thought to utter and think
While you displaced a truth in the air,

That though I loved them for their faults
As much as for their good,
My friends were enemies on stilts,
With their heads in a cunning cloud.

I hope that the truths displaced in the air in these pages have been displaced towards their proper locations; I hope that in all I have been saying my head, too, has not been in a cunning cloud. I remember Dylan Thomas's own head, benignly calm, as it looked in a photograph of his death-mask which a close friend of his, the poet Ruthven Todd, brought to show to Thomas's friends in London : it should have made me think of two lines of Thomas's, not well known :

And when blind sleep drops on the spying senses,
The heart is sensual, though five eyes break.

17 · NORMAN MACCAIG: FOUR POEMS EXAMINED

Akros, III no. 7 (March 1968): special Norman MacCaig number (Kinglassie, Cardenden, Fife, Scotland).

I METHOD

I possess four volumes of Norman MacCaig's poems, *Riding Lights*, 1955 (this was a Poetry Book Society recommendation and the winner of the Scottish Committee of the Arts Council's award for poetry, 1953–54): *The Sinai Sort*, 1957: *A Round of Applause*, 1962: and *Surroundings*, a Poetry Book Society Choice for 1966. I want to have a close look at one poem from each volume, rather as one might do in a practical criticism class – I shall choose poems that contrast with each other, for one of MacCaig's obvious qualities is his variety, his skill in a number of modes. There are three distinguished modern poets whom MacCaig often reminds me of: Edwin Muir, Louis MacNeice, and William Empson. I know, from conversations with them, that Muir and MacNeice, poets with few affinities except a certain deep withdrawnness of temperament, both greatly admired MacCaig. They also both tended to look on the short poem as, in its mode, a sort of emblematic riddle. But Muir was by temperament a slow introvert, dominated by sensation and thought. Muir worked outwards from inner intuitions towards emblems of these; MacNeice worked inwards from vivid impressions of the external world to reach at an inner state of himself which was not, like Muir's inner states, calm and transparent, but knotted and opaque. Muir worked from a deep experience of suffering to an assertion of peace; for MacNeice a vivid outward awareness of the pleasurable, 'the moment cradled like a brandy glass', heightened an inner tenseness and distress. I don't know whether William Empson has read or likes MacCaig – he reads and likes very few modern poets – and I know Empson too intimately to think that I can fit his very strange temperament into Jungian categories; but the dominant modes of his poetry are, one might say, thought and feeling, intricate, arguing thought, often however bluntly stated, and feeling which combines a boisterous and jovial appetite for life with moments of profound repulsion. Of other poets I have known Empson resembles most, in his proud and impatient assertion of his own opinion, Hugh MacDiarmid, one of MacCaig's closest friends. There is a fierceness in Empson and MacDiarmid that there is not in Muir or MacNeice, a bitter impatience with the intractable substance of life. MacCaig seems to me to owe nothing at all technically to MacDiarmid, but no doubt, for such a long and such a close friendship with such a quarrelsome man, there must be a deep affinity of temperament. One should add that one sees these multiple affinities with poets of very different kinds without feeling that MacCaig is a facile writer or a master of *pastiche*. What one does feel is that he is a poet involved – but is this not true of all good poets today? – with the mysterious double nature of the self as subject and object. He is a searcher and a prober, and in the old Scots sense a makar: a skilled craftsman who can try on, effectively, a number of deeply contrasting modes and styles.

(2) A MUIR-LIKE POEM

Let me first take a poem from *Riding Lights*, MacCaig's volume of 1955. I choose this by no means as the best poem in an excellently various volume, but as illustrating some modes of procedure that MacCaig has in common with Muir. It is a riddling and an emblematic poem on the vocation of the poet, on the possible inhumanity, or maybe the human impossibility, of the poetic quest:

TAPESTRY

The wood was waves, not trees.
The sorrowful hunter passed
Between the crying stems,
Seeking the never lost.

Great deer and little, hid
In their own branches, lay
Close to the surfy ground,
Their bodies still, eyes slow.

Knowing that he was
A symbol gave him strength
To pursue another loveless
And terrifying myth.

Between a life and a life
He moved, knowing well
No great deer would plunge off
Into the possible.

Let us accumulate a number of little technical observations, which may perhaps add up in the end to a fuller knowledge of the poem. The title, 'Tapestry', tells us that we are to picture static pictures on a tapestry, melting into each other, as in the mode of medieval romance, which offers endless variation and repetition, unlike drama, which offers situation, complication, unravelling; in this mode the thing we are seeking is never lost, everything is heraldic. The thickety wood of medieval romance is the same sort of symbol as the sea, with the endless variation and repetition of its waves. The hunter always pursues, the deer are never caught, the story is never begun or ended; one may think of the parallel images of static pursuit and sacrifice, the quest never consummated, in Keats's 'Ode on a Grecian Urn'. And perhaps the words 'loveless' and 'terrifying' here might be paralleled with Keats's 'Cold pastoral!' Art offers us our only images of the eternal, but it is a cold, a loveless, and a terrifying thing compared to life; and yet the quest of the true artist is to transform art magically into life. The cold figures on the vase for Keats become almost living figures; MacCaig's hero sees living deer, 'Their bodies still, eyes slow', and pursues his quest between 'a life and a life' – the life of the poet and the life of the poem, the life of the flesh and the life of the images,

> ... *knowing well*
> *No great deer would plunge off*
> *Into the possible.*

Rhythmical movement and a very careful and sparse decorum of diction make the effect of this poem rather than, in spite of its title, anything very vividly or precisely pictorial. A three-stress line, very common in Yeats, picked up often by Muir: 'The *wood* was *waves* not *trees* ...' Quatrains, with the second and fourth lines off-rhyming: *passed, lost: lay, slow: strength, myth: well, possible*: the first and third lines in the last stanza are also off-rhyme, *life, off,* and this fuller off-rhyming in the last stanza perhaps gives it the feeling of a full concluding statement. Yet notice that the effect of off-rhyme in itself is to mute any assertiveness: full rhyme in English, especially in short lines, has often a rather clashing and harsh assertive effect. There is a kind of minor consonantal linking, also, between the end-words in the first and third lines of the first two stanzas: *trees, stem: hid, ground.* Most of the words in the poem are monosyllables: leaving aside little words like *the, was, not, and, in,* and so on one counts from the beginning *wood, waves, trees, passed, stems, deer, hid, own, lay, close, ground, still, eyes, slow, strength, myth, life, life, moved, well, off.* Of the two-syllable words three important ones are present participles, *seeking, knowing, knowing*: when we notice this it underlies our feeling that this is a poem about seeking and knowing, about seeking poetic knowledge. The other two-syllable words are *hunter, crying* (participal in form but a verbal adjective), *little, branches, surfy, bodies, loveless, symbol.* The two three-syllable words are *sorrowful* and *possible,* the one four-syllable word is *terrifying.* Its unique length in the syllable-pattern of the poem draws special attention to *terrifying* which acts as a climax to the two earlier emotive adjectives *sorrowful* and *loveless.* There are three kinds of noun in the poem: *wood, waves, trees, hunter, stems, branches, deer, ground, bodies, eyes* are names of tangible things; *life* is the name of an abstract idea so familiar that it is not thought of as abstract: *symbol* and *myth* are sophisticated names for literary techniques, here mainly to draw the reader's attention to the fact that this is a symbolic poem about the nature of myth: the idea of the poet as hunter is the symbol of man's sorrowful, loveless, and terrifying pursuit of myth. At the end of the poem, *the possible* is a name for a set of very high-level philosophical abstract problems. The poem begins in the language of romance, *The wood*, and ends in the language of the metaphysics of logic, *the possible*.

In this apparently very simple little poem then there are three layers of reference: man as a primitive creature, a real hunter (the sorrow, the lovelessness, the terror are because he loves the creatures, the deer with 'bodies still, eyes slow' whom he must slay): a man as a symbol-making animal and an actor out of symbolic roles, a hunter after truth, say, in a large forest or sea, the huge intractable and untrackable universe in which he makes his small clearings, pursuing myth, an inescapable archetypal image: and man as a reasoner, a logician, forced to recognize that the great images will not transform themselves into actuality,

> ... *plunge off*
> *Into the possible.*

Yet is this logical pattern, which one can work out of the poem, what makes the poem work? One thing that worries me is that the equation of wood and waves in the first topic sentence doesn't seem to me to be necessary for this logical pattern: what the topic sentence makes possible is the one descriptive (rather than emotive) adjective in the poem, 'surfy' in 'surfy ground' and this seems to me extremely felicitous not in the logical pattern of the poem but because it reminds me of the feel of mossy moorland under my feet, the springiness of forest rides. Similarly, these little and great deer, the most actualized image in the poem, in the second stanza, 'Their bodies still, eyes slow' seem to me real deer not tapestry deer, seem something like Marianne Moore's real toads in an imaginary garden. Without the concreteness of 'surfy' I think the other main adjectives might add up, 'sorrowful', 'loveless', 'terrifying', to a set of emotional *clichés*. Similarly 'crying stems' works for me because of an association (not logically in the poem) with branches broken off and crying out in pain as in Dante's Wood of the Suicides. The poem, in the way I have worked it out, is statement disguised as symbolism – the *use* of the words 'symbol' and 'myth' tip one off that it is not a real symbolic poem, by definition inexhaustible and finally impenetrable, like Blake's 'Tiger' – but these two little bits, 'surfy' and the picture of the crouching deer, that give it life – 'plunge off' has something of the same active concreteness – come in, giving life, against the grain as it were of the predetermined pattern. I don't think this makes it a bad poem: I see MacCaig as very much a conscious planning mind in making poems, but with enough sense to let the little rough bits come in that enable the poem to 'defeat the mind', in Crichton Smith's phrase, or, in Bernard Spencer's, permit a 'twist in the plotting'. He lets a poem twist a bit askew against itself, and this is a strength, if it has a planned strength to twist against. He lets loose associations also work: playing *waves* at the beginning against *the possible* at the end. I thought of Eddington's definition of the basic substance of the universe as *waves of possibility*. This is what the universe consists of, not *trees*, not discrete solid objects. I even wondered if there could be a subdued half-conscious pun on *wood* and *would*: that which man, the myth-hunter, *would* have. I have been too fancy, I know, about a distinguished but slight poem, top-heavy in my commentary, but this kind of probing can at least suggest what a peculiarly tricky and delicately balanced object even a slight poem can be.

(3) AN EMPSON-LIKE POEM

What marks what William Empson calls the 'argufying' as distinguished from the 'imagistic' poem is an *if–then*, consequential clausal pattern (in grammar), a feeling of bluff commonsensical confrontation of an irrational situation (in tone). Here is an example from *The Sinai Sort*, 1957. Notice how the first line, like the first line of 'Tapestry' is a slightly baffling topic sentence, stating something paradoxical or difficult or multivalent in meaning as if it were plain common sense:

SENSE ABOUT NONSENSE

Hard feeling is true exercise for wit.
Can you, exploring all your passion's graces,
Do nothing but submit
To its harsh weathers and on all your faces
Write down in wrinkles what you feel of it?

Wit does not slide such weather off, but makes
Another image of it that, more civil,
Confesses such mistakes
A god might answer for, or the very devil.
So human beings argue with earthquakes.

Wit gives them tongues, reducing them so much
(Though roofs still fall) that in his death's confusion,
With feeling for a crutch
He limps himself to hell in the illusion
The earthquake understands his double Dutch.

And a case stated is a comfort. So,
Are you, lost in love's graces and disgraces,
To suffer only, and go,
Witless and wandered, through collapsing places
That may be heaven or hell for all you know?

'Tapestry' was analysable but unparaphraseable; this, on the other hand, perhaps more baffling in the end, is a very good poetic imitation of witty and paradoxical prose discourse. Take the first line:

Hard feeling is no exercise for wit.

The first line of 'Tapestry',

The wood was waves, not trees,

fuses or equates symbols: this line is not so much an equation as a pregnant confusion of cognate concepts. 'Hard feeling' could be one's own feeling about the hardness of one's fate – one's experience of suffering – but 'hard feelings', in ordinary idiom, are more usually feelings of undue resentment against others. 'Exercise' can be what an athlete does to keep himself in trim or what somebody who has a leg broken and mended does. Most men almost mechanically accept suffering, do not use suffering to strengthen the muscles of their intelligence, and the suffering of most men is written passively in the wrinkles, the lines marked by pain on their faces.

The second stanza says that 'Wit' does not 'slide such weather off', does not cure the grief of growing older and deepening one's wrinkles and one's heartache, but it can make suffering more 'civil', more civilized or 'polite', less animal and brutish. 'Civil' is used in a Hobbesian seventeenth-century sense, as in the phrase 'Civil Society'. (There is something of a pastiche of Donne's diction as well as of his mode of argument running through the poem.) Wit makes us aware of errors and blunders in our conduct that are superhuman, that a god or a devil (both lower case, not God and Devil) might well be reproached with, or asked to account for. When man brings his full intelligence to bear on his own misery and grandeur he reproaches himself, but feels a sort of awe of himself, as Job argued with God. The last line of the stanza,

So human beings argue with earthquakes,

reminds us of the great Lisbon earthquake which inspired Voltaire's *Candide* and, indirectly, Johnson's *Rasselas*. Lisbon was the most pious city in Europe; God chose to destroy it. As Voltaire was questioning Optimistic Deism, MacCaig here is questioning Optimistic Humanism: and is asking us to bring our intelligence to bear on what is inscrutable and destructive in the heart of man.

The third stanza says that the power of Wit ('Wit' and 'Witless', occurring at the beginnings of lines, have capital letters, as 'god' usually has, but not in this poem) reduces the moral scope of human earthquakes though it cannot prevent them having their results, roofs will still continue to fall. (Put it this way: associate Hiroshima with what Freud called the death-wish, and it will remain as great a disaster, but it will fit into a rational picture of human nature.) 'With feeling for a crutch' – leaning on emotion, or sensibility, or in the widest sense on love – man limps away to the hell of the fate his conscious destructive drives have brought upon him, but with the illusion, at least, that the unconscious, the id, understands what the conscious, the rational self, the ego, is saying about it. But in fact we cannot communicate with the unconscious, with the dark destructive drives in us; to these earthquake-forces all rational language is 'double Dutch'. The language of Wit is double Dutch in that it is a fusion of contrary or even contradictory ideas. There is a sense also of something like Orwell's NewSpeak. The more God (or the powers in man that man cannot control or assimilate, and that therefore appear to him either Divine or Diabolic or a fusion of the two) appears cruel and unjust, the more Man will think that God is listening to him, the more ready he will be to limp off to Hell (with 'feeling', the pressures of the Super-Ego and the Castration Complex, as a crutch) mildly and submissively. One is reminded again of Carlyle on the Calvinist God : that if he thought God had predestined him to Eternal Damnation, he would march off briskly to Hell like a soldier.

But this submissiveness, the fourth stanza suggests, is not the right tactic :

> And a case stated is a comfort. So,
> Are you, lost in love's graces and disgraces,
> To suffer only, and go,
> Witless and wandered, through collapsing places
> That may be heaven or hell for all you know.

What is the case that has been stated, and how is it a comfort? It seems to be that accepting everything that happens as predestinate (whether through God's will or the darkness of Human Nature hardly matters) makes one something less than a man, a cripple using 'feeling as a crutch' : a modern version of Holy Willie, using one's intellect to justify a horrible dogmatic system. One loses one's wit or even wits ('Witless') and sense of direction ('wandered'). One is caught in a labyrinth or maze of 'love's graces and disgraces' – love's mercies and shames and disasters, and the erotic sense of 'love' seems closely relevant here, though neither the Freudian libido nor God as Love can be excluded. One wanders idiotically and directionlessly through 'collapsing places' no longer even worrying about one's last end. The places

> may be heaven or hell for all you know.

The ultimate feeling of this powerful small poem, then, is the opposite of the feeling of Eliot's lines in 'Burnt Norton' :

> Heaven and damnation
> Which flesh cannot endure.

The poem might claim to be powerful indirect plea for the interests of Flesh against those of heaven and damnation; for intelligent striving in that actual world which, in Dr Johnson's phrase, we can 'enjoy or endure'. But if the message is in the end an anti-Calvinist one, it is presented with a Calvinistic gloom and rigour. One is reminded a little of Dunbar's 'Meditation in Winter' which after a set of powerful thoughts and images of winter, sin, and death strangely calls in as a redressing agent not heaven but the cycle of the year, the change of weather.

> *Come lusty Simmer, with thy flouris,*
> *That I may live in some disport!*

Let us pull ourselves together, not, at least, be 'Witless and wandered'. Do not let *us* collapse, though everything is collapsing round us. Let us prefer, at the worst, Wit's exercise to Feeling's crutch. It is a humanist message, but a hard one.

(4) A DUNBAR-LIKE POEM

I shall end with two poèms that need briefer comment, because they need only to be sensitively read to be properly appreciated. From *A Round of Applause*, 1962, I will take a poem – I think I broadcast about it once on the Third Programme – which is emblematic in intention, physical and objective, and which combines the 'rhetoric', the 'aureate' diction we associate with Dunbar – words like *golden, crystal, silver, shine*, phrases like *tawny brooches*, metallic images – with a humour that is Dunbar's also and with a loving feeling for animals that is more like Henryson. But this feeling for the creatures is in a long Scottish tradition :

BYRE

> *The thatched roof rings like heaven where mice*
> *Squeak small hosannas all night long,*
> *Scratching its golden pavements, skirting*
> *The gutter's crystal river-song.*
>
> *Wild kittens in the world below*
> *Glare with one flaming eye through cracks,*
> *Spurt in the straw, are tawny brooches*
> *Splayed on the chests of drunken sacks.*
>
> *The dimness becomes darkness as*
> *Vast presences come mincing in,*
> *Swagbellied Aphrodites, swinging*
> *A silver slaver from each chin.*

And all is milky, secret, female.
Angels are hushed and plain straws shine.
And kittens miaow in circles, stalking
With tail and hindleg one straight line.

Apart from the glitter words I have noticed, there are the little scritchy mouse-words, *squeak, scratching, skirting*: the more violent kitten-words *glare, spurt*, or, not violent but precise, *miaow, stalking*: and such felicities as the contrast of the thin and delicate sense and sound of *mincing* with the embodiment of the cows as *swag-bellied Aphrodites*. The sense of something holy brought in in the first stanza with *heaven, small hosannas, crystal river-song* is confirmed in the last stanza by the line with a touch of George Herbert or Henry Vaughan in it:

Angels are hushed and plain straws shine.

The poem is funny, affectionate, at once brilliantly ornate and beautifully accurate in its diction; and in its final mood devotional, with a sense of centuries of ancestral country pieties behind it. The accuracy and delight – the kittens as

... tawny brooches
Splayed on the chests of drunken sacks

– prevents a veering into sentimentality, as Burns veered with his mouse. But there is an intimacy, warmth, and homeliness that makes it apt to recall Burns, and that makes the poem plainly traditionally Scottish in feeling. This is a sort of thing that many Scots poets do, and that no English poet exactly does. Auden, for instance, writes brilliantly about animals, but never in a mood or tone resembling this.

(5) A MACCAIGISH POEM

In the most recent volume, *Surroundings*, 1966, I notice a technique which is at once more austere and more informal than that of the earlier volumes from which I have chosen poems; as if MacCaig had reached a stage of self-confidence when a reflection that occurred to him, put down as one might put it down in a note book, at once became poetry, because of the sureness of his hand. One is no longer reminded of other men's manners or mannerisms. Many of the poems are in short lines and free verse; the poem works out a line of thought and there is no ornamentation. I will choose one almost at random. It is about the poet and reality, as my first example 'Tapestry' was, but marks an enormous advance. It does not feel like 'literature' any more:

NO CONSOLATION

I consoled myself for not being able to describe
Water trickling down a wall or
A wall being trickled down by water
By reflecting that I can see
These two things are not the same thing:
Which is more than a wall can do,
Or water.

— But how hard it is
To live at a remove
From a common wall, that keeps out and
Keeps in, and from water, that
Saves you and drowns you.

But when I went on to notice
That I could see the pair of them
As a trickling wall or as a wall
Of water,
It became clear that I can describe only
My own inventions.

— And how odd to suppose
You prove you love your wife
By continually committing adultery
With her.

Instead of the deer in the tapestry the poet is now concerned with the plainest of things in the common world, and is no longer a loveless hunter. He realizes, as the French poet Francis Ponge does, that the plainest things, a pebble say, have never been described. The distinction between water trickling down a wall and a wall being trickled down by water is not a distinction which, for instance, a camera could record, but neither is it a mere difference of empathy or of the willed direction of our perceptions; we would all make a sort of distinction, in an easier case, between a steep hillside with a thin water track running down it and a small watercourse running down a steep hillside. Usually we do not attempt to describe but use a language of literary convention which we hope will call up similar feelings to our own in the reader though it can never exactly recreate our perceptions for him or, perhaps, after a time, for ourselves. MacCaig *refers* to what he cannot *describe*, and consoles himself with the thought that, unlike the wall and the water, he is reflective and perceptive discriminating consciousness. Yet the poetic consciousness cannot feed on itself. The water and the wall are the reality, with their human uses and dangers, which the poetic imagination needs to brace itself against. What the imagination can do is make fantasy out of reality, create fusions that are not in reality, make the water into a wall, or make the wall trickle like water. Nature or reality is like one's wife; the poet has a whorish imagination and is able to be loyal to his wife, nature, by continually transforming her in his fantasy into somebody, or something, else. Plain and bare and unaffected, this poem nevertheless contains everything about the strange relationship between imagination and reality that is to be found, for instance, in Wallace Steven's *Adagia* or *The Necessary Angel*. The bare style makes it all sound not, as Stevens sounds, like a daring and paradoxical postulate but like a plain obvious truth.

Choosing at random, I think (but one never really chooses at random) that I have demonstrated in MacCaig over the last 12 years or so not only a range of skill but a growth, a growing into sureness. The first three poems I looked at were all in a sense *performances*, tuned to certain modes and expectations : in that last poem we have the privilege of seeing the artist's note-book turned into art, the sketch or jotting becoming picture, of overhearing the poet apparently talking to himself, but, look, the bare and simple self-communion is a *poem*. The epistemology of poetry, or the poem which seeks to know what it is to make or be a poem, is one of the great new poetic subjects; MacCaig will be found to have made his contribution towards the poetic criticism of poetic knowledge.

18 · KEITH DOUGLAS: A POET OF THE SECOND WORLD WAR

Chatterton Lecture on an English Poet for the British Academy, 1956, read 14 March 1956; from the *Proceedings of the British Academy*, XLII, Oxford University Press, London.

My first words this evening should be to thank the Council of the British Academy for the great honour it has done me in asking me to deliver the second annual Chatterton Lecture, on the Meyerstein Foundation, and to explain the considerations which guided me in my choice of a subject. The conditions of Meyerstein's bequest are very generous. There is to be an annual lecture, by a critic who on accepting the invitation to lecture has not yet completed his fortieth year; and the lecturer can talk about any English poet at all, so long as the poet is no longer living. Nevertheless, such a posthumous generosity as Meyerstein's does, it seems to me, impose an almost personal gratitude on its beneficiaries; there is no harm, at least, in trying to devise the sort of lecture that Meyerstein might himself have enjoyed listening to. I never met him; but from friends of mine, much younger than himself, who knew him well, I have learned that one of his most striking characteristics was his interest in youthful poetic promise. Indeed, Chatterton, after whom these lectures are named, and of whom Meyerstein wrote the definitive biography, is the very type of the young poet of almost incalculable promise, cut down like a flower. Keith Castellian Douglas, who is my subject today, had a rather longer span of life than Chatterton. He was killed in action 12 years ago, three days after the beginning of the invasion of Normandy, at the age of 24. I feel that Meyerstein, if he were with us, would enjoy listening to an account of such a young man, who did fine things, and who might have done finer things still if he had lived longer, more than listening to the most scholarly account of, say, the later poems of William Wordsworth.

There is, however, another, and in this case a rather ironic, reason why Keith Douglas seems to me to be a peculiarly appropriate subject for a Chatterton Lecture. Chatterton is a symbolic figure, an emblem of unfulfilled renown, in a double sense. We have all heard of him; and few of us have really read him. He lives in our imagination as a legend; he lives in Wordsworth's great lines from 'Resolution and Independence',

I thought of Chatterton, the marvellous boy,
The sleepless soul that perished in his pride ...

He does not live for us, in the same way, in his own lines. He has, of course, no lines of his own so great as these two of Wordsworth's; but it is not only that, it is that we hesitate to look into his works lest, after being moved by the drama of his life, we should find them profoundly disappointing. Keith Douglas's life was not a tragic life like Chatterton's; it was a full, happy, and adventurous life, though cut short violently and early. Yet there is a real sense in which Douglas's life, like Chatterton's, might stand between us and his poems.

Douglas is remembered today (if, indeed, the English general reader remembers him with any vividness at all) as a war poet. He is remembered as one of three young English poets of great promise and early fame – the other two were Alun Lewis and Sidney Keyes – who all perished in the Second World War. Now, the attitude of the English public to war poets is an odd one. Poetry is what the English do best, but it is only, I think, in war-time that they remember that; it is only in war-time that they clamour for new poetry, that they ask, 'Where are the new young poets?', that they buy eagerly volumes and anthologies and periodicals devoted to new verse. Good young English poets, during a war, are published easily; so, I am afraid, are other young poets who are not so good; and in fact the sense of exile, the novelty of a foreign scene, the stress of action do, during a war, stir many young men into trying to express themselves in verse who, in quieter times, would never think of themselves as poets. And, in fact, so long as a war continues, so long as many of our young people are overseas, we find that we can read poetry by young men in the forces, even if it is not quite successful poetry, with sympathy. At the least, it will have a documentary interest; it will have the interest of an exile's letter home. That documentary and sentimental interest, alas, soon fades, once a war is over; and with it there tends to fade, however unfairly, our interest in the more genuine poetry which a war has produced. How often, today, do we open the works of Alun Lewis or Sidney Keyes? And yet, during the last world war, critics were right to praise them.

From the point of view of his post-war reputation, moreover, Keith Douglas was unfortunate in the time of his death; he ought to have died a year or two earlier. He was killed, as I have said, in Normandy in 1944. He had not yet published a volume, though some of his earlier poems had been published, along with some of the early poems of J. C. Hall and Norman Nicholson, in a kind of three-man anthology, *Selected Poems*, in 1943. But he was known mainly by what he had published in periodicals and war-time anthologies; and anthologies soon go out of print, periodicals are soon mislaid. It was not till 1947 that Douglas's prose book, *Alamein to Zem Zem*, was published, with some of his war-poems (sometimes in inaccurate texts) at the end. It was not till 1951 that Douglas's old Oxford acquaintance, John Waller, and myself were able (at the request of the late Richard Marsh) to produce a careful and correct text of Douglas's *Collected Poems*, arranged in reverse chronological order. The poems, by that time, had no longer the impact of news; they had not yet acquired the impact of history.

It is true that, in 1951, Keith Douglas's *Collected Poems* were well received; Ronald Bottrall, I remember, wrote a particularly perceptive review in the *New Statesman*. Yet they appeared in an unfortunate year. The year 1951 marked something like a watershed between two movements in contemporary English poetry. The prevailing mood among the younger poets of the 1940s, or at least among a fairly coherent group of them, was what was often called the mood of neo-romanticism. It was a mood that owed a great deal to poets like Dylan Thomas and George Barker; it is carried on today by a poet like W. S. Graham. It was a mood that preferred evocation to description, images to statements, feeling to thought, colour, one might say, to line. It was a mood, also, to which Keith Douglas had almost nothing to offer. I remember a typical new romantic poet of the 1940s, Tom Scott, telling me that he found Douglas's poetry hard, cold, and dry. Since 1951, indeed, a whole new school of young poets has come into notice that does share Douglas's ideals of precise and disciplined statement in verse: I am thinking of poets like Philip Larkin, Elizabeth Jennings, Philip Oakes, Kingsley Amis, Gordon Wharton, Bernard Bergonzi, John Wain. But these new young poets do not share Douglas's temperament. Their attitude to life is more negatively ironical than his, or at least more constrained and more hesitant. For in a sense, though not in the cant sense of the 1940s, Douglas *was* a romantic poet.

Keith Douglas's mother – and it is a great pleasure and honour for me, and I am sure for all of us, that she is able to be present with us this evening – wrote to me the other day, reminding me of an excellent short statement, called 'On the Nature of poetry' which Douglas, in 1940, contributed to *Augury*, an Oxford miscellany of prose and verse of which he was one of the editors. It is worth quoting in full. It was written, we must remember, by a boy of 20; and the qualities that come out in it are, I think, not only Douglas's simplicity and sincerity, his remarkable lack of undergraduate pose, but also his penetration. It might be a statement by a very mature man. It owes, I think, here and there, just a little to Croce:

> Poetry is like a man, whom thinking you know all his movements and appearance you will presently come upon in such a posture that for a moment you can hardly believe it a position of the limbs you know. So thinking you have set bounds to the nature of poetry, you shall as soon discover something outside your bounds which they should evidently contain.
>
> The expression 'bad poetry' is meaningless: critics still use it, forgetting that bad poetry is not poetry at all.
>
> Nor can prose and poetry be compared any more than pictures and pencils: the one is instrument and the other art. Poetry may be written in prose or verse, or spoken extempore.

For it is anything expressed in words, which appeals to the emotions either in presenting an image or picture to move them; or by the music of words affecting them through the senses; or in stating some truth whose eternal quality exacts the same reverence as eternity itself.

In its nature poetry is sincere and simple.

Writing which is poetry must say what the writer has himself to say, not what he has observed others to say with effect, nor what he thinks will impress others because it impressed him hearing it. Nor must he waste any more words over it than a mathematician; every word must work for its keep, in prose, blank verse, or rhyme.

And poetry is to be judged not by what the poet has tried to say, only by what he has said.

These aphorisms seem to me to be true; and perhaps Keith Douglas's criticism of many of the new romantic poets of the 1940s might have been that they wanted to be judged by what they had tried to say, not by what they had said, that they did not make words work hard enough for their keep. His criticism of our immediate contemporaries, the poets of the 'New Movement' of the 1950s, might be perhaps that they are not sincere and simple enough; that they too often say what they have observed others to say with effect, or what they think will impress their hearers because it impressed them hearing it. That would apply, for instance, to the many attempts by young poets in the last few years to imitate Empson's attitudes and catch his tone. Thinking as he did about poetry, Keith Douglas could obviously belong, in the strict sense, to no 'school'. And when I say he was essentially a romantic poet, I am referring not to his formal ideals about poetry, but to his personal temperament.

Thus, Douglas's attitude to war was, though humane and deeply compassionate, a heroic attitude. It had nothing in common with the humanitarian, pacifist attitudes of contemporaries of his like Nicholas Moore or Alex Comfort or Douglas's friend, John Hall. He was a good soldier, and in a sense he enjoyed his war. He enjoyed, at least, the exercise of the will in action. He was an officer, and an efficient officer, who enjoyed the responsibility that went with his rank. In that, among our poets of the last war, he was almost unique; Alun Lewis and Sidney Keyes were both also officers, and conscientious ones, but neither of them was a natural soldier in the sense that Keith Douglas was. And much more typically the soldier-writer of the last war tended to be, like myself, the sergeant-major's nightmare: the long-haired private, who could not keep step, who not only looked like a bloody poet, but turned out to be one: a great nuisance to his superiors generally till he could be parked in an office with a typewriter. Douglas, on the other hand, was physically and temperamentally adapted to war. It was a rough game that he was good at playing. Again, he was a very intelligent man, as these aphorisms on poetry prove, but not a man, I think, who had much use for intellectual chatter. The two or three times I personally met him, I do not remember our exchanging a word on any abstract topic. Whatever else he may have pined for during the war years, it will not have been evening parties in Chelsea.

Douglas, in fact, was a cavalier. Riding was almost his favourite sport, and in war he thought of his tank as if it were a horse. There is a poem, written at Enfidaville, in Tunisia, in 1943, which gives us, I think, some leading clues to his temperament. I shall read it in full:

ARISTOCRATS

'I think I am becoming a God'

The noble horse with courage in his eye
clean in the bone, looks up at a shellburst:
away fly the images of the shires
but he puts the pipe back in his mouth.
Peter was unfortunately killed by an 88:
it took his leg away, he died in the ambulance.
I saw him crawling on the sand; he said
It's most unfair, they've shot my foot off.

How can I live among this gentle
obsolescent breed of heroes, and not weep?
Unicorns, almost,
for they are falling into two legends
in which their stupidity and chivalry
are celebrated. Each, fool and hero, will be immortal.

The plains were their cricket pitch
and in the mountains the tremendous drop fences
brought down some of the runners. Here then
under the stones and earth they dispose themselves,
I think with their famous unconcern.
It is not gunfire I hear but a hunting horn.

In that fine last line, as Sir John Waller remarks in his notes to the *Collected Poems*, there is an echo of Roncesvalles. And the aristocratic morality, evoked in this poem, was the morality to which in the depths of his nature Keith Douglas was most profoundly drawn. He was an aloof, gay, and passionate man. He loved risk. The state of the world, and perhaps the nature of man, and perhaps his own nature in its depths, filled him with profound sadness; nevertheless, for him the sadness of human existence was a kind of destiny that had to be bravely and lovingly embraced. He was as far as can be from a nagging or carping attitude to life. And this partly explains the obscurity of his present reputation. The new poetry of the last five years has in itself many virtues of reticence and control; but it does not express, in its spirit, precisely these generous, aristocratic virtues.

Keith Douglas was born in 1920, in Tunbridge Wells. When he was eight, his father left his mother, and the boy never saw him again. Thus he acquired very early that earnest and sometimes rather anxious sense of responsibility that is found often, for instance, in the eldest sons of widows. At 11, he entered Christ's Hospital on the Nomination Examination, and from then on was able to pay for his education through scholarships. He took an active part in sports and amateur theatricals at Christ's Hospital, and also did well at lessons, though the headmaster thought him lazy. Already, as a schoolboy, he was writing very accomplished verses, and at 16 sold a poem to Geoffrey Grigson for *New Verse* – a hard nut to crack. He made many friends at Christ's Hospital, though he also seems to have been considered, especially by some of the masters, rather 'difficult'. In 1938 he went up on a scholarship to Merton College, Oxford, to read English, and was lucky enough to have Edmund Blunden assigned to him as tutor. He soon became one of the best known of undergraduate poets. The years just before the last world war, and just after its beginning, were, in fact, rather a good period for Oxford poetry: Douglas's contemporaries included Sidney Keyes, John Heath-Stubbs, John Short, and J. C. Hall. John Waller, another Oxford poet of the period, and the future editor of Douglas's *Collected Poems*, published some of Douglas's best early work in his war-time Oxford magazine, *Kingdom Come*. Douglas at one time was editor of *Cherwell* and helped to prepare for Basil Blackwell the undergraduate miscellany, *Augury*, from which I quoted his aphorisms about poetry. He was one of the poets included in the anthology *Eight Oxford Poets*. His years at Oxford seem to have been happy and successful. He made lots of friends, many of them women. The exotic beauty of four of these is commemorated in an unfinished fragment, of which this is one version:

TO KAISTIN YINCHENG OLGA MILENA

Women of four countries
the four phials full of essences
of green England, legendary China,
deep Europe and Arabic Spain, a
finer four poisons for the five senses
than any in medieval inventories.

In giving you this I
return the wine to the grape
return the plant her juices
for what each creature uses
by chemistry will seep
back to the source or die ...

Douglas had early joined the Oxford O.T.C., partly for the sake of the free riding it offered, and thus he was liable for service on the outbreak of war. He was not, in fact, called up, till fairly late in 1940. He trained in various places in Great Britain and in June 1941 was posted to the Middle East, transferred to the Notts Sherwood Rangers Yeomanry, but seconded to a staff job at base. He disliked this, and on the eve of El Alamein ran away to rejoin his old regiment, who welcomed him. He fought with them in a Crusader tank from El Alamein to Wadi Zem Zem in Tunisia, continuously, except for one interval of hospitalization and convalescence in Palestine, after he had been blown up by a land-mine. He kept a diary, and the book he made out of it, *Alamein to Zem Zem*, is probably one of the very few accounts, indeed, of fighting in the Second World War likely to rank, as literature, with classics of the First World War like Sir Herbert Read's *In Retreat*, the war chapters in Robert Graves's *Goodbye to All That* or Siegfried Sassoon's *Memoirs of a Fox-Hunting Man* and *Memoirs of an Infantry Officer*. The book has two great qualities: visual immediacy, and an almost frightening emotional detachment. 'I observed,' Douglas says, 'the battles partly as an exhibition – that is to say, I went through them like a little child in a factory – a child sees the brightness and efficiency of steel machines and endless belts slopping round and round, without knowing or caring what it is all there for. When I could order my thoughts I looked for something more significant than appearances; I still look, I cannot avoid it, for something decorative, poetic, or dramatic.'

The qualities of Douglas's prose in *Alamein to Zem Zem* – the brutal vividness of presentation, combined with an apparent almost icy detachment – are to be found, of course, in even greater concentration, in the poems he wrote in the Western Desert and during periods of leave in Cairo or convalescence in Palestine. These he published almost as soon as he had written them, sending many of them on airgraphs to M. J. Tambimuttu's *Poetry London*, giving others to his friends Bernard Spencer and Lawrence Durrell to put into the excellent magazine they were bringing out in Cairo, *Personal Landscape*. At the end of 1943 Douglas was posted home to train for the invasion of Europe. And with that posting the history of his career, as a poet, really comes to an end. His last completed poem is called 'On a Return from Egypt'. I shall read it to you later; it expresses very beautifully both a clear premonition of death, and a bitterness at the foreknowledge that he will not be allowed to survive, to write the poems he might have written:

> And all my endeavours are unlucky explorers
> come back, abandoning the expedition;
> the specimens, the lilies of ambition
> still spring in their climate, still unpicked:
> but time, time is all I lacked
> to find them as the great collectors before me.

This premonition did not affect his outward cheerfulness; Tambimuttu, one of his closest friends and warmest admirers, tells us of Douglas's gaiety when he dropped into the offices of *Poetry London*, the pleasure he took in riding in Hyde Park. Douglas was killed in Normandy on the 9th of June 1944. Shortly before his death he had managed to get some information from be-hind the enemy lines, and for this he was mentioned in dispatches. In an obituary article, in *Poetry London*, on Douglas, Tambimuttu wrote:

> I can say without any hesitation that Douglas's view of life and his actions were the most sound and realistic that any man of our generation can come to. He accepted the greatest gifts of this life and lived with passionate sincerity. His conclusions about life in action are the most mature any poet has arrived at in this war ... Douglas lived the poetry he believed in.

I want now to consider Keith Douglas's poems. And here I am confronted with a difficulty. If he were a very famous poet, much of whose work I could rely on most of you having read, I could simply allude to poems familiar to you, and make observations and judgments on these, illustrated by occasional quotations. But he is not a very famous poet; and the obvious alternative would seem to be to take rather a few poems, perhaps only three or four, out of his quite large output – 140 pages of poetry *is* quite a large output for a man of 24 – and to read these aloud, and go into them in some detail. But, on the other hand, can the examination of three or four poems, however carefully chosen, give us a proper notion of any poet's range? Fortunately, some sort of compromise is, I think, possible. Douglas's poems fall into a number of distinct groups, and any later group is always more interesting and important than the group that immediately precedes it. The poems that he wrote at school are mainly important in that they show us a boy patiently learning his craft. The poems that he wrote at Oxford have more depth and subtlety, but they have something in common – both in their charm, and in their occasional weakness – with all undergraduate poetry. They are very 'literary' poems. In the poems which Douglas wrote during his period of military training in England, we begin to feel that he is biting deeper into experience; or that experience is biting deeper into him. Finally, the poems written in the Middle East are, of course, Douglas's most important achievement. If we take these groups in turn, we shall get a fairly accurate picture of his development.

There is, however, one more group still: the group of poems Douglas was never able to finish. The most important of these is a poem, or a set of frustrated beginnings of a poem, called 'Bête Noire'. This, as it sounds, is not anything achieved. It is a succession of hopeless attempts to grapple with an intractable subject, the subject of what Douglas called, in con-versation and in letters, 'the beast on my back'. It is the subject of what any of us colloquially might call 'the black dog on my back': or in more ambitious language, it is the subject of what Freudian psychologists call, or used to call, the Death-Wish and Jungian psychologists call the Shadow. I imagine a Jungian psychologist would say that Douglas was very much aware of his Shadow, in a sense at times almost obsessed with it, but that he had never properly accepted it, or come to terms with it, and that therefore, in spite of the impression he gave of being far more mature than his years, he was not, when he died, yet a fully integrated personality. There was, as it were, a crucial and painful experience still to come, of which he had a kind of poetic premonition. The Shadow, in more homely terms than those of the psychologists, is the sudden awareness, which can be a blinding and shattering one, of all the nastiness, all the ulterior self-centredness, in our own motives and in those of others. To accept the Shadow is, in Christian language, to accept the possibility of Damnation and the reality of Original Sin. The Shadow, if we try to suppress our latent awareness of it – most people of a liberal morality and of progressive views try to do this, most of the time – can, as it were, irrupt upon us. And the moment of its irruption is the moment when we feel not only that we have never loved anybody properly, but that nobody has ever loved us, that love is a lie.

If you have read, for instance, either of Philip Toynbee's two excellent experimental novels, *Tea with Mrs Goodman* and *The Garden to the Sea*, you will agree with me that the character, or the archetype, Charley, in both of them, who sneers and jeers at everybody, who distrusts the sincerity of every vow and the purity of every motive, is an excellent personification of the Shadow. He is horrible; yet he is an irreducible element in each of us with which we have to come to terms if we ever wish to become whole beings. If we do come to terms with him, recognize him as having a function, he ceases to be the Devil, and becomes something manageable and even comic, say, Mr Punch. Douglas, I think, found it excessively difficult to come to terms with his Shadow just because he was such an unusually good man. He had high principles, and he always acted on his principles. As a boy, his first thought was of what he owed to his mother; as a young man, of what he owed to his country. His personal interests he had concentrated on high and wholesome things, on love, and poetry, and comradeship, and adventure. So it seemed to him inexplicable, I suppose, that he should have these black despairing moods. What had he done to deserve them? He had certainly never shirked any duty or danger, he was incapable of a mean act, and yet his black beast was liable to pounce upon him at the most unexpected moments, like the sense of guilt of a very bad, or the sense of inadequacy of a very weak, man. On his bad days, it could spoil everything :

> ... *It's his day.*
> *Don't kiss me. Don't put your arm round*
> *And touch the beast on my back.*

Had Douglas survived, given this obsession with the Shadow, and given also the strain under which he had laboured as a fighting soldier and the iron self-control which he had always exercised, given the roaring guns and the dead men and the buckled tanks in the Western Desert, I think that, a few years after the war, he might have had a bad breakdown. He would have emerged from that breakdown, I imagine, having come to terms with the

Shadow, and with a new depth as a poet. 'Bête Noire', as I say, is an unfinished poem, a failure; but in its light, or against its darkness, all Douglas's other poems must be read.

I shall be fairly brief about the poems Douglas wrote while still a schoolboy. In a schoolboy's poems one does not look for originality of thought or feeling. One looks for adroitness in handling words, for signs that the handling of rhythms, the shaping of phrases, gives a young poet pleasure. Here is the poem which Douglas at 16 sold to *New Verse*, a short poem which says nothing very much, but says it very agreeably:

DEJECTION

Yesterday travellers in summer's country,
Tonight the sprinkled moon and ravenous sky
Say, we have reached the boundary. The autumn clothes
Are on; Death is the season and we the living
Are hailed by the solitary to join their regiment,
To leave the sea and the horses and march away
Endlessly. The spheres speak with persuasive voices.
Only tomorrow like a seagull hovers and calls
Shrieks through the mist and scatters the pools of stars.
The windows will be open and hearts behind them.

The Oxford poems, written between 1938 and 1940, deserve, of course, much more attention. There are about 30 of them. They show, as contrasted with the school poems, a growing range and suppleness. But most of them are still very much 'occasional' poems. There is about them, occasionally, a slightly self-indulgent melancholy and a youthful romantic morbidity. One of the best of them, 'Leukothea', is about a beautiful dead woman. Her beauty was so supernatural that the poet imagines it has resisted corruption in the ground. A bad dream disillusions him:

So all these years I have lived securely. I knew
I had only to uncover you
to see how the careful earth would have kept
all as it was, untouched. I trusted the ground.
I knew the worm and the beetle would go by
and never dare batten on your beauty.

Last night I dreamed and found my trust betrayed
only the little bones and the great bones disarrayed.

That is good partly because it is so beautifully phrased, but good partly also because, I think, one finds oneself, half consciously, reading into it a meaning far deeper than the fantastical surface meaning. One thinks of the parable, in the Bible, of the buried talent. One thinks of people who fling themselves, from some practical compulsion, into the thick of the world, but dream always of reaching a stage when they can afford to cultivate some gift, to pursue some vision, which meant much in their boyhood, and then, when they have their chance, find that the vision has faded, the gift has decayed. It is Yeats's theme in a shorter, sharper, more completely bitter poem:

> Toil and grow rich,
> What's that but to lie
> With a foul witch
> And after, drained dry,
> To be brought
> To the chamber where
> Lies one long sought
> With despair?

'Leukothea', however, is rather exceptional. More typically, Douglas's Oxford poems express a mood which most generations of undergraduates must have felt, and Douglas's own generation, waiting to go to war, particularly poignant. There is the sense of magical years, soon passing, but for that reason to be treasured all the more highly; there is the special sense of the magic of Oxford as a place:

> This then is the city of young men, of beginning,
> ideas, trials, pardonable follies,
> the lightness, seriousness, and sorrow of youth ...

Already, however, towards the end of Douglas's Oxford period, his contempt of poetry was becoming more mature. He was trying to say more, and to friends who had liked his early lyrical smoothness it seemed that the new style he was developing was a rather harsh and rough one. Answering such a criticism from his friend, John Hall, Keith Douglas, when a soldier, wrote:

> In my early poems I wrote lyrically, as an innocent, because I was an innocent; I have (not surprisingly) fallen from that particular grace since then. I had begun to change during my second year at Oxford. T. S. Eliot wrote to me when I first joined the Army, that I appeared to have finished with one form of writing and to be progressing towards another, which he did not think I had mastered. I knew this to be true without his saying it.

The nature of the change in style, and the degree of the progress towards mastery, can be seen in two poems, the two most successful ones, out of the comparatively small batch which Douglas wrote during his period of military training in England. One of these, called 'The Prisoner', is addressed to a

Chinese girl called Cheng. There is in it a new depth, a new intimacy, a new painfulness:

> Today, Cheng, I touched your face
> with two fingers, as a gesture of love;
> for I can never prove enough
> by sight or sense your strange grace,
>
> but motherwise my hands return
> to your fair cheek, as luminous
> as a lamp in a paper house,
> and touch, to teach love and learn.
>
> I think a hundred years are gone
> that so, like gods, we'd occupy.
> But alas, Cheng, I cannot tell why,
> today I touched a mask stretched on the stone
>
> person of death. There was the urge
> to break from the bright flesh and emerge
> of the ambitious cruel bone.

The other important poem of this training period, 'Time Eating', might be described as metaphysical. This, like 'The Prisoner', gives us a hint about some of the deep sources of Douglas's *bête noire* obsession.

> Ravenous Time has flowers for his food
> In Autumn, yet can cleverly make good
> each petal: devours animals and men,
> but for ten dead he can create ten.
>
> If you enquire how secretly you've come
> to mansize from the smallness of a stone
> it will appear his effort made you rise
> so gradually to your proper size.
>
> But as he makes he eats; the very part
> where he began, even the elusive heart,
> Time's ruminative tongue will wash
> and slow juice masticate all flesh.
>
> That volatile huge intestine holds
> material and abstract in its folds:
> thought and ambition melt and even the world
> will alter, in that catholic belly curled.

But time, who ate my love, you cannot make
such another; you who can remake
the lizard's tail and the bright snakeskin
cannot, cannot. That you gobbled in
too quick, and though you brought me from a boy
you can make no more of me, only destroy.

Nothing in Douglas's earlier writing had led us to anticipate the melancholy gusto, here, of his metaphysical wit:

That volatile huge intestine holds
material and abstract in its folds:
thought and ambition melt and even the world
will alter, in that catholic belly curled.

There is something of the passionate ingenuity of Donne in these four lines, combined with something of the eloquent directness of Dryden.

During the period of his army training in England, Douglas began, there-fore, as it were, to reconnoitre himself in depth. But his main reputation will probably rest on the best of the thirty or so poems which he wrote while on active service in the Middle East. These are uneven; there are, in almost all of them, if we compare them to his Oxford poems, certain technical rough-nesses, of which Douglas was quite conscious. For he is not seeking merely as in 'The Prisoner' and 'Time Eating' to probe new and painful depths of personal feeling, but to absorb into his verse raw material which might, of its very nature, seem intractable to poetry. 'Cairo Jag', for instance, which I shall now read to you, will remain, to anybody who served in the Middle East dur-ing the last war, a vivid piece of documentation. It brings it all back, so to say. But is it, in the ordinary sense, a *poem*, is its painfulness resolved? Do its images merely pile up brutally or do they work, in the end, into some large reconciling pattern? It is a marginal case among Douglas's poems: cer-tainly very memorable, but not certainly very good. I leave you to judge:

Shall I get drunk or cut myself a piece of cake,
a pasty Syrian with a few words of English
or the Turk who says she is a princess – she dances
apparently by levitation? Or Marcelle, Parisienne
always preoccupied with her dull dead lover:
she has all the photographs and his letters
tied in a bundle and stamped Décédé in mauve ink.
All this takes place in a stink of jasmin.

But there are streets dedicated to sleep
stenches and sour smells, the sour cries
do not disturb their application to slumber
all day, scattered on the pavement like rags

afflicted with fatalism and hashish. The women
offering their children brown-paper breasts
dry and twisted, elongated like the skull,
Holbein's signature. But this stained white town
is something in accordance with mundane conventions –

Marcelle drops her Gallic airs and tragedy
suddenly shrieks in Arabic about the fare
with the cabman, links herself so
with the somnambulists and legless beggars:
it is all one, all as you have heard.

But by a day's travelling you reach a new world
the vegetation is of iron
dead tanks, gun barrels have no flowers or berries
and there are all sorts of manure, you can imagine
the dead themselves, their boots, clothes and possessions
clinging to the ground, a man with no head
has a packet of chocolate and a souvenir of Tripoli.

So it was. And the only moral comment Douglas allows himself to make in the poem is that so it was:

it is all one, all as you have heard . . .

And, when we have read the poem carefully, we realize that he means by that not only that it is all one in Cairo, that the shrieking Marcelle is at one with the shrieking cabman and the legless beggars, the squalor is universal, but also that it is all one between Cairo and the Desert: moral death and disorder match physical death and disorder: Marcelle's photographs and letters of her dull dead lover exactly match the dead soldier's packet of chocolate and souvenir from Tripoli, are as futile, and pathetic, and meaningless, and ultimately enraging. It is the kind of poem which Pope or Dryden would have written in neatly antithetic heroic couplets, Cairo in one line, the Desert in the next. Douglas leaves it as a jumble, giving us one clue that will enable us to sort it out for ourselves. We *can* sort it out, but we still wonder if it is a good poem; it is, at least, a very bold and original experiment.

It is interesting to contrast 'Cairo Jag' with the poem that immediaely precedes it in Douglas's *Collected Poems*, 'Behaviour of Fish in an Egyptian Tea Garden'. While in the Middle East it was Cairo which focused all Douglas's negative emotions, which made a satirist of him. But 'Cairo Jag' fails, if it does fail, because it lacks that 'coolness at the centre' which Saintsbury noted as the mark of a great satirist like Dryden; it is too near hysteria. 'Behaviour of Fish in an Egyptian Tea Garden' is urbane, detached, even gay in tone. A single metaphor is brilliantly sustained, and in sustaining it Douglas can bring to bear all his powers of visual fantasy. Yet the effect is more properly satirical, more damaging to its object, than that of 'Cairo Jag' :

> As a white stone draws down the fish
> she on the seafloor of the afternoon
> draws down men's glances and their cruel wish
> for love. Slyly red lip on the spoon
>
> slips in a morsel of ice-cream; her hands
> white as a milky stone, white submarine
> fronds, sink with spread fingers, lean
> along the table, carmined at the ends.
>
> A cotton magnate, an important fish
> with great eyepouches and a golden mouth
> through the frail reefs of furniture swims out
> and idling, suspended, stays to watch.
>
> A crustacean old man clamped to his chair
> sits coldly near her and might see
> her charms through fissures where the eyes should be
> or else his teeth are parted in a stare.
>
> Captain on leave, a lean dark mackerel,
> lies in the offing; turns himself and looks
> through currents of sound. The flat-eyed flatfish sucks
> on a straw, staring from its repose, laxly.
>
> And gallants in shoals swim up and lag,
> circling and passing near the white attraction;
> sometimes pausing, opening a conversation;
> fish pause so to nibble or tug.
>
> Now the ice-cream is finished, is
> paid for. The fish swim off on business
> and she sits alone at the table, a white stone
> useless except to a collector, a rich man.

One has doubts that *that* is a good poem.

But Douglas's temperament was not that of the satirist; it was, as I have said, a romantic temperament, in its ardour, though without that passion for self-deception, that indignant refusal to see things as they are, which we sometimes associate with the idea of romanticism. In the desert, he could still find release, in poetry, for the positive ardour of his mind. He need not merely be a satirist. He could address his Muse, partly as a lost, cruel mistress, partly as the moon :

I listen to the desert wind
that will not blow her from my mind;
the stars will not put down a hand,
the moon's ignorant of my wound

moving negligently across
by clouds and cruel tracts of space
as in my brain my nights and days
moves the reflection of her face.

Skims like a bird my sleepless eye
the sands who at this hour deny
the violent heat they have by day
as she denies her former way:

all the elements agree
with her, to have no sympathy
for my tactless misery
as wonderful and hard as she.

O turn in the dark bed again
and give to him what once was mine
and I'll turn as you turn
and kiss my swarthy mistress pain.

One is very often aware of Douglas's reading – one is aware, there, of how well he knew Wyatt:

as she denies her former way –

without ever feeling that he is writing pastiche.

I earlier this evening read to you one of Douglas's poems of action, 'Aristocrats'. It was not a mere poem of action, but a poem in praise of chivalry. He is never merely a descriptive poet: and his best poem of action, 'Vergissmeinicht', is like the earlier 'The Prisoner' essentially a poem about love and death:

Three weeks gone and the combatants gone
returning over the nightmare ground
we found the place again, and found
the soldier sprawling in the sun.

The frowning barrel of his gun
overshadowing. As we came on
that day, he hit my tank with one
like the entry of a demon.

Look. Here in the gunpit spoil
the dishonoured picture of his girl
who has put: Steffi. Vergissmeinicht
in a copybook Gothic script.

We see him almost with content
abased, and seeming to have paid
and mocked at by his own equipment
that's hard and good when he's decayed.

But she would weep to see to-day
how on his skin the swart flies move;
the dust upon the paper eye
and the burst stomach like a cave.

For here the lover and killer are mingled
who had one body and one heart.
And death who had the soldier singled
has done the lover mortal hurt.

Always look in a poem like that, which moves you, and which might seem to move you merely by its material, by what it rawly presents, for the handling. Douglas, I think, never wrote a more skilful poem than this; or one in which his skill is more modestly subdued to the total effect he is aiming at. What gives us the effect, for instance, in the first stanza, of the tanks lumbering bumpily and relentlessly on is a kind of wheeling motion in the stanza itself, repetitions and a concealed rhyme:

Three weeks gone and the combatants gone,
returning over the nightmare ground
we found the place again, and found
the soldier sprawling in the sun ...

What saves the stanza about the dead soldier's appearance from being merely repellent is, again, the deliberate formality of the syntax and the choice of a literary adjective – 'the swart flies', not 'the black flies', and an objective precision of statement, without emotional commentary, that gives an effect of icy pity:

But she would weep to see to-day
how on his skin the swart flies move;
the dust upon the paper eye
and the burst stomach like a cave.

And in the last stanza the effect of aesthetic distance, of the whole experience being held in control, is clinched by the eighteenth-century antithesis:

> *And death who had* the soldier *singled*
> *has done* the lover *mortal hurt.*

I shall not attempt to 'place' Douglas as a poet: I think that four or five of the poems I have read to you this evening would have to be considered very seriously indeed by any anthologist attempting to produce a representative selection of the best poems, written by the younger English poets, over the past 25 years; and I think it would be hard, among poems by younger poets of the 1950s, which have attracted much attention in the last few years, to match these four or five poems. But what is specially and sadly interesting about Douglas is the sense that his development was continuous and steady; the sense that, if he had been spared – he would be now in his middle thirties, if he were alive – he might well be, today, the dominating figure of his generation and a wholesome and inspiring influence on younger men. He had courage, passion, and generosity. These are three qualities that our age generally needs. I said, earlier, that I would read to you his last completed poem. In it, he foresaw his death; in it, he sighed for the flowers that he would not now pick; it makes a better peroration to this lecture than any possible prose sentence of mine:

ON A RETURN FROM EGYPT

> *To stand here in the wings of Europe*
> *disheartened, I have come away*
> *from the sick land where in the sun lay*
> *the gentle sloe-eyed murderers*
> *of themselves, exquisites under a curse;*
> *here to exercise my depleted fury.*
>
> *For the heart is a coal, growing colder*
> *when jewelled cerulean seas change*
> *into grey rocks, grey water-fringe,*
> *sea and sky altering like a cloth*
> *till colour and sheen are gone both:*
> *cold is an opiate of the soldier.*
>
> *And all my endeavours are unlucky explorers*
> *come back, abandoning the expedition;*
> *the specimens, the lilies of ambition*
> *still spring in their climate, still unpicked:*
> *but time, time is all I lacked*
> *to find them, as the great collectors before me.*

The next month, then, is a window
and with a crash I'll split the glass.
Behind it stands one I must kiss,
person of love or death,
a person or a wraith,
I fear what I shall find.

19 · THE POETRY OF THOM GUNN

Critical Quarterly (The University, Hull), III no. 4 (Winter 1961).

Thom Gunn is often classed as a Movement poet but though he first became known about the same time as the other poets of that group, around 1953, he belongs to a younger generation. He is seven years younger than Kingsley Amis and Philip Larkin, four years younger than John Wain, three years younger than Elizabeth Jennings. Born at Gravesend in 1929, the son of a successful Fleet Street journalist, Herbert Gunn, Thom Gunn was educated at University College School in London and at Trinity College, Cambridge. At Cambridge he had the sort of career which often precedes literary distinction, editing an anthology of undergraduate verse, being president of the English Club, and taking a first in both parts of the English tripos. The Fantasy Press published his first pamphlet of verse when he was still an undergraduate, in 1953, and his first volume, *Fighting Terms*, in 1954, shortly after he had taken his degree.

His second volume, *The Sense of Movement*, came out in 1957, published by Faber's, and won him a Somerset Maugham Award. Between 1954 and 1957, he had been teaching and studying at Stanford University in California, being much influenced by Yvor Winters. He used his Somerset Maugham award to spend some time in Rome. His most recent volume, *My Sad Captains*, came out this year. He now teaches English at Berkeley in San Francisco. He visits England reasonably frequently, but nobody could call his poems insularly English. Italian painting, Californian scenes and characters, Greek mythology, French literature and philosophy frequently give him the pegs to hang his poems on. In his work there is nothing of the insularity or the distrust of cultural or philosophical themes that, in different ways, marks Amis and Larkin. He resembles these two only in his admirable care for lucidity of poetic thought and language. He is not weakly jocular as these two sometimes are, nor on the other hand has he the humour which is one of their strengths. He is often a witty poet, in the sense of being concise and epigrammatic, but he is never heartily familiar in tone. He keeps at a certain cool distance from the reader. His poetry also is less a poetry either of acceptance of society, as Larkin's is, or of sharp social criticism, like that of D. J. Enright, than a poetry of firm assertion of the romantic will.

With Larkin, he seems to me the best poet of the group that became known around 1953, and a contrast with Larkin may help to bring out some of his central qualities. What Larkin seems to me to be repeatedly saying in many of his best poems is that a sensible man settles for second-bests. One of Larkin's best poems, for instance, is about being tempted to give up a safe, dull job for the sake of wild adventure and firmly, and the reader is meant to feel rightly, resisting the temptation; several other good poems, on the other hand, are about being tempted by love or by the spectacle of happy domesticity into some permanent kind of emotional relationship, but retreating, since Larkin as a poet needs a kind of freedom which is not wild, but which does depend on a firm cutting down of the number of one's personal relationships and emotional commitments. Larkin, one might say, is the poet of emotional economy. The title poem of his volume *The Less Deceived* (a poem about a girl being kidnapped and raped in the mid-Victorian age) is both about how we should not waste our sympathy where it cannot help and also about how the young man in the story may have felt an even sharper grief than the girl's when he had done his wild, fierce, wicked thing and burst into 'fulfilment's desolate attic'.

Larkin's tender poem about old horses at grass seems fundamentally to be about the idea that such real freedom as most of us can hope to enjoy in life will be the freedom of pensioned retirement, with no continuing social function, with enough to eat, and with some pleasant memories. His poem about looking at a girl friend's snapshot album is fundamentally about how cherished images are in some ways better than difficult continuing relationships; and the poem about the flavourless town where he grew up is, on the other hand, about how we should not fake up pleasant memory images where there are none. The total effect is that of a certain bleakness. When I think of Larkin I always think of Henry James's great short story, 'The Beast in the Jungle' : about a man who is so overshadowed by the sense of some nameless horror or terror that may jump on him if he takes risks with life, that he never takes any risks. When the beast does jump, it jumps, not as actual terror, but as the sudden awareness that a long life crippled by fear and caution has been wasted. The hero has never dared the high dive, never swum at the deep end. And it is too late now. There is a splendid relevant sentence of Elizabeth Bowen's : 'One is empowered to live fully : occasion does not offer.' Larkin's poetry is about not affronting the unoffered occasions. Gunn's is about snatching at occasion, whatever the risks, and whether it offers or not.

Outer order and personal stability, for Larkin, depend on our swallowing our gall. Gunn refuses to do this. I am proud to remember that, in 1953, when he was still an undergraduate, I included three early poems of his in an anthology called *Springtime*. The three poems I chose happened to illustrate, luckily, certain themes and attitudes that were to be recurrent. The first, about the world of the Elizabethan poet, began

> It was a violent time. Wheels, racks and fires
> In every poet's mouth, and not mere rant ...

Gunn insisted in this poem that the heroic attitude, which he sees as behind all notable poetry, should be stimulated, not quenched, by a threatening age. It is the poet's business to make tragic sense of it all :

> *In street, in tavern, happening would cry*
> *'I am myself, but part of something greater,*
> *Find poets what that is, do not pass by*
> *For feel my fingers in your* pia mater :
> *I am a cruelly insistent friend;*
> *You cannot smile at me and make an end.'*

The second poem was called 'Helen's Rape' and what it expressed might be called a nostalgia, though tinged a little with irony, for the kind of primitive violence that sees itself as moved by a divine force. This poem began :

> *Hers was the last authentic rape:*
> *From forced content of common breeder*
> *Bringing the violent dreamed escape ...*

The 'forced content' (meaning constrained contentment but carrying an over-tone of enforced *containment*) is that which Helen enjoyed as an ordinary *hausfrau*, a 'common breeder' or junior matron, with Menelaus. The 'violent dreamed escape' is Helen's rape, or abduction, by Paris, but she had dreamt of a more genuinely divine abduction, or rape, like that of her mother Leda or of Europa. The real age of the gods is already past, and though Paris was in-spired by Aphrodite, or moved by a divine madness, he had to soothe common-sense critics, and to pretend that he abducted Helen for political reasons, in retaliation for a similar abduction by the Greeks of a Trojan princess, his aunt. At the end of the poem, Gunn brings in the idea that only a simulacrum of Helen was taken to Troy and that the real Helen was wafted to Egypt. And yet even a distant Helen would know the harrowing griefs which even her image had brought on Troy.

So, at least, I interpret the very difficult last stanza :

> *Helen herself could not through flesh*
> *Abandon flesh; she felt surround*
> *Her absent body, never fresh*
> *The mortal context, and the mesh*
> *Of the continual battle's sound.*

The reference might just be, however, not to the legend of Helen in Egypt but simply to the idea that because Paris was only a hero, not a god, his carnal love could not transform her carnality into the divine. I think Gunn possibly ought to have put a comma after 'fresh'. If the reference is to Egypt, the meaning will be : 'Though bodily transported to Egypt Helen could not remain unaware of the havoc which Paris's love of her body had wrought :

even absent in Egypt she felt herself surrounded and sullied ('never fresh') by the lust and violence of the Trojan war.' Or it may be that a comma should not be added after 'fresh' but omitted after 'body' and that what she felt surrounding her Egyptian body was the 'mortal context', the circumstances of death, which are never fresh, not so much in the sense that they are not refreshed or refreshing, but in the sense that they have been there from the beginning, they never started.

The puzzles of such a stanza suggest that though Gunn is learnedly lucid he is never likely to be a popular writer. The reader of this short poem is expected to have a very detailed knowledge of Greek mythology, as the reader of the one about Elizabethan poetry needs a detailed knowledge of Elizabethan literature and history. They were the only two poems in *Springtime* to which I felt I had to add notes.

The third poem I chose, 'Carnal Knowledge', stated a third recurring theme, the idea that sexual love can rarely, whether or not this is a good thing, break down, or merge, the essential separateness of two people. The stanzas had an excessively clever Empsonian refrain,

You know I know you know I know you know,

alternating as,

I know you know I know you know I know,

but in the last stanza this was truncated:

Abandon me to stammering, and go;
If you have tears, prepare to cry elsewhere –
I know of no emotion we can share.
Your intellectual protests are a bore
And even now I pose, so now go, for
I know you know.

This was a more awkward, a more undergraduate poem than the others, and I feel that even today Gunn is never quite at his best when he writes of personal relationships. But implicit in the poem, though not brought cleanly through, was a theme which he was soon to use more powerfully, not a half-regret at the great difficulty of breaking down separateness, but a horror at the idea that such a breaking down, such a merging, should ever be possible at all.

I included in another anthology, *Poetry Now*, a poem which expressed perhaps less humanly but certainly more powerfully than 'Carnal Knowledge' this horror of merging. Two men have been sharing a bed (or the two men may be different aspects of the poet's one personality) and one of them gets up in the small hours, looks out at the moon, and declaims:

'Inside the moon I see a hell of love.
There love is all, and no one is alone.
The song of passion deafens, as no choice
Of individual word can hold its own
Against the rule of that anonymous noise.
And wait, I see more clearly; craters, canals,
Are smothered by two giant forms of mist
So that no features of the land remain.
Two humming clouds of moisture intertwist
Agreed so well, they cannot change to rain
And serve to clean the common ground beneath.

Singing there fell, locked in each other's arms,
Cursed with content, pair by successive pair,
Committed centuries to lie in calms
They stayed to rot into that used-up air
No wind can shift it, it is so thick, so thick!'

The ringing voice stopped, but as if one must
Finish in moral, stumbled on and said:
'In that still fog all energy is lost.'
The moonlight slunk on, darkness touched his head.
He fell back, then he turned upon the pillow.

It will be noted that in this passage, as in the earlier passage about Helen, the word 'content' which generally carries a strong pro-feeling in English poetry ('sweet content'), carries a strong anti-feeling; similarly the word 'calms' instead of suggesting 'calm after storm' recalls the rotting, glistering sea on which the ship lay becalmed in 'The Ancient Mariner'. Literary reminiscence and counterpoint is one of Gunn's main instruments. The giant lovers transformed into clouds might remind us of Ixion attempting to embrace Juno, but the line,

Singing there fell, locked in each other's arms,

gains extra force if one recalls Paolo and Francesca. The line that gives the moral, 'In that still fog all energy is lost,' recalls an urgent line of Spender's: 'Drink here of energy, and only energy.' The attack, however, as in Spender's case, is not so much on the stuff of which romantic love is made as on its self-centredness and stupefying effect. The clouds could dissolve into rain and 'clean the solid earth beneath', or the self-centredness of love, perhaps, could be translated into a socially useful emotion or at least a psychologically useful one; the 'solid earth beneath' may be the permanent personality and the twisted cloud figures projections of an attempted romantic escape from that. When the speaker turns on his pillow at the end, he may perhaps be turning not towards the sleep of exhaustion but to make love; in which case, perhaps, he has not found his own eloquence practically persuasive. But the love, as between two men, would be, by definition, sterile. This seems to me one of the most powerful of Gunn's early poems, with an almost Dantesque quality of visionary horror.

I know, however, few people who share this admiration. And I know of many admirers of another early poem from *Fighting Terms*, which strikes me as comical, but unconsciously so (Gunn, as I have said, has plenty of wit of the severer kind, but almost no humour). We have seen that separateness, self-sufficiency, energy even as something that inspires to restless movement with no clear purpose, are positive values for Gunn; so, sometimes, and it seems to me less attractively, are domination and ruthlessness. The early poem which strikes me as unconsciously self-parodic is called 'A Village Edmund'. Edmund is Edmund in *King Lear* and we are to think also of Gray's 'village Hampden' in the *Elegy*. Edmund is admittedly the most humanly sympathetic of all Shakespeare's villains, but Gunn's 'rough and lecherous' village counterpart of him seems to me, as it were, a Tony Hancock part :

> *One girl he fancied as much as she fancied him.*
> *'For a moment,' she thought, 'our bodies can bestride*
> *A heaven whose memories must support my life.'*
> *He took her to the deserted countryside,*
> *And she lay down and obeyed his every whim.*
>
> *When it was over he pulled his trousers on.*
> *'Demon lovers must go,' he coldly said.*
> *And walked away from the rocks to the lighted town.*
> *'Why should heaven,' she asked, 'be for the dead?'*
> *And she stared at the pale intolerable moon.*

What spoils this as serious poetry is not, however, so much the callowness of the attitude as the weakness of the writing; the melodramatic novelettish language of the girl; the stiltedness of phrases like 'obeyed his every whim' : the conscious manly toughness of the line about pulling his trousers on, and the at once coy and trite narcissism (for I take it the poet is emotionally identifying himself with Edmund) of 'he *coldly* said'. The pale intolerable moon of the last line, for that matter, is very much out of some old romantic property-box. Gunn's failures of tone and feeling do not come from an excessive chumminess or prosiness (as, say, Amis's or Larkin's failures of that sort might come) but from an occasional self-admiring melodrama or sentimentality. They are more like the failures of Stephen Spender (who seems to me a better poet at his best than he is generally made out to be, and who seems to me also temperamentally in some ways not unlike Gunn, who has gone out of his way in one poem to attack him); in many ways, in fact, Gunn is more like a 1930s than a 1950s poet. His are poems without a Muse, or the Muse rather is a male Muse, village Edmunds, warriors in byrnies, black-jacketed James Dean characters roaring through small American towns on motor-cycles. But a fine intellectual discipline can make something universal out of this, as it might seem in itself, somewhat dubious material.

Let me take an example of what seems to me a very notable success on Gunn's part, the first poem in his 1957 volume, *The Sense of Movement*. This is called 'On the Move' and these young men on motor-cycles are vividly the topic but savingly in the end not the theme of the poem. The theme, rather, is Sartrean existential humanism. I want to examine in turn the last three lines of each of the five eight-line stanzas. In these last three lines, in each stanza, Gunn presses from particulars towards a persuasive generality, which becomes progressively more firmly defined; he presses towards the stating of a moral. In the first stanza, the poet vividly observes birds on the edge of a dusty American road, birds which 'follow some hidden purpose', while the poet himself is vainly 'seeking their instinct, or their poise, or both'. He sums it up:

> *One moves with an uncertain violence*
> *Under the dust thrown by a baffled sense*
> *Or the dull thunder of approximate words.*

'Baffled sense' is not there, or only partly, what it might be in Keats, sensuous apprehension baffled by trying to reach beyond itself, but baffled intellectual apprehension; the baffled sense of what it is all about.

In the second stanza, the boys on motor-cycles, anticipated already in the first stanza in the dust and the scariness of the birds, roar by. And we are told of them in the last three lines:

> *In gleaming jackets trophied with the dust,*
> *They strap in doubt – by hiding it, robust –*
> *And almost hear a meaning in their noise.*

The baffling dust here becomes a trophy, a prize, of pointless speed; and the noise of the motor-cycles (in communication theory *noise* is contrasted with *sound*, and means any interference with the transmission of the message) becomes paradoxically for them a kind of communication. Very often in Gunn apparently simple and ordinary words like 'meaning' and 'noise' can, in their juxtaposition, carry in this way a lucid paradox.

In the third stanza, Gunn points out that the motor-cyclists are not riding towards any known goal but as fast as possible away from a known and frustrating background. It is they who scare the birds across the fields but it is inevitable that even a right natural order should yield to even a subrational human will. And there is this to be said for the motor-cyclists, that they are emblems of a larger human condition:

> *Men manufacture both machine and soul,*
> *And use what they imperfectly control*
> *To dare a future from the taken routes.*

The idea behind these admirably compact lines is Sartre's that man creates himself, creates his 'soul', by arbitrary but important choices. His choices cannot be made in complete foreknowledge of their consequences ('use what they imperfectly control'). But what is even more worrying is that the *general* consequences of all possible choices might be thought to be boringly worked out already. This abstract philosophical idea is beautifully translated into properly poetic language. The 'taken' routes are at once the routes daringly taken, or undertaken, by the young motor-cyclists to create a future and they are also the routes, the roads there on the map, which would not be there at all if they had not been 'taken' dully by generations of men already. Again, very plain, apparently obvious words produce a paradox.

The fourth stanza justifies the choice of the motor-cyclists as at least a partial solution of the human problem. Man is not necessarily at odds with the world because he is not purely an animal. Nor is he damned because, half, but only half an animal, he has to rely not on 'direct instinct' but on movements – say, movements of history or politics – which carry him on part of the way, even though in the end movement 'divides and breaks';

> One joins the movement in a valueless world,
> Choosing it, till, both hurler and the hurled,
> One moves as well, always toward, toward.

What one moves 'toward' is not to be abstractly defined, but one is moving away from that which one has found valueless (but there is also the Sartrean idea that value is imposed by choice, not there in the world to compel choice). One may be moving towards value.

In the fifth and last stanza, the cyclists vanished, the 'self-defined astride the created will'. (Again notice how a philosophical concept is beautifully translated into a poetical conceit, the 'manufactured' soul finding its emblem, or symbol, in the 'manufactured' motor-cycle.) The cyclists are right, for Gunn, to burst through and away from towns which are no homes either for the naturalness of birds or the stillness of saints who, like birds, 'complete their purposes'. The justification of these 'rebels without a cause' is that our civilized world, the world, say, which Larkin sadly accepts, has in its frustrating complication no home for either naturalness or holiness. And when one is, however restlessly and violently, 'on the move',

> At worst one is in motion; and at best,
> Reaching no absolute, in which to rest,
> One is always nearer by not keeping still.

Gunn is not in any ordinary sense of the word a religious poet, but he is (both in the ordinary and to some degree in the literary sense of the word) a metaphysical poet. The kinds of metaphysics that interest him are very different from those that interest Eliot, say, yet there are obvious broad affinities between the pattern of argument in this poem and some of the patterns of argument in *Four Quartets*.

I have thought it better in this article to examine what one might call the broad human interest of Gunn's poetry, taking three or four sample poems as pegs to drape my exposition round, rather than to review, or re-review his volumes in detail, or to go in detail into the verbal texture of his work. Swiftness, directness, lucidity, beautifully exact dramatic or logical construction in a poem, mark his work much more than richness of imagery or any sort of lyrical cry; the kind of technical-appreciative words one would use about his verse are supple, muscular, 'on the move'. But his deep authenticity comes from range of curiosity, an undefeatedness of spirit, and a swift readiness to make choices, without any hesitant bother about how the choices will be socially taken. If Larkin is a fine poet born, in a sense, middle-aged, Gunn is a poet who should have a peculiarly direct appeal not for angry, but for fierce, young men.

20 · PHILIP LARKIN: THE LYRIC NOTE AND THE GRAND STYLE

(1)

Philip Larkin was born in Coventry in 1922. His father had a senior municipal post and sent his promising son to Oxford. He talks to my wife, when we meet him, of his first year at Oxford which was her third, and when she was President of the Literary Society, which he then attended assiduously. At 23, in 1945, he published with the Fortune Press his first volume of poems, *The North Ship*, much influenced by Yeats, and in 1946 his first novel, which had an Oxford setting, *Jill*. Both volumes were brought out by the Fortune Press, but the copyrights are now in the hands of Faber, for whom Larkin revised *Jill* drastically in 1964, 18 years after its first appearance. In 1947, Faber (Larkin was a close Oxford friend of one of the directors, Charles Monteith) brought out a second novel, *A Girl in Winter*. Carefully and sensitively written, and quite free of these affectations of style which make one refer to 'the novel of a poet', these two fictions confront some of the same material as the poetry: loneliness, difficulty in defining the nature of one's feelings towards situations and people, and compensatory fantasies. There is also humour, sometimes, as in the remarks in *Jill* on Edmund Blunden's lectures, of a rather aggressive sort: Edmund planned in advance neither the detail nor the structure of his lectures but it was fascinating to watch him fitting them together like a bower-bird out of any twigs, straws, scraps of moss that were handy. But I think the disarming sweetness which I loved in Edmund was one of a number of qualities like unconscious good manners (if they are conscious, of course, they are not really good) and knowledge of exotic places and alien cultures which Larkin's generation were thrice-armed against. They were so alert, that whole set of young people that was called 'the Movement', for the pretentiously fake that they sometimes slashed down the vulnerably genuine.

For my own rather crude tastes in the matter, not enough happens in these distinguished early novels of Larkin's: he is better with moods, or scenes or anecdotes evoking moods, than with events, and so is essentially a poet rather than a novelist. These early efforts created little widespread interest and Larkin was a mysterious figure whom one heard about, as working in places one would never dream of visiting, in these days of the late 1940s – Wellington, Shropshire, Leicester, Belfast – finally in the University of Hull where he is now Chief Librarian and has taken the opportunity to encourage young poets like Douglas Dunn. But it is interesting how an underground reputation spreads: I am proud to find myself in the list of advance subscribers to Larkin's second volume of verse, *The Less Deceived*, brought out in October 1955 by the Marvell Press, near Hull: I rub shoulders on the list not only with close personal friends of Larkin's like Kingsley Amis, Robert Conquest, Donald Davie, D. J. Enright, Elizabeth Jennings, John Wain, but with distinguished poets of a quite different vintage like Charles Tomlinson, C. A. Trypanis, Vernon Watkins; with scholar-critics either already famous or on their way to fame, A. Alvarez, B. Bergonzi, F. W. Bateson, Vivian de Sola Pinto, Bonamy Dobrée, Richard Hoggart, John Holloway, Frank Kermode, J. B. Leishman, L. D. Lerner; a budding politician Edward Du Cann, a budding philosopher A. G. N. Flew. One wonders how the news got so widely and variously around. *The Less Deceived*, ten years after *The North Ship*, when he was 33 made Larkin's reputation. Two more volumes, again published at ten-year intervals, have kept the reputation up and added to it: *The Whitsun Weddings*, published in 1964 when he was 42, and *High Windows* in 1974, when he was 52. If he reaches his seventies we may expect two more volumes, if he reaches his eighties three.

Faber have now acquired the copyright of all Larkin's poems, and also publish a book of jazz record reviews, on which I am incompetent to comment. His controversial book is *The Oxford Book of Twentieth Century Verse* which succeeds, but does not replace, Yeats's *The Oxford Book of Modern Verse*. Though I have been on friendly though not intimate terms with Larkin for years (he quite frequently visits Leicester) I was oddly touched when he chose a longish poem of mine as one of his 'singletons': a poem of my youth. But on the whole, especially comparing the whole-hearted and indiscreet fulness of Yeats's introduction with the brief evasiveness of Larkin's, and also preferring on the whole Yeats's minor figures to Larkin's (this is the test of an anthologist: anybody can make a safe conventional selection from the very great), astonished by printing errors in the first edition and some very odd choices of copy texts, I felt that this was a job done against the grain, by a poet of the first order who yet rates the reading of poetry rather low down in his list of pleasures, and who feels about many contemporary poems a certain blankness rather than either fury or delight. (In a guessing game and basing my guesses almost purely on his poems, not on my pleasant but intermittent and puzzling personal impressions of him, I would guess that Larkin rates above poetry, as a source of delight for himself, memory, the solitary contemplation of the moon through glass, spring, social observation of the sort that stirs one's imagination but does not involve one too much personally, music no doubt, jokes, those of the oblique kind which can be told quite safely to the person they are about. I have missed out, but it must come quite high, a pride and pleasure that Larkin must feel in the successful labour that produces, in his own poetry, such triumphs of unobtrusive skill; about death and love which, again on the evidence of his poems, I think worry him as much or indeed a little more darkly and persistently than they worry the rest of us, I fancy he would say that poetry, like patriotism, is no solution.)

I should add that this guessing game is very much that. I am growing slightly deaf and when I meet Larkin often do not quite catch what he is saying. When I do catch it, it is often funny. I should explain that he is a tall, thinnish man with a very large round impressive face, with round glasses. When I first came to Leicester I came on him, with no thoughts of expectations of meeting him, in a bar. I knew the face but who ... where ...? 'Don't you recognize me, George?' said Larkin. 'It's God!'

(2)

I want to demonstrate a certain lyrical and romantic quality and, with it, a metrical dexterity so subtly unobtrusive that, even while it worked on them, readers have failed to isolate it as a main factor in their pleasure. But I may be tempted to interrupt this illustration, from lovely but slight poems, by the wish to show, in three examples from what strike me as the three greatest poems in *The Less Deceived*, *The Whitsun Weddings*, and *High Windows*, Larkin's mastery, when he wants to display it, of 'the grand style'. He is a great poet (I did not recognize this in my carping remarks upon him in my piece in this volume on Thom Gunn) who does not choose to be writing obviously 'great poems' all the time. He rejected Yeats after *The North Ship*, turned to Hardy: but Hardy, with his utterly different tone of voice, is as great a romantic and lyrical poet as Yeats. People write as if in Hardy Larkin had discovered only *Satires of Circumstance*, in Betjeman only 'Miss Joan Hunter Dunn'. Larkin has of course written very good funny and satirical poems but they have been made too much a central focus of attention, as have a few poems of which the mood seems frankly nasty. Critics should allow Larkin as they allow Hardy (and ought to allow Betjeman, through his parodic gestures, as in 'Sir John Piers') lyrical delight and pathos. They should notice that Larkin can make words dance. He remains, even so, a poet of the world's actualities but these are not always glum: they include joy, agony, the celebration of the dead in mourning.

Let me illustrate what I mean by three short poems from, in turn, *The Less Deceived*, *The Whitsun Weddings*, and *High Windows*. Here is the poem from *The Less Deceived*:

COMING

On longer evenings,
Light, chill and yellow
Bathes the serene
Foreheads of houses.
A thrush sings,
Laurel-surrounded
In the deep bare garden

> *Its fresh-peeled voice*
> *Astonishing the brickwork.*
> *It will be spring soon,*
> *It will be spring soon –*
> *But I, whose childhood*
> *Is a forgotten boredom,*
> *Feel like a child*
> *Who comes on a scene*
> *Of adult reconciling,*
> *And can understand nothing*
> *But the unusual laughter,*
> *And starts to be happy.*

The early and middle 1950s was a period in which the young poets of the 'Movement' (in reaction, for instance, against the wild licences of a virtuoso like Auden!) were, like the 'drab' poets of the earlier Elizabethan age, teaching themselves to count iambic feet on their fingers: they had learned that the second syllable, compared to the first, must come down with a thump, and they thumped as hard as possible.

Larkin is the kindest of men but if he was silent about this nonsense all around him he was not, in a very great century of metrical innovation by men of genius, going to practise it himself. Here, on the contrary, Larkin is defying the 'new correctness' in pure stress-metre lines (rather like Anglo-Saxon half-lines) in which two stresses can be brought up right against each other,

> *A thrush sings,*

or at either end of the line,

> Feel *like a* child,

or offer, in a repeated line, alternative choices:

> *It will be* spring soon,
> *It* will *be* spring *soon* ...

Eliot had used the same metrical device in parts of *Ash Wednesday* but even that great poet had not used it with greater skill.

One must in talking about poetry approach content by way of form (the two are inseparable, but distinguishable) just as in approaching the novel one must approach form by way of content: and in the drama the two are always switching masks (so that a realistic play must pretend to be an allegory, an allegory a realistic play). The content moves us here because it has found its appropriate form. We have a transition from spring from the 'fresh-peeled' thrush's song, from the houses transformed by the 'chill and yellow' light to human icons with serene foreheads that somehow cancels and transforms the forgotten boredom of childhood (it is now forgotten *positively*: not sullenly resented because it offers nothing to remember, as in Larkin's shoulder-shrugging poem 'I Remember, I Remember' saved by its crashing last line:

> *Nothing, like something, happens anywhere.*)

Poems of pure happiness are rare in Larkin (as moments of pure happiness are rare in life). But this is a happy poem, not merely a beautiful one: notice how the poem begins with a rapid, shrill note like that of the thrush and modulates to a slower and richer tone as we come to the point of it all, human reconciliation.

In *The Whitsun Weddings* I find a shorter poem in the same metre, more complex and sad but making a declaration that happiness is why we should live in time, also: only, we cannot live for ever. I mark the stresses as I hear them, but some are arguable, except that there should be two, and on key words or syllables, to each short line:

DAYS

> *What are days for?*
> *Days are where we live.*
> *They come, they wake us.*
> *Time and time over.*
> *They are to be happy in*
> *Where can we live but days?*
>
> *Ah, solving that question*
> *Brings the priest and the doctor*
> *In their long coats*
> *Running over the fields.*

In the first six-line section 'days' is repeated three times and stressed each time: 'they' is repeated three times and stressed twice, exactly like 'are': 'live' is repeated twice and stressed once if we take, as I do, 'time over' as a compound adverbial phrase with the main stress on 'over' which thus becomes one of the two used once and stressed. 'Days' is in the middle of the first line, at the beginning of the second, the end of the last. 'Are' is the second word in each of the lines in which it occurs. 'Happy' with 'over' is one of the two words used only once and stressed (but 'over' perhaps is merely *part* of a two-unit word, 'time over'). 'Live', like 'where', is used twice but stressed only once, 'where' in the second line, 'live' in the sixth. 'They' has its two stresses in the beginning and middle of line two, governing first an intransitive, then a transitive verb. The repetition of the word 'live' enables the second and sixth lines to be reversed images of each other:

Days are where we live ...
Where can we live but days?

This formal analysis seems, no doubt is, tedious. But the elaborate repetition patterns make us accept childlike or primitive thinking: days are active and personified, they come and wake us but fundamentally they are thought of as a place (like the fields in the last four lines) we are to be happy in. Where else could we live but in the fields of days ('Sheep may safely graze ...').

The last four lines sinisterly change the note. The phrases *'that question'* and *'long coats'* are the only two in the poem where stresses are powerfully and rather threateningly juxtaposed. If I am right in thinking the question in the first six lines one asked by children (grown-ups know that there is a variety of possible answers and no final one: what, after all, *are* days for?) then the long coats (the priest's black one, the doctor's white one) explain partly that these figures look sinisterly tall to children (or to the innocent, not yet expelled from Eden). For the children, to raise the question is to eat of the fruit of the Tree of the Knowledge of Good and Evil. The priest tells them that there is another place than days they can be happy in, but can they imagine such a place? The doctor can add to the number of their days but at the same time they will learn from him that their days are numbered. There is no resemblance in style, and no conscious reference I would imagine (Larkin dislikes literary echoes as he dislikes what he calls the 'myth-kitty') but I do find myself thinking of Blake's *Songs of Innocence and Experience*. The first six lines are innocence: the last four are experience. Without contraries is no progression, but the directness of the progression here makes us very sad.

It is part of Larkin's temperament and formation that, as he grows older, his poetry grows sadder. In *The Less Deceived* the central symbol was the church in 'Church Going', whose social core for Larkin was not any religious belief of his own but the giving of ceremonial dignity to the three great moments of birth, marriage, and death: I well remember reading for the first time the stanza on which the cunningly modulated poem turns, the stanza that made me realize that Larkin was a great poet:

Or, after dark, will dubious women come
To make their children touch a particular stone;
Pick simples for a cancer, or on some
Advised night see walking a dead one?
Power of some sort or other will go on
In games, in riddles, seemingly at random,
But superstition, like belief, must die,
And what remains when disbelief has gone?
Grass, weedy pavement, brambles, buttress, sky.

The key poem, in that sense, in *The Whitsun Weddings*, is 'An Arundel

Tomb'. The aristocratic couple, who probably married for dynastic reasons, whose social position demanded a tomb where they would lie side by side, the earl's ungauntleted hand clutching his countess's hands, the stiff carving, the little dogs at their feet, how could they tell that these formal and necessary stone gestures, demanded by their heirs' position as much as by their own, should become a heart-breaking symbol – though a lie, or almost a lie perhaps – of the eternal persistence of chivalry, courtesy, love? :

> Time has transfigured them into
> Untruth. The stone fidelity
> They hardly meant has come to be
> Their final blazon, and to prove
> Our almost-instinct almost true:
> What will survive of us is love.

There are great assertions in Larkin. It is an 'almost-instinct' not a universal, unavoidable, unconscious true instinct: it is 'almost true', not absolutely or certainly true, merely on the very verge of being true. But that very hedging caution makes the last line sound like a trumpet:

> What will survive of us is love.

In *High Windows* everything is very much sadder (though occasionally, in an outrageous way, funnier than before). The central symbol is not the church, not the tomb of the dead pair symbolizing love, but that building which seems to dominate our imaginations today, the hospital: not so much death as dying, dying with a slow decay of the faculties –

> What do they think has happened, the old fools,
> To make them like this? Do they somehow suppose
> It's more grown up when your mouth hangs open and drools,
> And you keep on pissing yourself, and can't remember
> Who called this morning?

I cannot speak for a death in acute pain, which I do not wish to imagine, but I have stood by the bed of an old man of nearly 90 and felt his pulse and whether his heart was still beating and put my ear on his chest for any noise of breathing. He was like a baby who has to be fed and cleaned but he died in peace in a sort of coma. It is all natural, it may come to all of us if we live long enough. It does not deprive us of our dignity any more than having been a baby does. The old man had been comfortably and consciously alive, as we are in dreamless sleep: death was an almost invisible transition. I think it is poems like this which have distressed some readers of *High Windows*, as previous collections of Larkin's verse have not distressed them.

The great poem in *High Windows*, however, is certainly not this one. It is called 'The Building' and the building is a hospital and the subject is the anonymity for us today and I suppose one might say the bureaucratization of

death. (My old man, in the last paragraph, died at home.) I shall quote the
end which again like 'Church Going' or 'An Arundel Tomb' has the ring of
greatness :

> ... O world,
> Your loves, your chances, are beyond the stretch
> Of any hand from here! And so, unreal,
> A touching dream to which we all are lulled
> But wake from separately. In it, conceits
> And self-protecting ignorance congeal
> To carry life, collapsing only when
>
> Called to these corridors (for now once more
> The nurse beckons –). Each gets up and goes
> At last. Some will be out by lunch, or four;
> Others, not knowing it, have come to join
> The unseen congregations whose white rows
> Lie set apart above – women, men;
> Old, young; crude facets of the only coin
> The place accepts. All know they are going to die.
> Not yet, perhaps not here, but in the end,
> And somewhere like this. This is what it means,
> This clean-sliced cliff; a struggle to transcend
> The thought of dying, for unless its powers
> Outbuild cathedrals, nothing contravenes
> The coming dark, though crowds each evening try
>
> With wasteful, weak, propitiatory flowers.

That last hanging line must have as much concentrated irony and pathos in
the sequence of adjectives – wasteful and weak they seem, but are they
propitiatory? all such wasteful weak offerings must fail to propitiate? it
is the very wastefulness and weakness that propitiates, that arouses the pity
of the gods? – as any in the English language.

(3)

I intended to illustrate Larkin's lyrical gifts with three successive short
poems from the three volumes I am looking at but I suddenly felt the need
to demonstrate his greatness. Nor do I feel now the need to demonstrate that
some poems in which the humour seems ill-natured express a tolerance, and
a sharp self-criticism, in the end. I will wind up by quoting and commenting
on the last of the lyrical poems, 'Dublinesque' from High Windows, that
caught my eye.

Like Webster, by Eliot's account, the later Larkin is 'much possessed by
death'. And one sees in a way his point, for in those hygienic prisons like the

one in 'The Building', under the efficiency of kind, indifferent hands, most of us are likely to die: unless, indeed, the whole system cracks, and dying with no care at all but the unskilled and ignorant care of friends and families, we find ourselves longing for that impersonal control we have dreaded. I hate hospitals, but would not like to die of starvation in the streets of Calcutta. We think less of all this than we imagine or suicide would be much more common. We think less of love also, less frequently and intensely, than those who utter their feelings in poems do. This may mean that we are sane and practical, and poets take things too intensely. But it may mean also that most of us are very imperfectly human, that we come under Wilfred Owen's commination:

> But cursed are dullards whom no cannon stuns,
> That they should be as stones ...

Nor, certainly, do our thick skins and our gift of cutting off sympathy at the nerve ends mean that poets are telling lies.

Of all Larkin's later preoccupations not dying, but death, and the celebration of the dead in the ritual of mourning, is the least painful and the most pregnant with consolation. 'Dublinesque' in its place and date and the music of its rhythmed speech recalls Joyce's *Dubliners*, and one feels that it is a poem Joyce himself might have written if he could have added the great human realism of his stories to his delicate minor talent for evoking mood in verse:

DUBLINESQUE

> Down stucco sidestreets
> Where light is pewter
> And afternoon mist
> Brings light on in shops
> Above race-guides and rosaries,
> A funeral passes.
>
> The hearse is ahead
> But after there follows
> A troop of streetwalkers
> In wide flowered hats,
> Leg-of-mutton sleeves,
> And ankle-length dresses.
>
> There is an air of great friendliness,
> As if they were honouring
> One they were fond of;
> Some caper a few steps,
> Skirts held skilfully
> (Someone claps time),

> *And of great sadness also,*
> *As they wend away*
> *A voice is heard singing*
> *Of Kitty, or Katy,*
> *As if the name meant once*
> *All love, all beauty.*

Here again as in 'Coming' and 'Days' is the line with two primary stresses (which are, of course, as in Old English metrics, the main sense stresses as well as the metrical stresses). But the movement feels different for there are more lightly stressed syllables and more strong secondary stresses. From his years as an assistant librarian at Queen's University, Belfast, Larkin seems to have picked up exactly not only the stress-patterns of individual Anglo-Irish words but the intonation-tunes of Anglo-Irish spoken sentences.

For instance, the English say 'stréetwalkers' but the Anglo-Irish say 'streètwálkers'. This makes all the difference to the music of the line

> *A* troop of *street*walkers:

pronounced in the English way,

> *A* troop of streetwalkers,

would sound like prose. Similarly, for the following sentence the common English intonation-tune would be: 'Some *cap*er a few *steps*'. The Irish pattern is

> *Some* caper *a* few *steps,*

and again the music here is saved. Similarly, in the second last line of the last stanza, the English emphasis might be with wretched results to the poem: 'As if the *name* meant *once* …' The correct Anglo-Irish speech prosody, which Larkin hears and wants us to hear, is

> As if *the name* meant *once*
> All *love, all* beauty …

I do not think the sense, in relation to the sound, needs any exposition. The sorrow comes in very simple and dignified words:

> *There is an air of great friendliness*
> *As if they were honouring*
> *One they were fond of* …

There is the shuffling dance, the clapping of time, the mourning for lost beauty, *les neiges d'antan*: none the less essentially beauty because it is the common beauty of Kitty or Katy of the Irish streets. I half-wonder whether, without the distancing of a Joycean past, without this disguise of Irish scene and intonation, Larkin would permit himself such a direct expression of heart-rending tenderness.

Still, having started off this collection with Yeats and Ireland I am glad to be back in Ireland at the end with Larkin and Joyce. Larkin's jokes and occasional sourness can wait for another day. From 1880 to, I would guess, at least 1980 we have had a century of terrible catastrophes and wonderful poets. Let me give thanks to the Poets, and to Larkin as the last I am greeting, at least.

NOTES

p. 11 It did, according to unpublished journals of Yeats, find brief fulfilment in 1907 – see the article by Professor Denis Donoghue, *New York Review of Books*, 1977.

p. 14 A good poet, Sheila Wingfield, Dowager Viscountess Powerscourt, described Yeats to me as what Irish servants call 'a half-sir'. 'Weren't his people flax merchants in Sligo?'

p. 15 But see earlier note based on Denis Donoghue.

p. 19 'Stare' is Anglo-Irish for a starling.

p. 55 The current use of the word 'gay' as a propaganda word to encourage the social acceptance of male homosexuality is a misfortune for poetry. I am all for the acceptance : I hate the narrowing of the word.

p. 74 But see note to p. 11. Professor Donoghue has a profound knowledge of Yeats's unpublished manuscripts. Yseult, incidentally, had been previously seduced by Ezra Pound.

p. 83 It seems to me now to have the quality of 'epic monotony' – in other words, to be rather boring.

p. 86 I would not now agree with this. Canto XIII, on Confucius, is the most beautiful and wise single Canto in the poem.

p. 88 I am not sure, as I was when I wrote this essay, of Pound's central sanity : some reports of his uncommunicative last years in Italy suggest that he had a sense of final failure, of having been on the wrong track.

p. 91 There *was* a rag-time tune with these words dating from Eliot's Harvard days around 1910 rather than from the 1920s. Rag-time historically preceded jazz.

p. 116 I cannot fit into the poem very easily the epigraph in Latin from Seneca's *Hercules Furens*, where Hercules kills his children in a fit of madness.

p. 126 Perhaps after reading this essay, Graves changed 'filthy ease' to 'drunken ease' in later printings of this poem. He has always avoided the striking line that destroys the unity of the stanza.

p. 137 I now think this is unfair. The preceding lines are 'Hunger allows no choice/To the citizen or the police.' What Auden meant is that a society where the cops and the robbers do not tolerate each other as humanly necessary will collapse into anarchy.

p. 144 I wrote this as an agnostic of deeply religious sentiments. I write now as an Anglican with few religious sentiments : I need the sacraments but hate the sermons and the false good-fellowship. In 1947, I was better and wiser.

p. 147 The scholar was the late Geoffrey Tillotson.

p. 201 Published, remember, in 1957.